Praise for
What Could Go Right

"*What Could Go Right* asks us to rethink the dystopian tropes of the future and instead to envision a more ideal world that we can build stronger together. With this new mindset, embracing the trends around us, and new tools for strategy and execution, we are empowered to build an inspiring sustainable future—for our own sake and for that of our children."

—**Kelly Dittmann,** global C-suite advisor, former chief strategy officer and sustainability managing director

"More than ever, especially in this time of so many crises, our world needs an inspiring vision to work towards. *What Could Go Right* challenges us to change our focus from the fear of dystopia to envisioning the world we want, and empowers us with the tools to build it."

—**Aarti Tandon,** CEO, Smart City Expo USA, World Economic Forum G20 Smart Cities Alliance member, Aspen Institute / ADL fellow

"This book is the perfect antidote for anyone who shies away from taking the positive risks of a life well-lived because they think too much about what could go wrong and not enough about what could go right. Justin Bean shares practical, actionable insights that will help us all face up to the daunting but not insurmountable challenges of an uncertain world."

—**Michele Wucker,** author of *The Gray Rhino* and *You Are What You Risk*

"Being able to envisage a positive future, with all the technology, creativity, and innovation required, is THE skill humans need to make this future come true. Justin's book contributes fresh green shoots of insight and inspiration to call positive envisaging to the fore of environmental and climate work. Justin's message will help create a thriving garden of environmental innovation, which is quickly taking over the old wood and climate-doomism so many of us are tired of."

—**Katie Patrick,** author of *How to Save the World*, gamification consultant, UN Environment Programme and Environmental Engineer + Designer

"Are we needlessly and self-defeatingly dour about our place in history and our prospects for the future? Justin Bean is so very right to point out that we live in fortunate times, and the future could be even brighter . . . if we wish. Read this book for a mental tune up / attitude check and find out about how to regularly work with optimists who are creating the change you're secretly wishing for."

—**Ryan Kushner,** founder of Third Derivative Accelerator and New Energy Network, author of *Accelerate This! A Super Not Boring Guide to Startup Accelerators and Clean Energy Entrepreneurship*

"Many entrepreneurs are wired to be motivated by seemingly impossible challenges, and climate change is the challenge of our generation. *What Could Go Right* works to paint a picture of what the world could look like once we've successfully transitioned to an abundant and decarbonized economy."

—**Cody Simms**, coauthor of *Levers: The Framework for Building Repeatability Into Your Business*, partner at MCJ Collective, former Techstars, Yahoo, and *New York Times* executive

"What a great read! Justin Bean's enthusiasm and optimism shine through in this well-researched and action-oriented tome. To quote the author: 'You have limited time to make an impact, so why not focus your limited time and energy on impacting the world in a positive way and feeling great in the process?' This book will help you do both."

—**Kate Drane**, founder and advisor to early stage climate startups, former director at Techstars, Breakthrough Energy, and Indiegogo

"In the face of complex global challenges, it may be our mindset that determines our outcome. In *What Could Go Right*, Justin Bean weaves together a compelling case for why we should choose vision over cynicism. Challenging the dystopian view of global change and disruptive technologies like AI and the blockchain, Bean leverages research and storytelling to ask: What if we could leverage these dynamic forces for the betterment of humanity? This is one of the best books I've read for being a changemaker in the modern world."

—**Peter Glenn**, clean energy entrepreneur and cofounder of EV Life, former Singularity University and Glassdoor marketing lead

"Buy *two copies* of *What Could Go Right*. One is your go-to guidebook to keep as you envision your best possible future. The other copy is for you to share with someone who you want to support on their journey!"

—**Jeff Fromm**, 5X Author, serial entrepreneur, cofounder of The Sustainable Development Group, contributor at *Forbes*

"Read this book if you want the future to be a better place, and you want to be part of building it."

—**Shannon Lucas**, bestselling author of *Move Fast. Break Shit. Burn Out. The Catalyst's Guide to Working Well.*, co-CEO of Catalyst Constellations, TedX Speaker, Former Ericsson, Cisco, and Vodafone executive.

"The right framing is key to the success of any idea and is a catalyst for taking action to attain any goal. While many others lament about the catastrophes of new innovations, I love how Justin frames the future of technology as opportunity. *What Could Go Right* is a north star for current and future leaders who want to have a positive impact on communities and society."

—**Aaron McDaniel**, author of *Global Class*, BerkeleyHaas professor and serial entrepreneur

"Justin invites us to envision, design, and get busy building the better future we want. He does this with what is not only an engaging read, but one that inspires us, informs us, and gives us the tools to make a difference."

—**Clint Wilder**, coauthor of *The Clean Tech Revolution* and *Clean Tech Nation*, editorial director at CleanEdge, contributing writer at NRDC and Environmental Entrepreneurs (E2).

"A groundbreaking guide to rethinking sustainable design and solving for the future amidst continual change. If you're facing today's problems feeling overwhelmed by the future, you're not alone. This book will lift your vision to a higher horizon and help you see—and design—solutions that reach beyond conventional thinking and into the emergent opportunities of tomorrow."

—**Ellen Petry Leanse**, bestselling author of *The Happiness Hack*, TedX speaker, leadership coach, former Stanford University instructor, Apple and Google alum

WHAT COULD GO ~~WRONG~~ Right

Designing Our Ideal Future
to Emerge from Continual Crises
into a Thriving World

JUSTIN BEAN

ISBN: 978-1-7326475-8-9
Ebook ISBN: 978-1-7326475-9-6

Permission to reprint images in this book were generously granted by Simpli5, Donut Economics Action Lab, Anthony Hodgson and Bill Sharpe, James P. Carse, and IDEO U.

For more information about the author, visit http://JustinCBean.com.

Editing and production by Jennifer Holder, Full Bloom Publications
https://FullBloomPublications.com

Cover design, interior design, and typesetting by Ryan Scheife and Jess LaGreca, Mayfly Design
https://MayflyDesign.com

Contents

Introduction

Effective Change Depends on Envisioning What Could Go Right

WHAT IS THE FULL POTENTIAL OF OUR HUMAN species? What wonders and experiences might we be able to create if we truly got our society, economics, and personal lives "right"? Given the challenges of ongoing crises we see around us today, and the social and environmental damage that they are projected to cause if we don't overcome them, what is the best approach to move ourselves forward? I've long sought answers to these questions, looking to science fiction, philosophy, economics, sociology, and technology-driven futurism. I've found that there are plenty of dystopian books, movies, and news reports written about our problems or the consequences of our technology that imagine in exquisite detail how horrible the future could be. But I found utopian stories or ideal projections rare, and often dismissed as naïve. This book seeks to help us envision and create this ideal world through exploring three main aspects:

1. The importance of envisioning *what could go right*— starting with an ideal vision of what could be, and how this approach transforms our mindset, empowering us to build a better future.

2. Technological and societal trends that are presenting us—impact-minded entrepreneurs, students, and communities—with opportunities to not only participate in this transformation but also to thrive by doing so.

3. An exploration of how we could meet Maslow's hierarchy of needs for society, with example visions of what ideal aspects of a society would look like.

We are living in a potent time. The many conflicts and institutional fragility we're experiencing reveal that while the conventional ways of doing things have helped us get this far, many no longer meet humanity's needs today or help us reach our potential tomorrow. This has been true for a long time, but in this Information Age the spotlights of mass awareness shine on just about everything. We all have the ability to see injustices and inequalities now, whereas before they were unseen, ignored, or easily covered up by the people who would care enough to take action. There is no hiding in the dark anymore. The ways we have traditionally operated on personal, social, and global levels are exposed—freshly revealing important aspects of our world that we don't like. Name any hot-button issue today or any crumbling system, and at the core of the struggle is our perception that the old system is inadequate for today's needs, desires, and human potential.

These conflicts put us in a hard position: We know past ways aren't working, so many people are fighting existing systems, but we don't yet have a vision of where we want to go. We have few concrete ideas of what the better alternative system would be, no idea what our daily lives would be like. If where we want to head remains a mystery, it will be very difficult to get there.

While today's efforts to fight the current system and raise awareness are an important phase in the process of change, if nothing new is actively implemented, we end up reliving the struggle. We're stuck fighting the same system all over again, just led by different faces. Maybe we replace leaders and think they're going to change everything for the better, but they usually don't, because the fundamental structures, incentives, and dynamics of our societies remain the same.

We also face deep worldview conflicts. These are usually resolved in one of two ways: (1) through extreme violence that brings out the most horrific sides of human nature or (2) by creating a better alternative that makes the old system obsolete, leaving it to fall away as we scale up and transition into something new. The second is a preferred peaceful and enthusiastic transition. But if no one can imagine this new way of being, there's nothing to work toward, no tangible steps are taken, and there's no basis for a peaceful shift. Without visions for what to build, we may escape war, genocide, and social unrest for a generation, but things still don't change in the long run. It's akin to trying to build a skyscraper with just steel and concrete, but no blueprint. While common sense says civil planners and architects are essential, most of us don't apply the power of vision to our own life path, the society we live in, or even the businesses we are so busy working for every day.

The only way to start setting goals and identifying tangible steps is to first envision the future we want to reach. Then we can work peacefully together to build new institutions, businesses, and solutions that meet humanity's needs in stronger and more resilient ways.

We live in a world of exponential change, so when we envision and build a better world, it must be one that can stand and flourish despite the many coming disruptions. But why are we building a better world at all? What benefits do we hope it will have? Consider these challenges, which are often perceived as insurmountable. Start imagining a world where we have resolved:

- The social inequities that cause so many of the struggles we see each other face

- Preventive actions and adequate resources to fight devastating diseases and weather disasters that result from climate change and encroachment on ecosystems

- Universal access to abundant food and water, as well as education, which reduces both health issues and the many effects of poverty that hamstring our lives, our progress, and our systems

But these are only the basics. If we truly envision what could go right, we can imagine ways of elevating every human being to their full potential through creative applications of technology, new ways of understanding value, and optimization of how we go about collaboration, government, and our economies.

The potentials for beneficial change are endless—and the essential step is to create visions of the world we actually want to live in. Rather than repeatedly posing the fatalistic, fearful, and disempowering question of what could go wrong, we must ask ourselves how good it could actually get. In other words, *what could go right?* This book focuses on envisioning a better world that you can work to create, provides some ideas for what the world of the future could look like, and shares how we can make our problems—and their underlying causes—irrelevant.

This book is not about naïvely ignoring the risks of our time or the real suffering that people face throughout the world; it's about creating a future that overcomes those risks and eliminates that suffering. It presents potential solutions to many of the problems we face today as a global society.

The world we are fed by social media, cable news, and apocalyptic movies would have us believe everything is terrible and will only be worse in the future. It behooves us, then, to understand these views rather than disregard them outright. This assessment of our future could become accurate if we don't out-imagine, out-innovate, and out-create the complacency, fatalism, and laziness of mind that could lead us to these futures. It's actually much *easier* to imagine worst-case scenarios than better ones, because the worst case is based on what we already know, whereas imagining the best possible outcomes challenges us to create—in our minds—new ways of living and operating that we haven't seen before. As we will return to again and again in this book, despite all of the challenges just discussed, we actually live in the best time in human history for innovation, creativity, and the actualization of a future that would be considered a utopia by today's standards.

I decided to write this book because I share the concerns of the people I see around the world, frustrated with the way things are, yet inspired by what could be. I've also been saddened by seeing well-intentioned and capable people paralyzed with cynicism before they even try to take action. I didn't want to sit on the sidelines and watch the world with apathy. I wanted to figure out what we can do to make it a better place, and who was getting it right. I was lucky enough to live in Japan, where I regularly rode the clean, fast, extremely punctual subways and bullet trains, wondering *Why can't we have nice things like this in the US?* When working in South Africa, I saw rapid adoption of renewable energy and resourceful innovations like solar water heating, home biogas digesters, and LEDs, while the US and Europe debated their effectiveness, despite plenty of positive examples. I wondered what it would take for these technologies to reach the world in time to reduce climate change and pollution. I traveled through China, seeing rapidly rising smart cities leapfrog the West within mere decades, but under an undemocratic regime with a questionable human rights record. How could we share the best of our cultures and countries, while helping each other overcome our common human challenges? What I realized was that many of the realities in these countries were created by people no different than you or I, but running different mind software—generating ideas of what was possible and what was expected. I wondered, what could we achieve by updating our visions and expectations of the future?

Throughout my professional career I have focused on making a positive impact through business, government, non-profits, or collaborations among them. I've also been privileged to work with organizations and leaders who are envisioning and creating new businesses, technologies, and ways of doing things that will propel us forward into a more sustainable, fair, abundant, and inspiring future. Through conversations with creative minds at *Fortune* 500s, startups, non-profits, and people around the world from Silicon Valley to the American South, from Japan, China and Southeast Asia to South Africa, the Middle East, and Europe, I have seen communities of people embracing and courageously building a better future. From new startups, technologies and solutions, to design-thinking competitions, grass-roots community building, and corporate impact initiatives, I've worked with amazing people on amazing projects. With this book, I seek to pull the insights from these conversations out of the boardrooms and whiteboards of the most innovative organizations I've worked with or studied, and bring them to you, the aspiring leaders of today and the future, regardless of where you sit. I hope that you can utilize these tools and ideas to envision our ideal future, get inspired, and feel capable, empowered, and able to go create it.

I invite you to read these chapters as the beginning of a conversation that leads to your own visions, collaborations, and action. There is much work to do, and it will not get done by simply absorbing this message. I ask you to read, reflect on, and enjoy this book, but primarily I invite you to use it to instigate your own solutions and commitment to doing what you can to help this world become a better place. When you do so with commitment, creativity, and persistence, I guarantee you will find more meaning, more like-minded people, and more purpose in your life—and I hope you will have a great time building the world you want to live in.

Chapter 1

The Mindset That Helps Actualize Your Ideal

WHAT PROPELS AND GUIDES US TO BUILD A BETTER future? A vision. What prevents us from getting started? Doubt and cynicism.

A vision is an aspirational description of what we would like to achieve, personally or as an organization. It serves as a clear guide for choosing our courses of action. Most often, we meet visions with these mindsets:

1. **CYNICISM:** We approach vision with suspicion because, deep down, we believe events turn out for the worst and people act only out of self-interest; therefore, the future is bleak.

2. **PESSIMISM AND FATALISM:** We believe that the worst will happen regardless of what we do. We want to confirm our hopelessness and lack of confidence in the future, so we selectively see the worst aspects of experiences, events, and people.

3. **OPTIMISM:** We want goodness to pervade reality and society, so we emphasize the more favorable side of events or conditions and expect favorable outcomes—usually because it makes us feel better

These mindsets affect the outcome of any vision. If we want the *ideal* outcome, the option that is most beneficial and fitting to a desired result, we need to shift our mindset to support it.

Leveraging the power of vision isn't Pollyanna optimism and it's not positive thinking. It's a strategic, tangible way to save us from a mediocre future at best and a downward spiral of violent conflict and extreme disruption at worst, so we can make a smooth transition toward a better world. This raises some questions: Why wouldn't we all form visions and work toward them naturally? Why do we often tend to approach change with cynicism?

The Temptation of a Cynical Mindset

Acknowledging risk and danger is an important part of our survival. While as a group humanity is a formidable species, alone we're easy prey. In our not-so-ancient past, being ostracized from the group could be a death sentence. We might get kicked out of the village, left on our own in the wild—which was life-threatening for a naked ape with few natural defenses. We are a successful species because we're social, and with the power of our combined minds, complex language, and opposable thumbs, we have the ability to create incredible innovations that give us an asymmetrical advantage over other animals. But like many other social animals, we're dependent on each other for everyday survival. So acceptance by the group feels like an instinctual imperative. Cynicism is a self-defense mechanism and a way of signaling to the group that we are not irresponsible in our thoughts and plans.

The thinking goes like this: If I'm being cynical and expressing doubts, even through humor, I'm signaling to my troop, tribe, group, or cohort that I'm not naïve, and I'm not going to waste our collective resources on things that aren't important. Playing it cool, being conservative in action, and betting on the worst-case scenario is generally the safe way to go. We're shielded from criticism and ridicule. But then the cynical mindset sinks deeper as we internalize it and start to self-police.

Cynicism becomes a shield for our ego, because the ego's primary goal is to help us match what we think we are to what we achieve in the world. Here's the internal logic: If I set my sights high and then get shot down, or I try to lead and get ridiculed, there will be a mismatch between who I think I should be and who I am. None of us likes being rejected and shut down, nor failing, and when it happens, it can be excruciating. Cynicism defends our egos against the horrible feelings that would result if we were to make a wild bet and fail. It works by cutting that possibility at the root—halting the imagination, envisioning, and dreaming that can put us at risk of vulnerability, rejection, and imperfect outcomes. As poet Suzy Kassem said, "fear kills more dreams than failure ever will."

Have you ever felt satisfied that you did not become seduced by a losing cause? When we predict the bad and are correct, we are comforted by our foresight. The result may be that we keep quiet, view others who dream too big as childish, and stifle the urge to instigate change under a pile of social shaming.

The dangers of taking this path are high, because through cynicism we:

- Abandon what we believe *could be* for the certainty of being right about what *isn't*

- Empower our negative aspects, which restrain our potential, and disempower our ability to overcome them

- Stifle other people who believe that we have the choice and the ability to make life better

- Betray our duty and agency as human beings to plan and act in ways that create a better world

- Allow wrongs to continue

- Perpetuate the oppression we purport to oppose

It's true that we get a little reward, a little shot of dopamine, from having accurate foresight and getting validation in hindsight. When what you've predicted occurs, you can pat yourself on the back. But this can also become a self-fulfilling prophecy. If you do end up predicting the worst future, and you do nothing about it, imagine having "I told you so" on the tip of your tongue—it's going to be the least satisfying *I told you so* in history, because without action, we all lose in the face of climate disasters and societal instability.

Of course, cynicism can be helpful in situations of persistent danger or extreme scarcity, as long as you act on your predictions to change the outcome. But that's not where the vast majority of the world is today. It is undoubtedly important to understand the source and nature of the troubles we face. This is a first step. But without a vision and plan of action to counter these troubles, a cynical mindset becomes impotent despair.

During this historical time of disruption *and* abundance of knowledge and resources at our fingertips, a cynical tendency is not going to lead us into a new world. Instead, it affects the decisions we make, and it could potentially lead us to vote or act out of fear, enabling authoritarianism, conflict, and people who are overly suspicious of each other, looking for the worst in everything. This isn't a direction we want to go as a society. On an individual level, cynicism causes the human potential in each of us to succumb to premature death while our heart still beats firmly in our chest—capable, but unwilling to achieve great things.

When the Stakes Are High, Change the Game You Play

Don't get me wrong. In a way, we can all be forgiven for being cynical. We live in a time of extreme risk, with existential consequences. I devote the end of Chapter 3 to describing the conditions that could tip us into civilizational collapse . . . or into a sustainable state and even thriving like never before. The stakes at this juncture in history couldn't be higher. For now, consider that when civilizational survival is on the line, it's not just you or me winning or losing—it's the entire planet and human civilization losing what has been built up over tens of thousands of years. If we truly descend into catastrophe and chaos, with climate-ravaged cities and the loss of ecological resources needed to support our lives, it's going to take a long, long time to rebuild. Environmental, economic, and social scientists agree—playing our collective game the same way we have for centuries simply will not get us through the coming disruptions. To adapt our systems quickly enough to succeed, we need to collectively think differently about the game we're playing.

The concept of finite versus infinite games was popularized by Simon Sinek.[1] What we often play today is a series of limited, finite games. A **finite game** has defined rules and is played by a person, business, or government for the sake of finishing and winning the game. These finite games are usually zero-sum games, where one player wins and the other player loses. A player can also mean a team or group. This is how we've been trained to think and operate through sports, competitive business practices, wars, and anything framed as "us versus them." Once there's a winner, the game's over; there is some reward for the winners, while the losers either get nothing or have something taken away from them. These games can be fun, and their rules are easier to understand, especially for short competitions in the name of entertainment. But when it comes to our society, economy, and lives, finite games are woefully inadequate and mislead us from understanding what kind of game we are actually playing.

Instead of accepting finite games, we can realize that we're all engaged in an **infinite game**—a game that lasts indefinitely, with the intention of continuing play as long as possible. Infinite games don't have well-defined rules, and the rules that do exist are fluid, so they can adapt to change over time. The players may or may not know they're playing, and the closest thing to winning is boosting the state of play over time so the quality of experience for players improves. We can shift from staving off destruction to learning with ferocious curiosity and reaching our full potentials.

The following chart sets the two games side by side.

Before we dive further into what playing an infinite game is like, let's look at what happens when two parties are playing against each other—but one approaches it as a finite game and the other plays an infinite game.

FINITE GAMES	INFINITE GAMES
Known "teams" or sides	Players are both known and unknown—everyone is playing
Defined by competition	Undefined collaboration and competition alike
The game proceeds according to fixed rules based on how it has historically been played	Without agreed-upon rules, the game opens up to innovation, creativity, and shifts in view
A clear achievement marks the end of a game	The point of playing is that it never ends
With clear winners and losers, someone comes out on top and others are defeated	There's no way to win except that the quality of play increases
Leads players and teams to seek what's best for "me and mine"	Supports playing to benefit others and the whole
Creates a focus on stats and status, whether customers, fans, points, profits, or power	Favors quality over quantity and focuses on a positive legacy

When an invading military force wants to subdue another nation's conflicting ideals, secure its resources, and then get out, they are playing a finite game to win (imagine the US wars in Vietnam or Afghanistan). But the other nation is defending their home, way of life, and all that is important to them. Their goal is to continue play beyond the war in order to survive beyond it, preserve their civilization, and have a say in their future. They are playing beyond the short-term, win-or-lose scenario. Therefore they fight completely differently because they're in it for the long haul—they're playing an infinite game.

Businesses are the main form of human economic activity, and they tend to play mostly finite games. They see themselves as winning or losing a quarter, a fiscal year, or a market. They usually perceive the impact of doing business as limited to raw materials, products, and services. Businesses know who their competitors are, what rules and regulations bind each other's actions, and what they are fighting over. When building their assumptions, the vast majority of businesses are not including the fact that they're operating within an ecological biosphere that enables the economy within which they play their game. Many costs, such as pollution or societal impact of the business, are pushed onto the ecology or society. These are known as "externalities" that are not recorded in the scores of the finite game. This can have negative impacts on the structure within which the business operates and, if the destruction is too severe, even end the play of the finite players.

Governments are supposed to bridge market failures and play the infinite games that enable businesses and citizens to play benign finite games, but too often they get sucked into the finite game of elections, losing sight of the bigger picture in favor of securing short-term finite wins. On the individual level, imagine a workaholic who ends up having a health scare, which awakens them to the fact that their finite game (their career) is jeopardizing their infinite game (their life), leading them to seek better work-life balance.

Preserving the balance between ecology and civilization is an infinite game, so for businesses to ever develop truly sustainable practices they must realize the game they are playing within is infinite—and that the end of the infinite game ends all finite games within it. The tragedy is that if we lose the infinite game of civilization within an ecological biosphere, all the finite games of the economy along with our personal wants, hopes, and dreams are canceled, and no further play is possible.

When envisioning the ideal future, outside of the paradigm and rules of the finite game, you can

- Perceive the impacts of your actions on the ongoing game, which enables you to better play the series of finite games within it.

- See the complexities and underlying trends of the environment you're playing in and better understand how multiple finite games relate to each other within the broader infinite game.

- Align your goals and mission to the infinite game so you're not starting a new venture within the limits of the current paradigm, or following the same trodden path that further contributes to the downfall of civilization. Instead, initiate a finite game that's *in service of* the infinite one—reaching sustainable human activities, impacting people's lives for the better, and enabling civilization to not only continue but *thrive like never before*.

What game do you want to play? Consider this an invitation to think about your life and place in history as part of an infinite game.

The other people you play with are also invited, and you can help others set aside the inherent limitations and dissatisfaction of playing us-versus-them and zero-sum games. These zero-sum setups are subtractive, not additive, not to mention inaccurate when the bigger picture is in view. It's okay to play smaller finite games within the infinite game; just know that you're doing it, and align it to the interests of at least not harming, if not nurturing the larger context within which you play.[2]

It's said that you miss 100% of the shots you don't take. Even a hard-working optimist who achieves only 10% of her goals has made greater strides than a cynic who is correct in his inaction or failures every time.

When we're imagining ideals and our desires to achieve greatness, unshielded by cynicism, we may be more vulnerable, but because we're more affected by the wrongs we see in the world, we also emerge unable to stand by and allow them to continue. These are appropriate responses to such problems. These feelings are vastly preferable to being apathetic about sad states of affairs, and therefore complicit in them.

Visualizing the Positive Will Shift Your Brain

From a psychological standpoint, when we envision positive outcomes instead of negative ones, we experience a fundamental change in our mental state. We shift from being governed by the *amygdala* within the limbic system of the brain, which is often called the "lizard brain." This is the area of the brain that governs emotions and memory regulation; it is responsible for the fight-or-flight reaction that gets activated in stressful situations, and it reminds you to fear situations where you've experienced danger or difficulty in the past. In a fearful or dangerous situation, your brain actually redirects resources to the amygdala and away from the frontal cortex, which manages higher reasoning. This reaction is known as *amygdala hijacking*.[3] Continued exposure to high levels of the stress hormone cortisol can even shrink the size of your brain, worsen visual perception, and damage memory.[4]

If you're thinking about your mortality because of climate change, social collapse, environmental degradation—all good reasons to be anxious—and you cynically decide there's nothing that can be done about them, you enter a mental state that actually makes you less able to think long-term, communicate with nuance, or be creative. Your brain limits the amount of energy available for creativity because it's worried about survival. By default, you will choose actions based on caution, fear, and self-preservation—actions that can be extreme. You either run as fast as you can, hit as hard as you can, or hide as quietly as you can. There is little room to listen to another perspective or meaningfully consider it. We can also appease in our social interactions, trying to calm down threatening people or animals so we can survive the encounter unscathed. But with this one-way approach, there's no way to peacefully instigate a mutually fair exchange, either. Essentially, cynicism limits your psychological resources, perspective, and potential.

When you take a positive approach that builds on visioning from a place of safety and positive outlook, envisioning the abundant outcomes you want, you'll engage more of your brain and more of its creative parts. This is what Katie Patrick, author of *How to the Save the World*, calls the "positive constructive imagination."

It catalyzes a feedback loop of dopamine rewards every step of the way as you get excited about a vision, attract people to your cause, and begin building that future.[5] Simply asking "What could go right?" gives you access to more options and frees you from fear so you can generate more desirable visions, products, movements, and possibilities, while being better able to consider a wider variety of options and perspectives. This happens because you feel safe. It opens the door to feeling inspired and engaged. You'll do more energizing work, be better at it, feel happier doing it, accomplish more of it, and have more meaning in your life.

Anyone who has seen a playground full of children knows it's undeniable that human beings are innately creative and energetic. When we are in a free, creative, and playful mindset, we feel more energized. We are freed up to be innovative and confident in instigating big things. We become more courageous in the face of changes and challenges.

When doing visioning activities, by turning them into creative play you can activate this sequence:

- Make a game of accomplishing your dreams and visions, and as new areas of your brain become available to you, you'll become more *excited* to think up positive visions.

- Because you're impassioned and inspired, and can see your vision playing out in the broader context, you'll become more *engaged*.

- You'll inject a lot more *energy* into your activities and communication.

- Finally, with new meaning behind your actions and a feeling that you're working on a problem of great importance, you'll become more *effective*.

The sequence is as infinite as the game, of course. As you play your infinite game, your view will become broader in context. *You will be better able to predict what's coming down the road simply because you're also* building *what's down the road*. Rather than just waiting for the future to happen or betting on what's going to occur, you are creating it. While a cynic can feel certain that we are all doomed, and justify complacency because of that feeling, you can feel that a better world is likely on the way because you're busy building it.

Seeing Into the Future You Will Create

When we look at ways of predicting the future path we should take in business, there's often a decision tree model[6] that says, "Okay. I've got options (A) or (B). If I choose option (A), what is the probability that either (a) would happen or (b) would happen? Then if I choose (b), what is the probability that (aa) will happen versus the probability that (bb) will happen?" You do this until you have a whole tree of many different decisions, outcomes, and risks, and then you figure out the most likely and advantageous outcome. Although a decision tree can be a great tool for planning and strategy, like much predictive data, it's also a disempowered way of looking at the world, because it focuses on circumstances and leaves you and your commitment completely out of the equation.

To follow along with probabilities like this, you'd have to be a disimpassioned robot algorithm. But with a vision in mind, you're dedicated to it, and more likely to inspire others to join your cause, so you're changing the probabilities and likelihoods all along that decision tree. When you plan for success and act in accordance with your vision, you make the desired outcome more probable. This will happen one way or the other, as you can't remove the human element from these predictions or plans. So don't let your cynicism try to predict exactly what's going to happen as if you don't have a role to play in it.

Choose the future vision you want to live in, and change those probabilities along the decision tree. This helps you create that future. Choose the lens through which you see the world, choose your frame, choose the game that you play. It's all up to you. You're playing a game one way or the other. But by setting a vision, you're more in control of which games you want to engage in, and you can be more deliberate about how you play. Then there will be a long-term path and strategy for accomplishing goals for the sake of humanity. Ultimately, we all have a stake in whatever you do. So ensure that your biggest stakeholders—humanity and the planet— will thrive as a result of your vision.

There's an Important Place in the Process for All Styles

How can we work together to envision or create something? A lot of the conflict that we think is fundamental to groups really comes down to a clash of styles. We each seem to experience each stage in the processes of creating, innovating, and changing differently. When we recognize that everyone's style contributes at some step along the way, conflict decreases. For example, if creative exploration in the beginning of a project isn't the way you enjoy thinking—if instead you enjoy figuring out why something won't work—don't worry, there's a time in the process for your type of thinking to add a great deal of value.

A helpful platform and work style assessment and model for thinking about what steps in the process of carrying out a project you are energized by and have strengths in is called Simpli5, offered by a company called 5 Dynamics, whose clients include Harvard, LinkedIn, and IDEO.[7, 8] The dynamics, or paths, in the process go like this:

1. **EXPLORE:** These are the creative people who love scouting out beyond the normal boundaries of everyday thinking. They think in holistic systems, sense relationship dynamics, and develop creative solutions.

2. **EXCITE:** People who are all about the people, networking, learning what makes others tick, and getting them excited about joining the team, getting people on board with the vision, and bringing people together.

3. **EXAMINE:** Examiners love to analyze, organize, and keep to schedules. They enjoy the puzzle of finding everything wrong with ideas, where the risks lie, and how problems might lead to failures. They like taking things apart, seeing how they work, and then putting them back together again, often with improvements.

4. **EXECUTE:** What energizes this group of people the most is, for lack of a better term, getting shit done. They want to check off the to-do list as fast as they can create them, measure performance, and hold themselves and others accountable to complete their commitments.

5. **EVALUATE:** This dynamic is not measured. However, it is a critical part of the overall process. This dynamic

is focused on continuous improvement and the key to success is to evaluate from the previous four dynamics, not just your preferred dynamics.

Breaking down the process this way makes it easy to see the value that everyone brings to the table. Without explorers, there would be no vision; without exciters, no one would know about it; without examiners, we would choose foolish paths; and without executors, we would still be meeting indefinitely to decide what we are *going* to do. Everyone has a role to play and a time to play it.

However, these differences in preferences are a key source of conflict on teams, whose members often jump around to different parts of the process based on individual preferences, making the team as a whole less effective. Thinking through this framework has three potential benefits. First, you will better understand which part of the process you enjoy and which step to bring your strengths to the table. Second, it will help you to accept the people who do not think the same way as you, support them, and allow them to shine when it is their time. Third, you will learn context that will help you interpret their ideas through your lens, engage with them during their part of the process, and be able to own your part when it's your time.

It doesn't matter whether you're an *executor*, who gets annoyed by people sitting around brainstorming all day (you just want to get moving!) or an *examiner*, who naturally sees all the different ways that each of these brainstormed visions is *not* going to work. There's a time for you in the stages that assess feasibility and viability. But during the exploration stage, free yourself to try brainstorming and have fun with it, or be okay staying quiet and letting others work out their part in the process. You'll have something to analyze later, and when you do, you'll have more background and a more interesting puzzle to analyze.

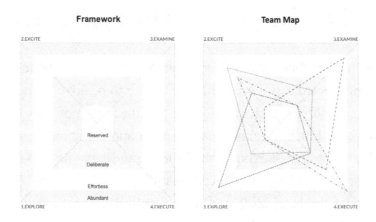

The Simpli5(R), 5 dynamics framework (left), with outlines of team members' scores overlaid as different lines (right) to show areas of overlap and complement to each other. A well-balanced team can be high-performing, but also create conflict due to different personalities getting energized from different aspects or phases of the work needed to complete a project. Understanding these differences and recognizing the value each team member brings to the team can alleviate conflict and enhance productivity.

If you are someone who is more excitement-focused, this framework will help you know when it is time for you to break out your metaphorical (or literal) pom-poms. You'll get people excited about the team's ideas so they can support whatever part of the process or project gets them invigorated. Just don't take anything and run too far with it yet, because it does need to be analyzed in order to be made feasible and viable.

Knowing that different styles relate to building a vision in specific ways can drastically reduce conflict between group members. When we make space for each step in the process, we can not only reduce conflict but also help people be more effective according to their own style. When teams can empathize with each other to recognize the value in all the steps, members are less likely to give in to the urge to change the process, grow cynical about any part of the project and people, or insist everyone skip ahead to their part of it.

The Gold Standard for Innovation

We've established that envisioning the positive outcome and working toward it is a more effective route to positive change and successful outcomes than following the linear path of cynicism or status quo. Much psychological research and many business case studies show that starting with the ideal, and most desirable, outcome is the best way to achieve true innovation.

Design thinking, developed at the Stanford d.school, is one of the most widely used models of product design, and can even be used for business, communication, or new systems design. Experts who've studied how to build products and businesses with this framework all agree that outcomes are better when we start with understanding the people we are designing for and we envision the ideal and most desirable scenarios. This Venn diagram summarizes the process.

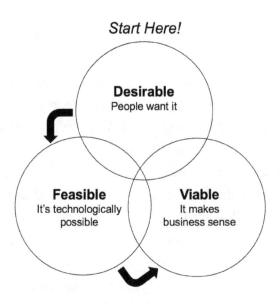

Design thinking seeks to unleash creativity by starting with what people want, without other constraints, then narrowing down to what is technologically feasible, and then if a business can be built to support development, support, and scale.

All successful projects, products, or services need to be desirable, feasible, and viable, and that order is deliberate—they always start with desirability. Feasibility asks the question, "Can it technically be done?" If you start any effort with feasibility, you limit yourself to your known or existing technologies, methods, and systems. You're not creating any new ways of creating a solution, nor are you looking outside your current understanding of what is possible. Viability asks the question, "What will be financially sustainable?" If you start with viability, you're first asking what customers are willing to pay for and how the project can be supported as a business. This also limits your field of view and will cause you to miss potentially revolutionary solutions and business models if you haven't figured out what people really want first.

When you start with desirability, you're asking, "What do people really want?" Freed from the constraints of feasibility and viability, you can imagine the ideal future, product, or solution. This will also force you to rethink what the underlying want or need is, not the existing product to meet that need. As Amory Lovins, a thought leader in the field of sustainability and coauthor of *Natural Capitalism*, is fond of saying: "People don't want oil and electricity; they want hot showers and cold beer." Once you've truly figured out what people want, you can then assess the gap between the technology available today and what needs to be built (feasibility), and then how much it will cost you to build versus how much people are willing to pay you for it (viability).

This approach is used by most major tech companies and successful product developers. It's a gold standard for design of just about any product, service, or system, and it can also be applied to social change. If you just follow historical design standards— whether for cars, apps, surgical tools, or great social causes—you're missing an opportunity to build a better future with a better lived experience for all who use your design. When you're envisioning a new product experience or a new social experience, you can imagine it as part of someone's ideal world. They are going to be impacted by this experience, and you can empathetically create the ideal experience.

Part Two of this book shares ideas for the kind of future you may want to design for. But first, let's look at why today's problems make this moment in time a perfect opportunity to get excited about meaningfully working to create the future you want to live in.

Part One

THE PERFECT CRISIS FOR CHANGE IS UPON US

WE THROW THE WORD "CRISIS" AROUND PRETTY casually these days, but it holds potent meaning. It comes from the Greek word *krinein*, which describes the absolute final moment a doctor has to decide which action to take to treat a patient. Past that point, the patient will die. There's been time leading up to a crisis, but suddenly if doctors don't take bold action, treat the patient, and decisively intervene, the patient will die. This describes where we're at today. Complacency and following the status quo for our society is likely to lead the patient—human civilization—to falter, largely die off, or even become extinct.

In meteorology, a perfect storm is the result of a unique combination of rare phenomena coming together to aggravate conditions. The issues we face as global, national, and local communities are coming together to create a perfect storm. I'm taking this common metaphor a step further by calling this a time in which we're facing the *perfect crisis*. True to the Greek origin of the word, these conditions are brewing all at once—and if we don't act to profoundly change things in this time of crisis, we could face collapse at all levels. But the good news is that the size of the opportunity is equal to the size of the challenge. The solutions to this crisis will also pave the way toward a more vibrant, thriving, inclusive world.

The trends of our time are coming together in exciting ways that make this decade perfect for nurturing the beginning of a major transition. Innovation is happening with great speed, breadth, and magnitude across almost every sector of our economy and society. The number of tools available to us, and our collective urgency for a more sustainable, just world has exploded, bringing disruption to existing structures, assumptions, and traditions long held by businesses, governments, and ourselves. If we move toward our ideal future quickly and effectively, we can finally overcome challenges that have held us back for decades. The perfect crisis is the moment when change is most ripe. That moment is now—let's discuss why and how we can seize it.

Chapter 2

Good News:
The World Has Gotten Better

DESPITE ALL OF THESE CRISES, THE WORLD IS actually in better shape than we think. We have already created a world that would be considered a utopia by those who came before us. Today, conditions that were utopian just centuries or even decades ago have become an everyday experience that we accept as normal. Consider the difference almost two centuries of innovations have made on key aspects of our lives (these are worldwide statistics).[1]

	1820	2015
EXTREME POVERTY	94%	10%
BASIC EDUCATION	17%	86%
LITERACY	12%	85%
VACCINATION	0%	86%
DEMOCRACY	1%	56%
CHILD MORTALITY	41%	4%

While Europe industrialized and reached a high living standard fairly early compared to other regions, it took several hundred years to occur, beginning with the Renaissance. It has taken more than a century for the US to get to where it is today. But China and Southeast Asia have pulled a billion people out of poverty within a couple of decades, showing how quickly change is accelerating. What's going to happen next in India, Africa, and the rest of the world? Not only are we able to do more, we're able to do it in a shorter period of time.

But we don't have to measure progress over centuries. Our world has changed for the better even in recent decades. The rates of extreme poverty, hunger, child labor, child mortality, death in childbirth, smoking, homicide, violent crime, nuclear arms stockpiles, and costs of clean energy have gone down significantly across the globe. At the same time, positive trends are rising: leisure time, life expectancy, education levels, literacy, and access to the internet.[2] But over and over we see examples of a disconnect between how people perceive the world and what is actually happening.

Perception Has Diverged from Reality

Since the mid-1990s through today, around 60% of Americans report believing that crime had increased in the preceding year, during one of the steepest declines in crime in history. In fact, violent crime in the period 1993 to 2015 decreased from 80 per 1,000 to 20 per 1,000.[3] This is also true throughout most of the developed world in Europe, Asia, Australia, and New Zealand.[4] The year 2020 did show distressing increases: about 3% for violent crime and 25% for murder; only time will tell whether our recent peace will hold, but these crime rates and those of 2021 were still far below the peaks of the 1990s.[5] (We will discuss strategies to reduce this in Chapter 8.)

In a 2019 study on race relations in the US, a majority of respondents, both Black and white, felt that race relations were bad (58%) and getting worse, especially after the election of Donald Trump (56%).[6] However, despite the fact that some racist people and rhetoric are more visible and vocal than ever, we've made enormous strides on racial equality for several decades, and we are continuing to improve on this front—although changes are still not happening fast enough. Positive gains against racism do not mean we should ever dismiss that it still occurs and that it is harmful or even deadly. We need to continue to press for change with urgency and not let despair lead us to hopelessness.

Improvements over recent decades have been steady—in 1942 only 32% of white Americans agreed that whites and Blacks should attend the same schools; by 1995, 95% agreed. We see similar magnitudes of positive change for interracial marriage, voting for a Black president, and support for the statement that Black people should have "as good a chance as white people to get any kind of job." However, we have also seen a rise in hate crimes, including against Latino and Jewish people, which hit a sixteen-year high in 2019.[7] This included sharp rises in hate crimes against Asian Americans after the rise of COVID-19.[8] The vast majority of Americans today would find it reprehensible that there is even any percentage of the population who doesn't strongly support racial and ethnic equality. But we must also recognize the progress we've made on this front, if for no other reason than to have hope and determination for the remaining struggle ahead. Learning how progress was made in the past can also give us examples to follow as we move equality forward in our time.

In relation to poverty, a study found that 52% of people believed poverty was rising, when in fact global poverty has declined over the last few decades and this trend is actually accelerating in recent years.[9] According to the same survey, 61% of people believed child mortality had stayed the same or increased, at a time when in reality it dropped by half over the last two decades, even in the least developed countries.[10]

When asked if the world is getting better, only a tiny fraction of people tend to respond yes, from 3% in France and Australia, to 6% in the US and 11% in Thailand. In developing countries people tend to have a more positive view of progress. In Indonesia and China, for example, 23% and 41% (respectively) responded yes. This may be due to steady economic growth in those countries, and an appreciation for new conveniences and resources that people in developed countries would expect to have. Similar to the progress listed in the opening of this chapter, when we zoom out, we can see that the overarching trend of progress in both our global society and local communities is extremely positive.

The Effect of the Internet as Global Witness

So if things are generally getting better in so many ways, why do we continue to think we're living in such a terrible and progressively worsening time? One reason we're at a point of so much conflict is that massive amounts of information are being shared about what's actually happening in our world—information that previous generations were not privy to. With the advent of technologies like smartphones, body cams, instantaneous sharing, and live streaming, more of us can see what's going on and instantly share it with local and global communities. Websites and news channels that shape our views of the world get paid for clicks and views, which are increased by sensationalism and extreme viewpoints. Adding to the challenge are the algorithms that decide what information we see, feed us more of what we click on, and drive us deeper into rabbit holes of fear-inducing or extreme information.

As we have seen in the widespread protests of recent years, many people are fed up, disenchanted, and angry about the inadequacy of yesterday's world to meet the needs of today's humanity, let alone our future. Much of this is driven by increased visibility into our problems. One example is the growing awareness of police brutality. It's not as if some police had just recently started discriminating against, violently harassing, and attacking Black people in 2020 when mass protests for George Floyd started and Black Lives Matter became a movement. While it has been happening for hundreds of years, it is getting harder and harder for authorities to keep this behavior out of the view of all communities, even if it's been apparent to disenfranchised communities for centuries. This visibility is at the heart of our perception that things are terrible, because our eyes are more open to the suffering, catastrophes, and unfairness that we may not have known about or paid attention to in the past. Yet visibility is a positive step, because it creates accountability, which is the first step to change.

We Perceive So Many Crises in Part Because There's So Much Change

There's conflict in change. And right now, we're going through a large transition, composed of many smaller changes. Whether we're talking about national politics, social and economic models, individual experiences or companies, so much of our world is in transition . . . and conflict. When trying to better understand how these transitions and conflicts work, I find the 3 Horizons model (based on the work of Anthony Hodgson and Bill Sharp) to be a helpful framework.

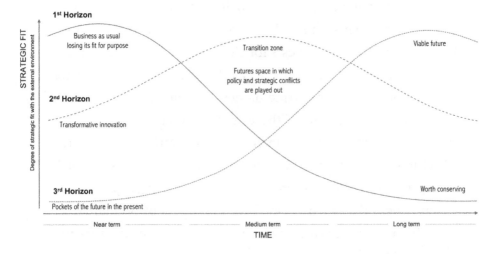

As business as usual begins to lose its fit for purpose (1st horizon), new innovations arise to facilitate the transition (2nd horizon), while pockets of the future appear in the present that could lead to a new abundance (3rd horizon). During the transition however, conflict and competition between the status quo and new alternatives peak before superior alternatives replace the previous status quo to create a viable future. Some aspects of the old world may be worth conserving and continue on in the new future.

The *first horizon* is the status quo, and like any status quo, it will decrease in relevance and effectiveness over time if it can't adapt to change or the changing needs of people. The *third horizon* is the fresh alternative, the new reality, the plan for a better future. Around the world, there are people who see the inadequacy of our status quo and feel a sense of urgency to create that new future. Examples span the issues of fossil fuels versus renewable energy, hierarchical management versus distributed and empowered teams, analog versus digital tools and systems, car-centric urban design versus hybrid walkable and transit-connected "urban villages," race-to-the-bottom labor practices around the globe versus empowered employees with safe and healthy workplaces—the list goes on. If the alternative is truly better and more viable, people will like it better and choose it instead, leading that third horizon to increase over time. The *second horizon* is the amount of conflict between the first (status quo) and third (the new and different future). As the first horizon declines and the third horizon increases, they reach a point of maximum conflict before adherents to the old paradigm see the benefits of the new one and finally embrace it.

No one can say for sure which aspects of our society are at this point of maximum conflict, approaching it, or just over the hump, but the tension and conflict between the old era and the new definitely seem to be on the rise. We do know that we are in crisis, in so many different areas of society, in many different sectors, and among social movements.

To illustrate, let's consider this 3 Horizons model in terms of fossil fuels versus sustainable forms of energy and transportation. When oil and coal came to dominate the industrial age, basically no one even gave a thought to sustainability—they focused instead on how to power a machine or move a locomotive. But as we discovered that the climate was changing due to our activities, sustainability entered our worldview, and it began threatening the market dominance of existing players. Efforts for sustainability were attacked defensively and proactively. Among other tactics, the oil industry funded disinformation research campaigns and tried to convince people that climate change wasn't happening or wasn't caused by human activities, in order to protect their business interests.[11]

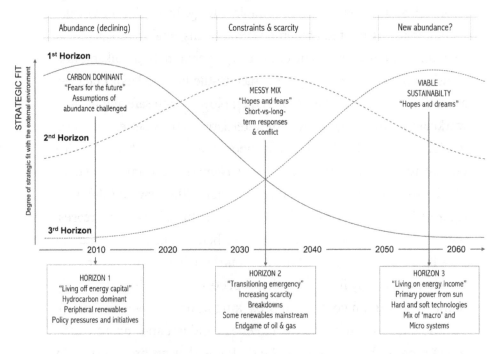

As the 1st horizon (business as usual) goes into decline, the 2nd Horizon (disruptive innovation) rises along with the conflict of scarcity, constraints, and new alternative solutions. As the new alternatives begin to become the norm, the 3rd horizon (emerging future) eventually rises and the 1st horizon dies out or peters out. This example shows the tension between declining unsustainable carbon resources (1st horizon) and rapidly rising sustainable energy and resources (3rd horizon), with the rising conflict of the transition (2nd horizon).

Between 1998 and 2005, ExxonMobil spent $16 million on advocacy organizations that sought to confuse the public on climate science.[12] In 1998 a $6 million campaign was also executed on behalf of major fossil fuel companies and the American Petroleum Institute, to mislead "a majority of the American public" that "significant uncertainties exist in climate science," also employing "independent scientist" operatives, think tanks, and public relations professionals to create the Global Climate Science Communication plan to spread disinformation.[13] It also undercut climate treaties like the Kyoto Protocol.[14] This is also a great example of companies playing the finite game (protecting their companies' short term financial interests) at the cost of the infinite game (stability of human civilization on Earth).

The conflict is still ongoing, but many companies and organizations are finally acknowledging that in addition to the climate benefits, it just makes good business sense to use renewable energy sources. For example they reduce long-term risk, provide new business opportunities, provide customers what they want, reduce fuel costs, reduce public backlash, and help enhance brand perception. As the general public has grown to recognize the value of clean energy, and its costs have plummeted, the topic has become less politicized. Renewables have become cheaper than coal and gas in many US states.[15] In fact, the conservative US state of Texas leads the country in nonhydroelectric renewable power, producing one-fifth of the total US utility scale energy, and more than one-fourth of US wind energy.[16] Some oil companies are investing in this pivot, such as BP, which announced in 2020 it would slash oil production by 40% and invest $5 billion in bioenergy, hydrogen, carbon capture, and electric vehicle charging points by 2030, while divesting $25 billion from its oil and gas refining business over five years.[17]

While renewable energy is moving up the curve on the second horizon and passing the maximum conflict stage, many of the examples I offer in this chapter are only now approaching it. The conflicts over them will get worse before they get better. For example, take the idea of universal basic income (UBI), in which people receive a certain amount of money on a regular basis, similar to Social Security but for all ages (we'll explore this in more depth in later chapters). The idea is not new; in fact, Martin Luther King Jr. was a proponent.[18] The concept was recently brought into the public consciousness, mostly thanks to Andrew Yang's 2020 presidential platform.

Despite the many potential benefits for society, if the momentum continues and UBI becomes more popular, there will likely be more conflict around it. This is because, like many of the examples in this chapter, basic income requires a mind-shift from systems that primarily benefit the centralized power we are so used to seeing around us to a more distributed, people-based economy. Many of these emerging economic models are more humanistic; they recognize the human element of an economy differently from the lenses we've been trained to see the world through. There's going to be a big conflict between the forces of established centralized power and the decentralized networks of empowered people of the future. This is similar to the struggle that occurred over the creation of Social Security, which was a radical—and some at the time thought reckless—program before it was signed into law by Franklin D. Roosevelt in 1935.[19] Similarly, UBI will need to be paid for, and if not done through some new money system like cryptocurrency, it may come at the expense of other government expenditures or require new sources of revenue—never a popular change for those footing the bill.

As I shared in Chapter 1, we can avert disaster and get to a better world much faster with the right visions for where we want to head. We waste time by staying too long in the conflict zone and fighting the opposition without a plan for what to build or energy left to build it. Add to this the increasing distractions of social media, entertainment, and 24-hour news, which makes us liable to lose focus and move on to battling the next conflict before we solve the causes of the last one. This in itself could be disastrous, because in our perfect crisis, we are short on time as it is, and we have limited resources to help us succeed.

It's Our Turn to Pioneer Positive Change

As we move forward to create an even better world than we believe possible today, we might imagine people further in the future looking back on us much as we look back on the Old American West. Not much more than a century ago, it had lawless bandits, manifest-destiny mentality that reinforced social and economic disparities, and forceful takeover of the land from its long-established inhabitants. Imagine traveling back in time, pulling up a stool at a bar in the Old American West to tell the people that within a century their tiny two-street town would become a sparkling city with serenely peaceful streets by comparison, that the diseases plaguing them would be long eradicated, that a global information network similar to a brain would connect all of humanity, and that most future Americans were able to fly around the world to enjoy visiting foreign lands. Now imagine the dismissive looks, and laughs, you would get for sharing this vision, not to mention a potential invite to a shootout at high noon.

The human experience a century into our future could easily sound just as incredible (and implausible) to us today. In a way, we're facing similar magnitudes of change, as well as the upheavals or conflicts that come along with that. If we can suspend our disbelief and envision a dramatically better world, we can actually achieve it sooner, assisted by the ongoing exponential development of technology, collective memory shared over generations and distance through books and the free global communication of the internet. Now let's explore these converging trends and megatrends so we can see the hope, and opportunity that's peeking above the horizon.

Chapter 3

Better News: A Changing World Is Full of Opportunities

OUR OLD WEST TRIP TO EXPLAIN THE MODERN world didn't go so well. Now imagine a visitor from 2100 explaining their world to us and how it came about. What patterns or similarities would you notice in how change was made? What kinds of events or innovations do you think catalyzed change and moved us forward?

Today we see technology all around us. It's on an exponential path of growth and advancement, with every new year showing us people who are inventing, creating, and enhancing technology at a mind-boggling rate. It's not only becoming more sophisticated and widespread, delivered into the hands of more people, but the costs of technology are actually plummeting. Whether it's computing power or artificial intelligence (AI) enabled devices, services, and data, technology is exploding. And with this explosion of technology meeting an explosion of need for solutions comes immense opportunity—for impact and for entrepreneurs.

You've likely heard a tech-buzzword soup about AI, blockchain, and the internet of things (IoT). By exploring what they are and how they're coming together for societal change, we can wrap our heads around what's happening and where we're headed. The burgeoning amount and variety of data in our world can feel overwhelming. Nearly everything electronic is giving off data that can be used to better understand how to manage a building, traffic, or parking; serve people more relevant ads; or change insurance premiums based on how well people are driving. These sensors, business and academic records, video files, machines, GPS location records, smart infrastructure like streetlights or traffic lights, mobile phones, and the amount of data they produce are feeding the ever more advanced and self-learning data science that we call AI, which in turn is being trained to become more advanced by the ever larger oceans of data. Everyone and everything is leaving behind a growing data trail for AI to analyze.

In his book *Life 3.0*, Max Tegmark says that in the first Industrial Revolution, we decoupled muscle from the human body or working animals, by making machines that did physical work. This liberated many of us from repetitive, dangerous, and unhealthy tasks, allowing us to specialize in more interesting work, leading to new innovations and business models. AI is enabling the decoupling of time-consuming or tedious thought processes from human beings so machines can carry the mental weight. AI-driven applications now go far beyond simply being faster calculators, unleashing amazing innovations capable of doing the grunt work that bores our minds, poring over immense amounts of research and information to distill the important insights we need to make decisions—and in so doing, enabling us—at least in theory—to not only accomplish more but to be the masters of our own time and mental space.

AI and IoT: Machines That Sense and React to the World

The best (and possibly nerdiest) guidance I've heard about AI is: "If it's called machine learning, it's probably coded in Python. If it's called AI, it's probably coded in PowerPoint." There is a lot of hype surrounding AI, much of it in the form of slick marketing PowerPoint presentations, so let's quickly define what it is we're talking about.

- **ARTIFICIAL INTELLIGENCE (AI):** The umbrella term for any machines that can "think," using mathematical algorithms and data science in some way.

- **MACHINE LEARNING:** A subset of AI algorithms that pull in data to improve their understanding and can iterate and refine actions over time to improve. These can be supervised (trained with human help) or unsupervised by humans.

- **DEEP LEARNING:** A subset of machine learning whereby the machine improves itself without help or intervention from humans.

- **NEURAL NETWORKS:** A way of processing data that attempts to mimic the human brain's neural networks, whereby each "neuron" in the network processes information with different weights and passes it along to other neurons for more filtering before reaching world-changing conclusions, such as "this is a picture of a cat, and that one's a dog." All joking aside, the same seemingly trivial types of innovations could also be trained for more important tasks, such as quickly recognizing what is cancer and what is not.

There's plenty of reason for hype. Moore's law is a widely known observation that the number of transistors on a microchip doubles every two years, while the cost drops by half. Every time we run up against a wall and declare that Moore's law is dead, a new innovation changes the way we go about designing and producing microprocessors and puts us back on the trend line eventually—the most recent potential game changer being carbon nanotubes.[1]

A relatively new but similar measure called *algorithmic efficiency*, or Moore's law for machine learning, assesses how much compute power is required by an AI to complete a task. A study found that this efficiency doubles every 16 months, actually outpacing Moore's law.[2] An example of this is image-recognition computer vision, which in 2019 needed just 2.3% of the computing power required in 2012 to complete the same task. It performed forty-three times better in just seven years! In addition, total computing power used by AI since 2012 has been growing *seven times faster* than posited by Moore's law, effectively multiplying the total power of AI in terms of total use, speed, and efficiency of resource use.

The evolution of AI is almost like a growth of an organism, as evolution originates with beings capable of self-sustaining and sensing the world around them. One day, long ago, a single-celled organism swallowed a smaller cell, which somehow survived. This smaller cell entered into a relationship with the larger one, taking in nutrients from the larger cell and providing its host with energy in return (the scientists who discovered this named it *mitochondria*). Once this larger cell had more energy, it started to grow sensors— tiny hairs and appendages—to understand the world around it. Later generations developed eyes to see and ears to hear. Through evolution, senses developed to the point of, say, the impressive visual faculties of an eagle, capable of seeing prey miles away. A similar progression is occurring in the machine and digital world. With all the information out there, coming from more and more sources, AI is growing more capable of making sense of that information. It used to be that I needed to type code to speak to a machine, but now I can simply talk to it. It will interpret those sounds, convert them into language in the written word, and then store them or take an action. Speech recognition is a commonly known form of AI, which has resulted in everyday digital assistants like Siri and Alexa.

By our giving awareness to nonhuman intelligence, machines can now sense the world. Through 3D LiDAR (light detection and ranging), lasers act as a kind of radar or sonar that gathers information from the world by measuring how long it takes for hundreds or thousands of lasers to bounce back from objects; then a computer-vision AI reads those 3D, real-time maps of the world (if you've ever seen an autonomous vehicle, those are the spinning cylinders). Like an organism with sensory faculties, the AI can now "see" what's physically happening. This has many uses, such as automatically counting and measuring people's bags as they board a plane. That is the most chaotic part of the boarding process and can lead to a lower on-time performance for airlines. With AI assistance, airlines can predict when they're going to run out of overhead space, so they start requiring people to check their bags rather than carry them on. This makes boarding faster and more efficient, and airlines gain better on-time performance and a better customer experience. The industry as a whole and our individual travel experiences can be boosted because a machine was able to perceive, analyze, and predict to give people more information. And some poor soul didn't have to stand there counting and measuring bags one at a time.

Another application is in smart cities. In the past, once every ten or fifteen years, cities put somebody out on a corner with a clipboard, a pen, and a tally counter. They counted every car that came by, and then they created a report for policy decisions—whether they should increase or decrease the time at a red light, speed limits, parking time limits, number of lanes, and so on. With computer vision on traffic cameras, those AIs can now understand the differences between vehicles; they can count the number of cars, trucks, buses, bikes, and other vehicles on the street and give us granular and continuous information about how the streets are being used. This provides better information for these policy decisions, as well as new matters like where to put in more bike lanes, change traffic lights based on real-time conditions, or take out a parking spot and put in a passenger-loading zone for an Uber or Lyft so double-parked cars aren't jamming up the streets.

This results in a dynamic or responsive city that more quickly iterates on policies and actions that improve our lives. It's one step toward establishing predictive cities where we know the likelihood of certain things happening. We will be able to change and respond to these probabilities to prevent negatives like accidents or crime, or encourage more positives, such as transportation options that reduce pollution and traffic, community events that help businesses thrive, and public health choices that help us live longer and healthier lives. In the transition that's taking place, the physical world itself starts thinking and either gives us better information to make smarter choices ourselves or simply takes action for us.

Blockchain: What Is Disintermediation, and How Will It Bring Everyone Into the Network?

When most of us hear "blockchain," we think of cryptocurrency or Bitcoin, but there are many more uses for it outside of money. With smart contracts, for example—which is what platforms like

Ethereum enable—machines or software can execute agreements and transactions between each other automatically. Today these are carried out by an apparatus of legal, financial, and insuring institutions to ensure trust between the people or organizations involved and to reduce their risk. But smart contracts work without the involvement of a third party or intermediary institution. Blockchains are stored not in a centralized database but in all computers, phones, or other nodes in the network, so it is difficult, if not impossible, to destroy, manipulate or hack them.

I caught up with Brad Davis, Blockchain Product Manager at Chainlink Labs, to ask his opinion on the topic and hear his vision for the potential of blockchain. Brad offered an inspiring vision on the potential impact of this technology, saying,

> Blockchain and the decentralized automation it enables is in its infancy. While Bitcoin is widely known around the world, the implications of smart contracts and distributed autonomous organizations are not yet widely recognized in the public sphere. But these will have profound impacts on the way we are able to exchange value with each other in the future, and the relationship we have to centralized institutions. As these technologies simplify how we collaborate and transact with each other on a peer-to-peer or person-to-distributed-network basis, we will be compelled to reconsider our need for many of the established and most powerful organizations and industries we rely on today. There is immense opportunity for all of us in realizing this transition.

Blockchains can also offer value through *tokenization*. The way tokenization functions is as we go about an activity or create value, a secure token is created for that specific good or service and provided to the user, which can be traded to someone else to transfer ownership. Nonfungible tokens, or NFTs, have recently generated a ton of hype (and income) for many people, tokenizing ownership of digital goods and making that ownership easily tradable. But it's not the technology that's revolutionary here; rather, it's the change in how incentives and collaboration can be structured. This is very different from today's economic model of a few powerful centralized intermediaries like banks and platform companies that create currency, set rules or prices, and eliminate users at will.

Let's say you provide a ride for someone using a smart contract, and that action provides you a Rideshare token for your service; then as more people use that Rideshare token network, they make it more valuable, similar to owning shares in an increasingly successful company. But this isn't just a shiny badge; you're also cashing out on it and getting paid. If Uber or Lyft were built on a distributed network based on blockchain and smart contracts, you wouldn't need much of an organization to manage it, because the system itself could be self-regulating, and everyone who is either a driver or a rider is participating in that system, growing, maintaining, and owning it. Arcade City is one such emerging alternative based on the Ethereum blockchain. Drivers and riders cut out the middleman (Uber or Lyft) to negotiate price, build a reputation on the platform, and transact rides independently with smart contracts, creating what is sometimes called a *distributed autonomous organization* (DAO). Much like a video game, drivers and riders advance in level through work and reputation, reducing insurance rates for drivers, to ultimately offer safer and cheaper rides.[3]

Another example of this is the internet browser Brave, which pays users in Basic Attention Tokens (BAT) for their attention using the browser. Essentially, it blocks ads on websites but replaces them with ads from Brave's network. The ad revenue is then shared with publishers and users. Brave has chosen this *reverse advertising model* to pay the users with BAT that can be traded for premium services or for the user's local fiat currency (read: real money). Instead of today's model, where the user is kept out of the transaction except to buy products and services, they are compensated through the attention economy, which pays users for their attention—the value they're bringing to the interaction.[4] STEEM and HIVE are other blockchain tokens that pay bloggers and social media users to contribute content and engage with content, similar to getting paid from Medium or Facebook for your contributions to the other network users.[5]

Automation: Leaving the Boring Work to the Machines

What could you achieve in life if you were George Jetson, with a staff of intelligent robots to help you achieve your goals? With the combination of automation, AI, and blockchain technology, you can now actually go out and attain a goal. A company called Fetch.ai created what they call *autonomous economic agents*. They're able to take a goal or objective—say, something as simple as "I want to get my hair cut once a month, and I want the best price for it, but I also want good quality"—and help you achieve it. When you tell the autonomous economic agent to figure that out for you, it will search user ratings to find the highest ratings, then search for pricing, and then consider distance to find the most convenient place for you. Then it will share its recommendations, or simply tap into automated calendars, set up an appointment, and essentially achieve a goal for you. It'll be intelligent enough to sift through the right types of data and figure out the right actions to achieve that goal. If you come back from your haircut and say, "All right, this haircut was okay, but I'd like to try something else," you can train it to improve over time, like any other search algorithm or AI.

Automation can do many jobs for us, making each of us many times more productive. It's as if we have staff working for us, but the employees are all AI of some kind or autonomous economic agents. Over time, they are becoming more and more adept at doing human jobs. As more of the economy becomes digitized and automated, it will require fewer people to accomplish more of our economic activity, with more of an impact. But this is only the beginning. With automation, tasks and goals that require large administrative structures can be easily managed by one person. By deploying more DAOs in combination with widespread increases in automation, we've got another quantum leap in what is possible.

There is much fear and hyperbole around the automation of jobs, and there is good reason and evidence to be worried that many jobs will be automated. But there is also an opportunity to create many more jobs, and ones that are much more stimulating, empowering, and meaningful, while making goods and services more affordable and available to everyone. Perhaps we should even be celebrating the potential for liberation from boring work and economic desperation, while accelerating these new opportunities. The vast majority of jobs that are automatable today are tedious, repetitive work that takes a toll on the human body without providing much real interest or satisfaction. However, the jobs ripe for automation tomorrow are people's livelihoods today. Given our current expectations for people to work within our existing system in order to make the money needed to eat and pay for housing, transportation, and other necessities, we feel understandably concerned about AI's potential to take away jobs. It's true that the jobs likely to remain—that defy attempts to automate them—call on what we as human beings are really good at—being creative, innovative human beings, working with each other, and leveraging our creativity. Einstein envisioned us working two to four hours a week while technology did everything for us, powered by abundant nuclear energy. But absent UBI and strong social supports that enable people to take entrepreneurial risks, Einstein's vision remains elusive. This conundrum has generated a heated discussion; in 2019 Andrew Yang became the first politician to discuss it in depth and bring up basic income as a solution.

With different economic models, safety nets like UBI, affordable healthcare, and updated incentive structures, automation could be heralded as the best thing to happen to humanity yet. The COVID-19 pandemic also showed how providing emergency basic income can reduce suffering on a massive scale. The "labor shortages" of 2021 and 2022 may turn out to stem from both a need for wages to finally meet workers' needs after stagnating for decades, and for many an extended time away from work after a very stressful few years.

Either way, we need to reconcile the interests of workers and employers in a world of automation. Technology continues to be a two-sided coin: It can create incredible abundance and benefits for us, yet always seems to threaten how we've always done things. Truly terrifying repercussions—like extreme widespread poverty and the dissolution of social contracts leading to terrorism and civil wars—could come if we're unable to adjust to the future as much or as quickly as necessary, as individuals and as a society. But we can avoid this fate by enfranchising all and renewing social contracts.

Economic Enfranchisement: Democratizing Money

Currently, the central government prints money and distributes it to banks. Banks then choose which businesses, homeowners, or organizations they believe are worthy of loans. That money is then used for the agreed-upon purpose—funding a new business venture, buying a home or car, paying workers to perform tasks, or theoretically creating some value for the society and economy. But what is considered valuable is chosen by the banks, based on their risk appetite and investment thesis. The theory is that prices and interest returns accurately reflect value, and that means value will be compensated for as the market balances for everyone's benefit. But that theory doesn't stand up to scrutiny in many cases where much of the value provided by people is not compensated with money.

There are huge amounts of work, services, and production unmonetized and unrecognized as economic value. In fact, in our economy today it is difficult to assign value via the pricing mechanisms we use for some of the most important activities. Parenthood is a great example. Our economic system recognizes no value for motherhood, so what if mothers likewise decided children had no value because they didn't pay? Of course, this is absurd, but it points out that there is much more value than what is valued economically. How long would our society last if all mothers and fathers simply walked away from their unpaid parenting work? Probably not long at all, and definitely not longer than one generation. Yet regardless of this immense value, their work is unrecognized by the present economic mechanisms, and they often work one or more additional jobs in order to make enough money to pay for their cost of living.

In fact, only a small fraction of the value that people create in the world is actually compensated for with money. The Organization for Economic Co-operation and Development (OECD) estimates that on average 29% of the work that men do goes unpaid, while 49% of the work that women do goes unpaid.[6] In a sense this means that the activity of human life is not accurately valued by pricing mechanisms, with some dire consequences—everything from low self-esteem to poverty, poor health outcomes, to staying in abusive relationships.

A Career Builder study found that 78% of American workers live paycheck to paycheck, and 25% do not contribute to a savings account.[7] More than half of minimum-wage workers are working two or more jobs. Disenfranchisement from our economic system can lead to a poverty trap that causes health problems or even higher rates of death that can persist for generations.[8] While a very small number of people today live a post-scarcity lifestyle, with no unmet needs (but of course still some unmet wants), most people still live in a scarcity-based economy where it is difficult to get ahead, let alone take on the risk of entrepreneurship or following their passion.

Research indicates that countries and states with strong social safety nets actually enable their people to be more entrepreneurial and take more risks—and there's a lot of appetite to take these risks.[9] A study by the University of Phoenix found that 63% of people under thirty wanted to start a business.[10] The Deloitte Millennial Survey reports that 80 to 83% of millennials and Generation Z feel that business should be measured in terms of social and environmental impacts, in addition to making money.[11] They also want business to innovate, improve people's lives, and emphasize inclusion and diversity in the workplace. This seems like a perfect combination of entrepreneurship and innovation meeting a desire to make a positive social impact with business. But to take entrepreneurial risks and survive in the process, these people need money.

We are used to a world where either an investment bank or group of well-off people form a venture capital firm to invest in businesses that are highly screened. In this way our current relationship to money is very controlled. In 2020, venture capital invested $164 billion in 10,862 companies.[12] However, this funding is still highly competitive, and many good ideas and teams don't get funded.

More solutions than ever are coming from the crowd, whether it's crowdsourced engineering for apps, creating digital software to solve our greatest problems, or even finding and providing investment capital. Crowdfunding is seeing an incredible boom. In 2009, crowdfunding raised less than $2 billion globally.[13] By 2016, it amounted to more than $34 billion,[14] and it is projected to reach $300 billion in 2030.[15] This capital is also reaching more businesses, projects, and social causes, amounting to nearly 6.5 million of these in 2019.[16]

This shift to crowdfunding is happening with platforms like Wefunder or StartEngine allowing people to invest as little as $100 to help entrepreneurs fulfill their creative visions. And thanks to Title III of the JOBS act passing in 2016, equity crowdfunding has become available to regular people without $1 million in assets or annual salaries over $250k. This means that everyday investors not only contribute money to something they believe in but also gain some ownership in the startup companies they help fund.

This technology-enabled equity could lead to a more balanced ownership economy that makes more people stockholders and business owners, instead of simply employees—fueling innovation more democratically, which could help bring a collective vision of our shared future to reality. Rather than returning to the new Gilded

Age that some have predicted we are headed for, we could reverse this course and give more people a stake in the economy they support, in addition to interest income—the biggest source of wealth for the wealthy. With the ability to crowdfund and participate in the ownership of startups that will become the next billion-dollar companies, more people will have financial returns from the economy surrounding them, not just paychecks. These are also better returns, with venture capital outperforming the S&P 500 for the last decade, and making life-changing returns for many.[17]

While this also includes more risk, the return to an ownership economy lets us own a little bit of the store down the street or the app we use to get a delivery from one farther away, so we have a stake in its success, similar to the initial idea of the stock market. We're going to patronize that store or app, we're going to tell our friends about it, and we're also going to support it. We're in the very infancy of where all of this technology, ubiquitous information, and new tools can lead us. What's more exciting than any one of these on their own is the impact we can create when they all come together.

A Converging Picture of Everything

The future is most exciting when all the capabilities converge, as they have enormous implications for society and our daily lives. While today electrification, rates of internet access, smartphone penetration, and the sharing economy may seem like old news, they have laid a foundation for a dramatic expansion of impact, when combined with ubiquitous sensors, AI, smart contracts, circular economy processes, and transparency. As the cost of intelligence and automation decreases, we could see dramatic improvements in everything around us—if we harness our power of vision to create the future we want.

When I say "everything," I don't mean all things will magically change overnight. But over a long enough time scale, nearly every human-conceived system could change. The implications of these technologies could lead to profound improvements in our world, so it's helpful to understand the potential impacts and find the opportunities as we design for our ideal.

Electrified Everything

Electric machines and motors are vastly more efficient than those that run on fossil fuels. In cars, for example, the process of refining crude oil into gas and transporting it for use entails an energy loss (read: waste) of 56%—and that's before you use it! Converting and transporting electricity entails a loss of only 5%, depending on how far you live from the generation. With gasoline, once it's in your tank, getting that energy to turn your wheels loses another 70%, mostly through creating heat instead of torque. With an electric vehicle, you lose only about 18% if you include charging and inversion. This means that you use only 16% of your gasoline for its intended purpose of moving your vehicle, versus electricity using 77%.[18] Even hydrogen cars, while much better than gasoline, only use about 33% of their energy for moving the car.

But where is this all headed? I spoke with Peter Glenn, founder of EV Life and an expert in startups and electrification, from renewable energy projects in Africa to his work with Singularity University in Silicon Valley. According to Peter:

> The mass electrification of homes and transportation has myriad benefits. For homes, renewable energy growth is exploding, both at the utility scale and distributed household level. With better management of demand response through tools like virtual power plants, our electricity can be cleaner and more resilient. Advances in storage and microgrids are better able to manage the volatility of renewables today.
>
> On the transportation side, Americans are finally getting excited about electric vehicles' superior performance, increasing availability of models, and the ability to save more than $1,000/year on fuel and maintenance versus gas vehicles. EVs can also offer "vehicle-to-grid" capabilities that, if authorized by regulators, could stabilize strained electric grids, deliver cleaner electricity, and offset billions in stationary storage investment.
>
> Altogether, the proliferation of batteries in cars and buildings provides opportunities for energy exchanges and analytics to ensure we can deliver cheaper and 100% clean energy before 2050.

Electricity is also much less expensive: On average a gasoline vehicle costs around $0.15 per mile for a 22-mpg car, while electric averages around $0.03.[19] As our energy grids and homes shift to more renewable sources, this type of energy will only become cheaper and cleaner, helping to combat climate change. It also means not spewing poisonous gasses at breathing level throughout our cities.

So, from an efficiency, cost, and public health perspective, it just makes sense to switch to electric, as many industries are doing today.

To continue with the example of transportation, there is a dramatic shift (no pun intended) toward electrification across personal, public, and freight transportation. Tesla's sporty cars, personal trucks, and semi-trucks have dominated the headlines in recent years, but these are only a part of the story. In China, for example, electrification of transportation is already widespread. In 2019, there were 425,000 electric transit buses in operation around the world—421,000 of those were in China, where the number is projected to rise to 600,000 by 2025.[20] In the US, most public transit buses still run on fossil fuels, but it's projected that by 2045 at least one-third of the country's 70,000 buses will be electric, according to the US Public Interest Research Group (PIRG.)[21] Two of Chicago's electric buses save the city $24,000 in fuel every year, providing significant taxpayer and Chicago air-breather benefits. These are not isolated trends. In fact, the US National Renewable Energy Laboratory forecasts that as much as 76% of vehicle miles traveled in 2050 could be electric.[22]

Aviation is responsible for around 2.5% of all emissions globally. Electrifying aviation would result in a 90% cut in fuel costs, 50% lower costs of maintenance, and a 66% reduction in noise for take-offs and landings, with none of the tailpipe emissions of conventional aircraft. While the electric aircraft industry is currently in its infancy, and expensive fossil-fueled fleets will not be retired overnight, the combination of rapidly increasing battery storage density, plummeting costs, and environmental regulations is predicted to cut aviation emissions 50% by 2050. Siemens predicts that by the same year, electric aircraft could be the standard solution for the industry.[23]

Electrifying the economy includes many other areas, including cooking, water heaters, remote generators, pumps, and other facility machinery, all of which is projected to increase overall electricity consumption as a share of all energy consumed from 19% in 2016 to 41% in 2050. But because of the efficiency of energy transfer from electric goods, overall energy consumption is projected to decrease 21% by 2050. As this is happening, more of our economic activity will become dramatically cleaner and less expensive, easing today's cost and regulatory constraints, which will enable new business models. Our vehicles and tools will also interface more with the digital world, enabling more insights, intelligence, and automation.

Insights from Everything

What the hell is a *zettabyte* (*Back to the Future* reference, anyone)? An average 700 by 1050-pixel image or a 415-page e-book is about one megabyte (MB). A zettabyte (ZB) is 1,000,000,000,000,000 of these 1 MB files. According to the analyst firm IDC, the totality of all data in the world, which it calls the *Global Datasphere*, was 33 ZB in 2018 and will grow to 175 ZB by 2025.[24] While almost half of this data is from consumers, the portion coming from enterprises is projected to increase to 64% by 2025, and much of this is driven by sensors.

Not only is there more data, but it's rapidly getting cheaper to store, send, and analyze. In 1967, a hard drive that could hold 1 MB would cost you around $1 million. Today that MB can be stored for the bargain price of around $0.00002. This increase in data combined with plummeting costs of both storage and sharing, enable the internet to be a thing, along with a vast array of data services.[25]

All this sensing means that vehicles, machines, public spaces, office buildings, public infrastructure, and more are essentially waking up—providing immense amounts of data that can give real-time visibility into conditions as well as analytics that can be used to better understand and plan how all of these can be used better and more efficiently.

While there are plenty of clipboards still in use, they are quickly being replaced by tablets and analytics platforms ingesting vast amounts and variety of data from nearly everything around us, helping us better manage these things to improve safety, operations, and user experience.

Intelligent Everything

Once things and spaces generate data, they can then start not only giving us real-time information and analytics to think about but also doing some of that thinking themselves. Thanks to all this data being generated, AI and machine learning are getting enough data to become more and more adept at understanding our world, or at least the sliver of it they are focused on. This means they will be able to skip some steps for us, to do the number crunching, review of massive datasets, and distill for us not only what's happening but also what it means in the context of all the other data we didn't want to spend hours poring over and digesting.

With this ability, it can then move from descriptive (what is happening) to predictive (what will happen) to prescriptive (what to do about what's happening or will happen). The biggest area where this is already occurring is maintenance and operations of machinery. For heavy industries, downtime of a manufacturing line, train, or oil well drill can cost the company thousands or even millions of dollars per hour.[26] However, other consumer, commercial, and governmental spaces are also becoming more intelligent, leading to what the research and advisory firm Gartner identifies as people-centric smart spaces, in which technology enhances the experience of the people in these spaces, while providing rich analytics to those who manage them to maximize safety and operational efficiency.[27]

In 2019, Gartner listed smart spaces as #8 in their top ten key strategic technology trends,[28] and in 2020 they were the organizing framework for the entire top ten. I saw this rapid growth up close and personal while working at a Fortune Global 500 technology company, where we combined sensors, 3D LiDAR, computer vision for video analytics, and AI to build smart cities, retail, transportation, factories, stadiums, and more. This part of the business grew by about ten times over the first five years I was there—while demand expanded into new industry after industry. I expect this trend to continue for years to come.

Autonomous Everything

Once the things and spaces around us have data flowing from them, and the intelligence to understand what *is* happening versus what *should* be happening, an increasingly attractive option is to skip making a human do what needs to be done, and instead have the machines take care of it. Machines are becoming more and more capable of performing more and more tasks, thanks to intelligent vision systems, smarter "brains," and more dexterous movements.

According to McKinsey, the capabilities and market adoption of robots have grown dramatically. In 1975, robots could carry around 6 kg and move in up to five directions. By 2015, they could carry 1,000s of kg and move in over thirty-two directions, and these numbers are increasing rapidly. The number of SKUs (products) available in the market went from just a few in 1975 to nearly 350 in 2020. Not only are robots getting better, they're getting cheaper. Prices dropped by nearly half from 1990 to 2015, while labor costs more than doubled in the same time period (more on this later).[29]

But automation isn't just about robots; it's also about information processing and actions. Back in 2017, an AI created by JP Morgan Chase called COIN (Contract Intelligence) set about interpreting commercial loan agreements and other mundane tasks. It completed in *seconds* what would have taken lawyers and loan officers 360,000 hours per year. Not only did it complete these tasks quickly, but it also avoided the human error that leads to loan servicing mistakes during the yearly interpretation of around twelve thousand new wholesale contracts.[30] In 2020, China's Alibaba joined the fight against COVID-19 by developing an AI that could analyze more than three hundred CT scans of a patient in twenty seconds to detect the coronavirus—a task that usually takes a human fifteen minutes.[31]

McKinsey also estimates that around 50% of current work activities are automatable with *technology available today*.[32] There's simply a cost curve for when it makes business sense to automate—and of course, there is the human impact of layoffs. But this doesn't even take into account how rapidly new technologies will emerge, cheapen, and be adopted. Add to these innovations the capabilities of smart contracts and intelligent autonomous agents, and you've got not only a smart ecosystem of AIs but ones that can transact with themselves on our behalf.

Automation will also decrease costs. When much of ride-sharing is eventually automated with autonomous vehicles, the price will drop significantly so that your ride could cost, say, fifty cents instead of six dollars. That enables new business models, like having advertising pay for your ride. Imagine if transportation worked like search engines, where you pay for your ride by watching an ad, or it's paid by the organization you're visiting, much like parking validation. This is just one example of how the attention economy will continue to grow. One way to reduce poverty is to give people more money. The other is to make whatever they need cheaper and more accessible to them. Automation can help drive costs down to make more of the economy affordable to all, increasing abundance for more of the world than ever. In fact, this technology will go a long way to reduce the inflation we saw with the supply chain shocks during the COVID-19 pandemic.

All of this could lead to a world in which human capability is amplified many times over, passing along both physical and mental tasks to automation, so that we can focus on strategy, creativity, or just enjoying our lives however we wish. It's the next chapter in a long story of specialization of humanity's labor. Consider that we used to spend hours hunting, curing meat and hides, growing crops and grinding grains to feed ourselves.

More recently our direct labor is distanced from procuring and preparing our own food and other necessities; we work in front of screens, serve fries, fix other people's property and machines, and drive each other around to acquire the means of survival. With everything automated, we will be called to specialize even further into what makes us human, in an abundant world where the necessities are cheap, clean, and easy. But will we all have a fair share in this world?

Distributed Everything

Currently, getting our collective needs met seems alienated from us by what are often perceived as giant, omnipotent organizations over which we have no influence or power. But that is falling away because of both the new tech and business models we've discussed and social media's ability to very rapidly expose information and catalyze movements of people for change.

We weren't always a species huddled around centralized cores of power. Ninety percent of human history was organized in hunter-gatherer societies,[33] with tribes and family groups operating as cohesive but loosely organized and mostly egalitarian units.[34] Our brains and those of our humanoid ancestors evolved this way, with communities that supported each other, respected women and men roughly equally, and generally aligned to our needs for nutrition, belonging, and community—which by many estimates resulted in happier people than today.[35]

However, let's not get too nostalgic—infant mortality was high, ostracization by the tribe would likely lead to death, and protection from the elements or warring tribes was minimal. Most estimates of civilization tell us that around ten to twenty thousand years ago the First Agricultural Revolution created food surpluses, which led to the concentration of power, specialization of labor, feudalist lords who demanded taxes for protection, centralized government, and eventually what we consider our modern capitalist economies, with some social support from government spending and enforcement of law. Because of this progression—as well as the Industrial Revolution, which drew populations into urban centers to seek work—greater wealth was amassed than ever before, and modern societies became centralized in terms of power, wealth, and control. However, all of these are shifting back toward distributed models—closer to our hunter-gatherer way of life, but empowered by revolutionary technologies and systems in a way our remote ancestors never were.

The sharing economy may seem like old news today, but that might just reflect the rapidity of its adoption—that it's become a routine concept to us so quickly. The barriers and assumptions that the emerging sharing economy seemed to test are rapidly diminishing, especially with millennials and younger generations. New areas of the economy are being taken over by collaborative consumption, and where a customer may have once gone to an institution or intermediary, now they often go to a platform or community to find the good or service they need.[36] Also, these disintermediated business models are expanding across countries that may have been laggards during Uber's early days, creating their own local versions. Despite the lack of novelty, growth is still going strong. PricewaterhouseCoopers estimates that of the five most applicable sectors—the sharing economy—represented only around 6% ($15 billion) of the traditional operating models of businesses in the same sectors in 2013, but will grow to 50% ($335 billion) in 2025.[37]

But distributed economies are not all about the sharing economy; they are about person-to-person or peer-to-peer transactions. While Amazon has become the world's most valuable brand,[38] one of its fastest-growing competitors is Shopify, which not only allows entrepreneurs to build their own e-commerce store but also provides options for them to outsource all of their products, delivery, marketing, and support—allowing anyone to create their own distributed, largely automated fulfillment business through drop shipping.[39] Startups using blockchain and automated approaches are integrating into Shopify to provide more services and automation for entrepreneurs. With equity crowdfunding, these entrepreneurs now have more options than ever to find funding for their projects and ideas, ones that wouldn't otherwise have made it through the filters of seasoned venture capital or traditional finance providers.

But what about the team you'll need? Services like Upwork, Thumbtack, and Fiverr can now help you find a distributed team of experts that can collaborate remotely—and effectively, as proven in the COVID-19 pandemic—including employees working for some of the largest and most complex companies in the world. All of this leads to more opportunity for innovation, more inclusiveness for people who were once unable to find a job with a corporation, resiliency in the face of rapid change, and the ability to gain more productivity from our physical resources, thereby reducing waste and pollution.

Ethical and Sustainable Everything

Just as the paradigm of the shared economy was rapidly adopted by today's rising generations of consumers, so are expectations for sustainability and ethics. For many people who may very well see some of the most catastrophic impacts of climate change in their lifetimes—who have also grown up with few naïve illusions about the selfish motives of corporations and governments, thanks to ubiquitous information and empowered, unfiltered reporters and bloggers[40]—the need for positive change in the world is not only clear to them, it's critical.

The seventy-two million US millennials (born between 1980 and 1996) and sixty-seven million Generation Z (born between 1997 and 2012) make up over 42% of the US population, and they are rapidly increasing in workforce size, economic resources, and political influence.[41] They are also adept at using and filtering social media, while building online communities that can remotely coordinate to collaboratively achieve goals—or bring down long-established careers and brands in a matter of hours or days. These generations vote not only with their dollars but also with their likes and shares.

While baby boomers and their parents are also avid users of Facebook and Twitter, many companies know that younger generations have more lifetime ahead to be their customers, and that they can lose their brand loyalty quickly. Companies are right to fear the fickleness of these generations, but the ones that understand them also see an incredible opportunity to gain loyalty. Millennials and Generation Z demand corporate social responsibility, reward brands that further social and environmental causes, and will turn on brands in a heartbeat if they are found to have acted unsustainably, disingenuously, or unethically.[42] With all the transparency of information available and readily shared on social media today, there is little room to hide for companies or governments that do not act in the interest of future generations or that stifle social progress and equality. The 2020 George Floyd and Hong Kong protests, among many others, have shown that people can move to outrage and action faster than ever before, and with better coordination.

For companies and governments that can demonstrate their ethical behavior and contributions to progress, this is great news. This combination of transparency, movement-building, and action could all lead to a more fair and just society in which even powerful individuals, companies, and governments are held accountable and are encouraged to contribute to the common good of society, while still operating successfully within a thriving economy.

Big companies and investors are also seeing the opportunity to invest in building a better future and finding ways to proactively join the fight against climate change and social ills. They also know this is a successful business strategy. In fact, Boston Consulting Group (BCG), a leading strategy consulting company, found that companies who integrate social impact into their core business not only attain the highest level of social impact but also achieve the highest levels of shareholder returns. BCG found that building a business around doing good is good for business in terms of returns, profitability, recruiting and employee satisfaction, and valuations. Investors rewarded top ESG companies (those committed to environmental, social, and governance ethics) with valuations that were 3% to 14% higher and margins that were 12.4% higher. Companies that take this strategy of integrating impact into their core business, open new markets, spur innovation, reduce costs and risks in supply chains, strengthen their brand and support premium pricing, enjoy advantages in attracting talent, and strengthen relationships with governments, regulators, and influential parties.[43] It seems that social and environmental impact is not only a risk-reduction strategy; it's also a business opportunity that companies can't afford to miss in the coming decades.

With regard to sustainability, entrepreneurs see opportunities to build new innovations and businesses,[44] while global banks like Goldman Sachs see efforts to increase adaptability and resiliency as the largest infrastructure build-out in history, which Goldman is happy to help finance.[45] Sustainable and ESG investing is also booming—it's now being offered by most mainstream investing banks and growing rapidly, further accelerated by the COVID-19 pandemic.[46] In fact, in Q1 of 2020, global sustainable funds received $45.7 billion of inflows, while the broader global funds saw outflows of $385.7 billion. These funds often beat the market and fare better during crises: During the COVID-19 pandemic, stocks with high ESG scores performed 5 to 10% better than ones with low ESG scores. The latter also saw significant decreases in earnings forecasts.[47]

With the full power of some of the biggest players in our global economy poised to solve our sustainability and resiliency challenges, and ethical business arising as the norm, we can achieve a truly great society. With our economic and social incentives better aligned to the health of our environment, long-term business health, and social progress, economic actors will be more likely to do the right thing, and do well by doing so.

These Trends Are Shifting Everything

All of these trends are heading in positive directions that present an opportunity for us to create an abundant and fair world that's rich with opportunity for all. Not all of these will progress at the same speed, and there will be setbacks and disappointments along the way, but the underlying trend line is clear: The future has the potential to be a place that we can be proud to live in and excited to wake up to every day. What might that be like? Let's explore some theories about what could go right—without overlooking what could go disastrously wrong if we do not align reality with vision. As we envision this future, remember that it isn't a prediction of what the future *will* be, but what it can be, if we are able to focus our energies away from dystopian despair and onto creating the future we want.

Chapter 4

Where This Could All Be Heading

IS PROGRESS INEVITABLE? NEVER. THE SPERM whale has had an enormous brain (much larger than ours), complex relationships, and abundant resources for around twenty million years. But no cities, nuclear energy, or spacecraft. Precious historical moments that produce technologically advanced species like us may come around only every four billion years, and only when conditions are perfect. Let's not waste this opportunity.

In our lifetimes, the future is coming together in such disruptive ways that for us to align with ideal possibilities, we may be forced to reframe how our economy works. A case in point: Energy is free globally, thanks to the sun. Ultimately, we have a free nuclear power plant in the sky, sending energy all the way to the earth at no cost to us. The sun is going to be reliable for at least another five hundred million to one billion years before it expands and boils away our oceans.[1] For now it's the source of all of our ecological and economic activity: Its heat warms our air, which generates the wind, which drives the waves in our oceans. It was the energy source for the plants and animals whose decomposed remains became the fossil fuels we now burn in our cars and factories. But we are shifting from spending energy capital (fossil fuels) to using energy income (renewables) to power our civilization.

With free energy from the sun being converted into electricity by solar panels, wind turbines, and other renewables, there is plenty of capacity for our economies to become fully electrified. Given this free fuel, energy infrastructure needs only to be built and maintained, essentially decreasing the cost of producing energy over the course of its life. The overall cost of renewable energy gets cheaper because it's drawing on free fuel sources from fixed infrastructure that needs minimal maintenance over time. Of course, it costs money to build a windmill or solar panel (fixed costs); this amortizes to a smaller amount over time as the asset produces energy and pays back. The costs of fuel, maintenance, and operations is called marginal cost, which could approach nearly zero over its lifetime. But this leads to big "what if" possibilities:

- What if automated production were powered by renewables and used recycled materials from automated recycling machines, and the supply chain and production decisions were made by AIs using smart contracts to trade with each other?

- What if these automated factories and robots recycled, remanufactured, and maintained the solar panels and windmills that powered them?

- What if, because of these forces, fixed costs and marginal costs of energy became essentially free?

With this approach, the marginal cost of production and operation of the overall system goes down to nearly zero over time. Combine this with automation and AI, and the effects could ripple through the economy and eventually lead to what Jeremy Rifkin termed the zero marginal cost society. That means we get to free or nearly free energy, which means free or nearly free power for our homes, vehicles that transport us, and production of many goods. According to a report by RethinkX, costs of energy, materials, food, transportation, and information will fall by a factor of ten, while production processes will use 90% fewer natural resources and produce only one-tenth to as little as one-hundredth the amount of waste.[2] This could profoundly change the structure of our economy and society, the assumptions we make about them, and the abundance of our world.

Financial Access for the Good of All

Our economy and our civilization are not all about energy and production, of course; they're also about human interactions and the incentives that drive them. Let's consider the actions people take and how we can return value to them for those actions. Think about all the time people spend sharing content on social media or blogs that is monetized only by the company providing the platform. If you create a series of posts on social media, you're providing value to the network of people, and revenue to the platform, but you're not getting paid today.

Imagine if Facebook paid you for your inputs, and that income increased not only as people engaged with it, but also as people found more value in it. A "love" response would be more valuable than an "angry" response. You could incentivize the spread of love, positivity, and whatever else will influence society for the better. Anger might be an appropriate response to a violation of someone's rights; however, love, understanding, and collaboration are what will help solve the problem in the end. Incentivizing that collaboration through platforms like Slack or Basecamp could build the bridge from perception and reaction (social media) to taking action (project management and communication software).

While this can sound like social engineering and get a bit creepy if abused, generally people want to incentivize the good in each other, and we naturally (and institutionally) do so anyway with social praise and stronger relationships for people who display positive behaviors, like awards and prizes, and corrective punishments for bad behavior, such as prison and fines. People also naturally want to do good. The vast majority of people, when you ask them, say they would like their work to be meaningful and to create positive effects in the world. In fact, 90% of people would take a pay cut to do something more meaningful, according to a *Harvard Business Review* survey.[3]

The prevailing perception seems to be that you can either make money *or* do good in the world. So what if we could change our incentive structures to provide money to people doing positive work, incentivize *that*, and shift away from the parts of our economy that actually incentivize people to do bad? With longer-term thinking, we could proactively create incentive structures to reward positive actions and discourage negative actions. "Vice taxes" try to disincentivize products like cigarettes and alcohol, while some governments are exploring "tax shifting" to not only discourage harmful products but also use the proceeds to subsidize healthy or responsible products.

In past years we subsidized many of the fossil fuels that are harmful to our environment and air, to the tune of billions of dollars,[4] while expecting renewable energy to compete in a free market. But this is changing. Many of the countries that subsidized renewables early on now have a stronger mix of clean energy, and this push has also catalyzed a market that has dramatically reduced prices, while driving innovation.[5] In a socially incentivized economy, there would be better incentives that lead to better behaviors and outcomes that benefit us all.

These types of incentives have the potential to shift corporations and individuals toward more responsible products and services that are in line with the health and happiness of their employees and society. That's what employees want, but often they feel that they must do work they don't see as a positive contribution to society in order to survive—which can lead to a world where the aggregate is destructive.

When we arrive at a world where necessities are nearly free and people are incentivized to do good—which the vast majority naturally want to do anyway—we'll have built a framework and engine for a more positive world. We are often told a story of the sacrifices needed to live in a sustainable world: that we will sit in dark, cold rooms, unable to go out and enjoy our lives because doing so creates too much carbon. Instead, all these technological solutions available to us are in line with a society that is abundant, where we can learn, grow, enjoy social time, create new knowledge, and start innovative businesses that give us a sense of purpose and meaning, all while contributing to building a better world.

Transparency: Light Is the Best Disinfectant

Technology and innovation are enabling a world where everything will be transparent, giving us an accurate view into what happens in the world—which can help us create a more ethical society. This is an important key to what's been missing, because malevolent power and corruption can flourish only in an opaque world. Institutions, just like people, do things that are unethical when they can keep them hidden from public view. As we get more eyes on such activity, we shift toward everyone needing to be ethical and sustainable. If an organization takes harmful actions, and everyone's able to see it, the power of human society can be brought to bear to reconcile the issue. If business and government actions are transparent, auditable, and viewable by everyone, then social power comes back to the people, who can demand more socially beneficial policies and courses of action. People themselves need privacy in their personal lives, but do organizations and people like politicians and police officers on the job—especially when the consequences of their actions are highly impactful?

Not only will people-driven corporations and governments have an opportunity to help create a better future, but with the distributed tools and finance we've explored, people from all over the world will have the ability to learn and create like never before. How many potential Einsteins or Elon Musks are spending their time and human potential just working to survive? Whether in the working-class neighborhoods of Nairobi, Delhi, Detroit, Houston, and Ho Chi Minh City or the high-rise offices of New York, London, or Singapore? How many of the next Maya Angelous, Salvador Dalis, Marie Curies, Banksys, or Lebron Jameses are not pursuing their gifts, but instead doing menial labor to survive or even just putting up with the boredom of rearranging spreadsheets in an office? Imagine the explosion of creative expression, technological innovation, and new startups that would erupt once these people were liberated from drudgery and empowered to work on their true passions. Today only a fraction of us truly have the ability to join the creative or innovation class, but with these new tools and information, imagine all the hands and brains we would have on deck to solve the challenges before us and also accelerate the construction of a better world. This century is our best opportunity in human history to make this a reality.

The trends we've explored here have the potential to lead to a world where the necessities and comforts of life alike are abundant and accessible; where production is ethical and sustainable, driven by an informed and empowered society. It is a world where readily available access to capital, powerful digital tools of creation and collaboration, and sophisticated ways of solving problems all come together to empower creativity and innovation for the betterment of everyone and everything we touch. In this world the competition is for the betterment of oneself and our collective world, with purpose and meaning readily available to all, and a culture that challenges us to engage in creating something new, collaborating with like-minded people, and creating the future together. Our current world would seem apathetic and barbaric by comparison, and we would look back not with nostalgia but only with thankfulness that we made it through these times unscathed.

The Future Could Also Go Terribly Wrong

This all sounds like a great world, but let's not be naïve—our future also has the potential to go very, very wrong if we don't take action to guide this path toward our desired sustainable and ethical world. Data and technology are simply tools that we can use for whatever outcome we choose. Those who lean toward authoritarian control and domination over human freedom could co-opt these technologies to create a truly nightmarish dystopia that would be very difficult to escape.

George Orwell's book *1984* described a totalitarian state that forcefully controlled people's bodies, relationships, and minds. Aldous Huxley's *Brave New World* showed us a false utopian society where people were so placated by materialism, mind-altering drugs, distracting entertainment, and commoditized sex that they grew to love and defend their enslavement. Neither of these stories captures anywhere near the possible scale and pervasiveness of human control that could be possible in the near future, but they got aspects of the risks right. Most haunting is the warning from Orwell: "If you want a picture of the future, imagine a boot stamping on a human face—forever." Because human civilization could go terribly for ourselves and future generations if we don't get it right in our time, we dare not ignore the negative potential outcomes. We must dedicate ourselves to work hard to avoid such a future.

China's current surveillance state is an example of how this capability can be used to force obedience in ways that are exceedingly creepy. In 2017, BBC reporter John Sudworth conducted an experiment: He and the local government agreed to feed his picture into the city's facial recognition system at a given time. He then went to an undisclosed location, where it took only seven minutes for the local police to find and arrest him.[6] Of course, if used ethically, these types of systems could keep our cities safe. But if abused and used opaquely, they can lead to extreme, unchecked power. The detainment and abuses of the Uyghur Muslim population in China is an early-stage example that could be considered mild, in hindsight, compared to just how terribly wrong this could go without meaningful oversight.[7]

A functioning democracy is based on informed citizens making informed choices. But human decisions are based on the information we receive. Those in power need not control the military's tanks and bombers if they control the information we use to guide our decision-making processes, and thus our society. Social media is already being weaponized,[8] and the potential for this abuse is profoundly disturbing. AI bots are currently monitoring social media and then being used to influence not only our purchasing behavior but our political worldviews as well. This contributes to the divisions we see in our societies to the point where it becomes destabilized; to a point where either we don't trust the governments or organizations that might actually have our best interests in mind, or our institutions become gridlocked, or we descend into civil war for reasons that might not actually be supported by facts.

In 2019 a Pakistani-based terrorist group attacked an Indian paramilitary convoy in Southern Kashmir, leading to airstrikes from the Indian military. Pakistan quickly weaponized fake news on social media, using old pictures of crashed fighter jets and injured pilots to cause confusion and chaos, and ultimately convinced the Indian citizenry to distrust its own government and withdraw their support. The US is also increasingly a target of social media weaponization intended to influence its elections from the outside and create chaos in order to divert attention from international affairs.[9]

Vladislav Surkov is a brilliant Russian propagandist and operative who brings Sun Tzu's famous *Art of War* approach to an entirely new level of sophistication, seeking to win wars through battles of the mind, without ever reaching a battlefield. He describes this as a "non-linear war," which was described well in Adam Curtis's documentary *Hypernormalisation*. The aim of this disinformation is to bewilder a population to a point where the only truth is power.

His aim is to undermine peoples' perceptions of the world, so they never know what is really happening. Surkov turned Russian politics into a bewildering, constantly changing piece of theater. He sponsored all kinds of groups, from neo-Nazi skinheads to liberal human rights groups. He even backed parties that were opposed to President Putin.

But the key thing was, that Surkov then let it be known that this was what he was doing, which meant that no one was sure what was real or fake. As one journalist put it: "It is a strategy of power that keeps any opposition constantly confused." A ceaseless shape-shifting that is unstoppable because it is undefinable.

. . . When political actors can't agree on basic facts and procedures, compromise and rule-bound argumentation are basically impossible; politics reverts back to its natural state as a raw power struggle in which the weak are dominated by the strong.[10]

This strategy could enable an organization to get ahead of perceived competitors. If it's a malicious government, it can be used in horrible ways. If it's a corporation, it can be used intentionally or unintentionally in ways that could be harmful or even catastrophic for our jobs, health, safety, and economic future over time

Add to this phenomenon the multiplier of productivity made possible by software, which helps one person do the work of a team, more so than physical goods, which are inherently limited. There is also the network effect: The work value of a network increases as more people are on it, making it harder for an alternative to succeed. Combining productivity with the network effect can lead to runaway success, otherwise known as the superstar effect, or winner takes all. For example, Facebook makes around $2 million in revenue per employee, versus General Motors, which makes around $700,000 per employee.[11] As a software business, Facebook can generate immense activity and wealth with fewer people—meaning digitization can also lead to more concentrated power and control by a few megalithic corporations. If these corporations are incentivized only to grow and attain more market power, they can behave in ways that would be classified as sociopathic if they were exhibited by a person, causing harm to countless people, the environment, and our economy.[12] We've even seen that well-meaning or neutral companies can actually cause harm to our mental and emotional health[13] through their techniques to capture our attention and get us "hooked" on their products.[14] But we do have techniques to combat this: Regulations, public backlash, voting with our dollars, and creating viable alternatives are several ways we can encourage corporations to be more benevolent.

Technology not only makes governments and corporations more powerful but also empowers individuals for better or worse. It will continue to become easier and easier for one person to kill a million people—although (thankfully) at present this is still extremely difficult. As technology becomes further embedded into our lives, the impact of hacks and control of that technology becomes more dangerous. For example, access to powerful AI that could tap into or attack the digital infrastructure that enables the food, water, energy, and financial logistics of our civilization could be used to harm both people and our social fabric, posing an extreme risk.

In fact, a US Congressional report recently found that if the electrical systems of the country were attacked with a high-altitude electromagnetic pulse (HEMP) weapon, this could wipe out the electronics we rely on for our society to function, leading to the death of 90% of the US population within the first year from starvation, disease, and societal collapse.[15] With enough know-how and willpower to make this happen, someone who is disenfranchised—ostracized from society—who has a violently passionate political viewpoint or a mental health issue, or who simply wants to watch the world burn, can do so. We must find ways of enfranchising such people, bringing them in from the cold, and helping them find community or emotional support—this will not only restore them but will make our society in general more healthy. We need to resolve the economic cruelty that many face, or we will continue to see a rise in joblessness, poverty, divisiveness, resentment, desperation, and crime—a recipe for terrorism, disaster, and human suffering on a scale never seen before.

A Connected World Is a Safer World

With great power comes great responsibility. Technology is getting more and more powerful and accessible by the day. This demands a society that has enough responsibility, wisdom, and compassion to handle all this technological power and steer its use into creating positive human and environmental impacts. Luckily, there are many positive trends helping us move in this direction. We're more connected across borders than ever, making it much harder for a government to build popular support for a war with a country where we can see the daily lives of people via social media or when we travel abroad, building affinity with them.

According to a Harris Poll, 87% of business travelers reported that traveling has made them more empathetic.[16] Until the

COVID-19 pandemic, more people were traveling than ever before, with 1.2 billion international travelers in 2015, predicted to reach 1.8 billion by 2025.[17] While the pandemic slowed down air travel significantly, eventually it will return to prior levels. These trends may seem superficial, but they are actually helping to create more of a sense of common humanity. We know that "others" are not a bunch of evil people when we see them living lives similar to ourselves, sharing their experiences with family and friends, or posting videos of their cats or dogs being goofy. It has been proven that when we are acquainted with people from "other" groups, it catalyzes empathy, support for their plights, less hostility, and solidarity. This finding is called *contact theory*. It's not enough to just see each other nearby; we must actually engage together in activities such as working or socializing.[18] Sounds like something we could all use more of after recent quarantines. Recall a time you've experienced this phenomenon—and imagine how you might scale this to more people.

Models of Societal Collapse Describe Familiar Conditions

If we had enough data to enable a working model of psychohistory— Isaac Asimov's fictional science from the *Foundation* series—we could study civilizations across many planets and their civilizations to predict when and how societies, including our own, would succeed or fail. However, we have no crystal ball, no affirmative science that accurately predicts when or how we'll approach collapse. Some researchers have attempted to find patterns in civilizational history with some success, but we must keep in mind that society and social factors are incredibly complex, so any conclusions are highly speculative.

One commonly cited phenomenon is the Thucydides trap, a term coined by political scientist Graham Allison referencing the ancient Greek historian, who observed that when the power of one state rises in the presence of another, previously dominant state, the outcome is war. Many observers posit that in the last five hundred years there have been sixteen of these cases, and twelve of them have resulted in war.[19] Today's most noticeable power conflict is between the historically dominant US and China, which are ratcheting up tensions after decades of relative peace. The good news is that three of the four cases in which a violent war did *not* result were the three most recent (USSR versus Japan, US versus USSR, UK and France versus Germany).[20]

Another researcher, Sir John Glubb, studies the rise and fall of historical Western empires over nearly three thousand years, going as far back as the Assyrians of 850 BCE, and as recent as the "fallen" empire of Britain. In his 1978 paper *The Fate of Empires*, he notes an empire life span range from 207 to 267 years, with the average around 250 years, or ten generations when using what he called "the human yardstick." He observed different common stages of empire and called out several aspects of the later stages, including frivolity; overall decadence; racial conflict; inability to absorb immigration peacefully; the arrogance of the "native" group, which often sees itself as divinely favored or genetically superior while blaming immigration for their woes; obsession with money versus the value of work; and the rise of overall pessimism.[21] Many of these conclusions could be influenced by Glubb's values and worldview at the time, but the commonalities are fascinating nonetheless.

More recent research on fallen civilizations by archeologist Phillip Trella has sought to better understand cycles of growth and disintegration by studying the remains of ancient cities. His research reveals both social and environmental factors. Discoveries of increasing numbers of remains of craft or luxury goods closer to the time of collapse hint at the rise of stratification and increased diversion of resources to serve an elite class. This created vulnerabilities among the classes below, as elites became ever more separated from the realities on the ground. The results were poor resource utilization and uwnsustainable practices, as well as disastrous decisions by out-of-touch elites who didn't understand the realities they had become separated from (such as resource scarcity, disgruntled workers, and unsustainable spending). The consequences were often overspending on maintenance and rivalries, destruction of ecological resources needed to fuel the cities, lack of resiliency in their systems, rising violence, ecological disasters that disrupted food or critical resource supplies, degradation of the average health and diet of the citizenry, and overall human suffering.[22]

Jared Diamond's *Collapse* similarly surveys a variety of civilizational downfalls and concludes that they can happen for a variety of reasons, including environmental degradation, population crashes, resettlement, loss of faith in political ideology, and internal conflicts.[23] Our modern parallels to these aging and collapsing societies can be unnerving, to say the least, but keep in mind that each researcher is viewing the data through their own lens and context. Diamond shifts the conversation from one that paints human societies as programmed machines to one that depicts them as systems of choice, where we can avoid these cataclysmic outcomes through better assessments of our situations and take appropriate action to redirect ourselves to a better path.

How Unique Is Our Existence?

As we zoom out to look at the larger picture, we may be playing out a pattern on this planet that has been experienced by life on others. The Fermi Paradox explores the unsettling gap between the high probability of there being life on other planets, given that there are so many stars and planets that could harbor life, and the fact that we haven't seen or heard from any aliens (at least as far as we can prove).[24]

This starts with the Drake Equation, which estimates that there should be at the very least a hundred million planets in our visible universe where life has arisen (others estimate a 38% chance we are entirely alone).[25] Many of these would have established civilizations thousands or millions of years before us, with any that endure reaching impressive heights by now. We would only have been able to detect these types of civilizations recently, for only a matter of decades—an infinitesimally small amount of time in a universe that is, by most estimates, over 13.7 billion years old.[26] The universe should be crawling with life, saturated by civilizations that have had millions or billions more years to develop and grow. So we must ask ourselves—where are all the aliens?

We find nothing so far, no ancient TV signals, no radio conversations, no verifiable visitors. This leads to the idea of a "great filter" (a term coined by economist Robin Hanson) that civilizations have great difficulty passing through—and that we may be approaching ourselves.[27] Perhaps we are playing out a pattern that has played out on millions of planets before us, growing our way toward a collapse of epic proportions, with the entirety of our existence to be seen only briefly, like a spark in the night sky, never to be seen again. If it exists, we are still at a point before reaching the filter today, and our species may represent one of the few chances for life and consciousness to continue on—if only we can get this right.

But what if there is no filter, and other life forms have simply become so advanced that we can't see their signals or don't recognize them as "life as we know it" anymore? Entertain, for a moment, a vision of what might happen if we did indeed prove that the unidentified aerial phenomena (UAPs, previously known as UFOs) people have reported in our skies were actually technologically advanced visitors. What if we could understand and replicate the tech that provides UAPs' purported capabilities of instantaneous acceleration, gravity-agnostic propulsion, utilization of a clean and powerful energy source, and extreme speeds? Some highly credible sources say we actually have evidence for this. In 2019, videos were released from the US Department of Defense (DoD) showing footage of UAPs from fighter jet cameras.[28] They released multiple examples of footage, and the DoD verified their authenticity, leading to very convincing evidence that they were in fact real. Now, this doesn't prove we are being visited by aliens, but it seems to show that there could possibly be ways of moving vehicles around using propulsion leveraging exotic physics that we aren't aware of today. Seeing this verified footage is a first step in accepting the possibility that vehicles could exist that can move from eighty thousand feet to a few feet above the water in a few seconds, verified by radar (evidence that unfortunately the DoD has yet to release).

Of course, this is impossible with what is available to the public today, but simply accepting that this type of tech is possible could be a wild card for our future. Innovators might be inspired by this to discover major advances in propulsion technology, energy, or physics. Having access to or being able to build this technology ourselves would present us with an incredible opportunity. History shows that things happen in ways we couldn't predict, with unforeseen consequences that create a new crisis cycle—or a new innovation cycle.

The unpredictable happens regularly, turning our best projections into feeble attempts at fortune telling. The internet is a recent example of something that today seems like an inevitability, but at the time came out of left field and changed forever our global landscape of communications, commerce, and technology. Technological innovations like affordable cold fusion or gravity propulsion could change everything. We could develop teleportation. We could create the replicators of *Star Trek*—a computer that can create anything from a sandwich to a cell phone for you in a matter of seconds. Wild cards could transform us in personal or spiritual ways: What if we confirm that we actually can communicate telepathically, maybe with technological assistance, or that life after death actually exists and we're able to track our passage, measure it, or somehow even connect to people who have passed away? What if we scientifically confirmed that there was no life after death at all, or that this reality really is just a simulation?

Today these examples live only in the realms of science fiction, but sci-fi has inspired generations to create the future that brings their stories to life. The simple act of planting ideas in the cultural imagination imbues us with the vision to guide the creation (or avoidance) of it in real life. One thing is certain—there will be wild cards in our future that go unpredicted but will enable new ways of living if we are creative enough to use them in ways that impact the world for the better.

Getting Beyond Predictions with the Choice to Create

Trying to predict the future, as we have done some of in this chapter, can be helpful, but it's ultimately not the best approach to reach the most ideal outcome. In a 1978 speech, political theorist, philosopher, and cofounder of the Institute for Social Ecology, Murray Bookchin observed: "Futurism is the present as it exists today, extended into the future. I don't believe that we have to extend the present into the future. We have to change the present so that the future looks very, very different from what it is today."[29] The only way we can do this is to design the ideal future we want to live in and build that future without being limited by the mental constraints of trying to simply extend the present.

Ultimately we need to guide the development and application of technology to avoid the dystopian outcomes I briefly shared in this chapter. If it were a battle, we would not be able to defeat big, centralized, entrenched powers or armed governments using guns and direct fighting. We don't stand a chance with weapons—and violence only creates more of the same, while undermining the goals for which we are fighting. Instead, if we truly want to shift to a better world, we need to create and implement it faster together than others can divide and destroy. The only way we will direct the next shift into something positive is through *building an undeniably superior alternative*. We shouldn't waste our energy fighting the old world; instead, we should make the old world obsolete, and naturally, collectively move to that better world we create: piece by piece, person by person, sector by sector, country by country.

The Case for Urgency

One thing seems to be clear from all these studies and theories: We have a narrow window of time to make the right changes, as we may not again get the chance to be at such an advanced stage of civilization that can achieve such great heights. It has taken four and a half billion years for life to get to this point, where we have intelligent, technologically advanced animals on the earth (humans this time around, but perhaps dolphins could evolve hands and develop technology in the next iteration). Our species has made an incredible impact on the planet, and right now we're seeing the beginning of some of the worst effects of this power. We're in a stage where the earth's ecosystems and the biosphere we depend on are responding to the massive amounts of carbon and greenhouse gasses that we've been putting into the atmosphere since the industrial age began. So much of the old technology we created and have become dependent on has created unforeseen problems for the world.

If we don't act on our new knowledge and instead just continue with the old world status quo, we're moving toward eventual collapse. A collapse that appears closer and closer the more we learn about ecological and social systems. Between now and then, we have time to create a viable future, but it is short. If we are not successful, perhaps in another couple of centuries or eons we'll be able to get back to where we are today. But we are dangerously close to missing our window for changing the way we interact with the environment and ecosystems our lives depend on. This time, right now, is critically important to ensure that we have a future. And since you're alive right now, *your* work and effort are essential. We have an incredible and ever-growing wealth of tools and resources at our fingertips to work with, more than any generation has enjoyed. Now is the time to build the next phase of humanity's future, and we are lucky enough to be a part of it.

Can we really rise to the challenge? When we take a look at the changes humanity has demonstrated in the past, we see how truly capable we can be.

Chapter 5

The Past Innovations That Got Us This Far, in a Tradition We Must Continue

THE YEAR WAS 1934. THE GREAT DEPRESSION had ravaged the United States. Unemployment was starting to turn around but was still at a painfully high rate of 22%. Nearly a quarter of Americans were out of work, and to make it worse, weather and drought in the Midwest had destroyed thirty-five million acres of farmland. Hundreds of millions of acres were at risk, and many people were in danger of starvation, while the misery drove others to take their own lives in increasing numbers.

Not only were things terrible in the United States, but there was uncertainty abroad as well. At this time, Hitler had declared himself Fuhrer, Stalin was massacring people in Russia, and throughout China the Chinese Communist Party was battling the Chinese Nationalist Party. America's position in the world was uncertain. This was a time of chaos, change, and desperation for people around the world.

People were on edge and terrified of what could come, having already endured World War I and a deadly global pandemic. While the Roaring Twenties brought innovations and a new Gilded Age, the economy collapsed in 1929. So there they were, in a moment of dramatic uncertainty, without clarity about what the future would bring.

Although times like this are undeniably unnerving and can cause us to anticipate the worst possible outcomes, global history shows that when we have overwhelming crises to solve and new technological advances to draw on, we tend to create new solutions and find new ways forward. Tough conditions in the past have led to inspired urgency that not only helped us effectively address the problems at hand but also laid the foundation for opportunities we would continue to build on. We are still benefiting from the legacies of the historical changes we will discuss in this chapter. These stories are evidence that this moment is perfectly ripe for us to innovate and push forward into a new and better world, just as our forebears did.

The Road from Depression to Abundance

President Franklin D. Roosevelt was in a truly difficult situation as he tried to figure out how to rebuild America. He decided that the route to recovery was a series of programs he famously called the New Deal. He set out to create a new social contract with American workers and American companies to push for organic development in a way that would rebuild trust and the infrastructure of America. It would indeed lay the foundations for growth and a return to abundance, beyond anything the world had ever seen before.[1]

In our history classes, many of us learned that the New Deal was a monolithic government program that used brute force and threw money at infrastructure and employment projects to get the economy moving. But in fact a large part of the New Deal was critically reliant on the private sector and making investors feel comfortable putting their money into building the future of America by reducing their risk.

FDR did that by creating the Reconstruction Finance Corporation (RFC), which acted as an intermediary and a guarantor of loans from the private sector. Private companies and private investors put their money into the investments managed by the RFC, and these investors saw private returns with guarantees from the US federal government. This helped reduce uncertainty and fear for the investors. It funneled money into businesses that were deemed fundamentally sound but were operating in a depressed economy and didn't have the inflows of capital they needed to carry out business operations, employ people, and do their part to help get the economy moving again. The RFC ended up being a very successful program, despite some criticism. It started to restore the confidence of the investor class, create more jobs for the working class, and provide the capital needed for the entrepreneurial class to create the jobs, solutions, and innovations that forged a path out of the Great Depression.

The Federal Housing Authority helped funnel that investment money into building homes and getting people into them. The Rural Electrification Administration similarly helped to reduce the risk for investors by bringing electricity to rural areas that had not yet been connected to the grid. There was little private financial incentive for utilities to build the infrastructure to bring electricity to rural America, but this program enabled them to reach these areas. That began bringing rural America into the modern economy. It also created many new opportunities for entrepreneurs and businesses to serve the rural community through media like radio (and later, television), once they could access these, thanks to electricity. It took a lot of smart work and building the right incentives for the capital of the private sector to fund electrification, as well as connection to telephone lines and more. All of these programs, along with the later ramp-up in production for World War II, worked together on a fundamental level to unify the country into one economy.

There's an overlooked story to be told from this era, though—the role of entrepreneurs. When everything collapsed after the twenties, entrepreneurs were stranded with great ideas but no money. They are a vitally important source of innovation, helping economies rebuild and adapt from the bottom up, one business and livelihood at a time. Who else would create the future through the invention of new products and services? It doesn't just happen with the money investors hold. Government programs alone don't do it, although they can help create conditions that nurture entrepreneurship. Programs like unemployment insurance, Social Security (essentially a UBI for retirees, but paid for in advance), and other social safety nets helped entrepreneurs take the risks they needed to, knowing that they wouldn't starve if they failed. The future was built by entrepreneurs, employees, and businesspeople who took the government-backed money from newly confident investors and programs to build and run their businesses. They could employ people to make new products, which were sold to customers who now had money to buy new products and services, thanks to the increasing number of jobs that brought increasing incomes.

This virtuous cycle empowered the innovative and entrepreneurial class and was a major factor driving progress. Whether within small business or big companies, entrepreneurs saw solutions to problems as opportunities. In this way, the effort to end the Great Depression became an era that transformed the way we live.

The New Deal was ultimately successful: The economy got moving again, then doubled over the course of World War II and continued to create long-term growth and innovation. It created an enormous middle class in the United States. Quality of life was unmatched anywhere in the world, with the fruits of growth shared with more of the population than ever before. The ideal for those who came home from the war was to settle down, raise a family, and carve out their own piece of the American Dream. With the middle class expanding faster than ever, the war machine was largely converted to a consumer products and services machine. In many ways we are still benefiting from these efforts today, and we can take many lessons from this experience as a society. Of course, the economic impact of mobilizing the country for World War II should not be underestimated— nor can we ignore the human suffering this global conflict created. Perhaps the New Deal would've been enough to get us to the same place, without all of this human suffering. But what can be said for sure is that a vast amount of wealth and opportunity was created in that period as the US successfully built its way out of the economic crisis. Obviously global war is never an appropriate or humane solution to economic troubles, and we should strive to find ways of proactively building infrastructure and products that serve to create a better world for humanity rather than destroy what it has already built.

The Eventual Chinese Miracle

Now let's cross the Pacific and reach back even further to 1861. China had just suffered a humiliating defeat by the British in the Opium Wars. It sought to rebuild through many sweeping efforts— but, try as it might over the course of a century, success eluded this ancient society despite the learnings of its rich history.

The Chinese leaders first looked externally for models to build better conditions for their society. The Xinhai Revolution in 1911 was partially an attempt to essentially mimic US democracy and Western-style institutions such as legislative, executive, and judicial branches of government to ensure separation of power. But this approach failed to take off. The Chinese didn't see the same types of industrialization and growth that their neighbor Japan was starting to experience. After being closed to the world for over two hundred years, Japan was opening up its economy and society to globalization. Development came rapidly, and this longtime rival became increasingly antagonistic toward China. China was watching closely. Westernism in Japan was becoming popular—everyday people and political leaders alike began adopting Western clothing and modernizing their technology. China wanted to emulate this, but even with political reforms and a popular slogan of "only science and democracy can save China" the Xinhai Revolution failed, without the desired benefits ever reaching the people.

After WWII the Chinese Workers' and Peasants' Red Army rose up and sought to emulate the Soviet central planning model instead. This was essentially an attempt to force a revolution to create a new society based on this model. However, this effort to import a governing style just didn't work for China, and after thirty years under this system the country decided to seek a more homegrown approach.

By 1978, more than a century after the Opium War, poverty in China was stuck at roughly the same level. China again looked to reform itself, but this time by designing its own model, having seen no fruit from efforts to create a grand new society through its many direct attempts at revolution. China began to look inward. Instead of emulating others, its leaders considered internal dynamics and culture and created a model based on who it was and what it needed to grow and modernize. This started with building a solid foundation through agrarian innovation, constructing immense amounts of infrastructure supported by a stable and involved governmental system, then moved to empower the industrial and financial sectors through new tools to scale and participate in global commerce, eventually leading China to become the advanced economy it is today.

Instead of trying to skip over fundamental sources of stability by simply imposing political ideology, China saw that they needed to get their own house in order and develop their capacity to be a modern economy, starting with agriculture and then moving to industry and eventually high technology. It seems that there is an organic quality to how industrialization develops. The same patterns emerged of their own accord in the UK, US, and Japan. Especially for countries with a large population, a sustainable and productive agricultural sector is needed for a society to move into industrial development, manufacturing, and then begin to lead through modern technology and digital products.

China has finally emerged from a series of failed experiments, and by looking at who they truly were and what they needed, they have lifted 815 million people and counting out of extreme poverty, which fell from 88% in 1981 to 0.7% in 2015. China's story is one of extraordinary economic transformation.[2] This amount of wealth creation and social mobility in such a short time is unprecedented in the history of the planet. It shows how poised the modern world as a whole is for huge turnarounds, massive advancements, and powerful change.

What Causes, and Limits, Democracy

More recently, the Asian Infrastructure Investment Bank, founded in 2014, is similar to FDR's Reconstruction Bank, as it funnels private and public money into building infrastructure that helps develop economies throughout greater Asia—a region that is home to nearly 61% of humanity. China will not only be a center for developing Asia but will also build new connections between Asia, Europe, and Africa, creating routes for goods and economic activity, and let's not forget political influence. China is positioning itself very well in the world, for its own interests and those of its friends.

When we look at the economic history of China since 1 CE, we can see that China has historically been one of the largest economic powers in the world, responsible for about 30 to 40% of the global share of cumulative GDP up until the mid-1800s, when Europe and the US began to industrialize.[3] To China's cultural mindset, the rise of America and many other Western countries is really just a short blip on their screen of history. The Chinese see their country's recent growth and prominence as a return to its rightful place as the true leader of the world.[4]

As a gigantically populous country with thousands of years of civilizational history, philosophical roots, and scientific achievements, China is a longtime contributor to human civilization. In this century, AI is a strategically important technology to excel in globally. While Chinese investments in AI surpassed those of the US in 2017, the US reinvested in 2018 to take the lead and is projected to pull further ahead in the coming years. These investments will result in amazing innovations in robotics, sustainability, and other kinds of technological and social innovation. In fact, thanks to AI $15.7 trillion is projected to be added to the global economy by 2030, and the US and China are on pace to receive 70% of this windfall.[5]

These economic benefits are enormous, but how far will China and other world leaders take this power? In Xinjiang, in north-western China, this technology has been used against the Uyghur population in ways that can only be described as Orwellian sur-veillance and imprisonment that enabled terrifyingly inhumane treatment.[6] China is an authoritarian state, and as long as it remains so, it cannot develop to its full potential. Studies of the rise of democracy in the UK, US, and Japan show that democracy isn't the cause of industrialization, but rather a consequence of it. As coun-tries modernize, distribute more resources, and grow a middle class, the people gain more power and demand more rights and more say in the political and economic process that they're a part of.

China is struggling to find a balance that its population will accept. One of their original needs was to ensure stability by any means, especially with the recent history of regular revolutions. They've taken a heavy hand to ensure this stability and ensure ongo-ing unification of the country. This continues today, as we've seen in Hong Kong, in Xinjiang, and further back in Tibet and Beijing's Tiananmen Square. Taiwan could be next to feel that heavy hand—and become a flashpoint for a larger conflict with the US. This conflict would be a disaster for both countries, their people, and the progress that the interdependence and collaboration of these superpowers have helped advance in the world.

The next challenge for China will be how they reconcile the freedoms of their people with the need for stability. As the Chinese population becomes economically and technologically enriched and sees the freedoms enjoyed by much of the Western world, they will inevitably seek more freedom and self-determinism. This dynamic is creating a tipping point, as we have already seen in Hong Kong and other regions. In Hong Kong, in reaction to the 2020 National Security Law that passed after months of pro-democracy protests, 39% of businesses surveyed by the American Chamber of Commerce there said they planned to move assets, capital, or operations out of the city, and 53% of people surveyed had plans to move.[7] While China has progressed impressively over recent decades, their authoritarian model is being increasingly challenged not only by foreign partners and competitors but more importantly by its own people. To continue to flourish moving forward, China must find a way to respect human rights and freedoms while still maintaining an effective political apparatus that achieves its ambitious economic development goals. While China's increasingly loud criticism of the messiness of Western democracy and vulnerability of openness has its merits, unfavorable views of China have reached historic highs in recent years, mostly due to questionable ethics and poor human rights records.[8]

As we build the more egalitarian, global economic system that I shared in the last chapter, this will most likely catalyze political enfranchisement and democracy, which will lead to stability. We have seen this in other countries that have embraced shared growth as they developed, such as the Nordics, Canada, Japan, New Zealand, Singapore, and South Korea, which all score highly on the Human Freedom Index and Quality of Life Index.[9, 10] This seems likely, except in countries that have become rich from oil or other monolithic sectors of their economies where the wealth generated can be funneled directly to the ruling class without being shared. Many of these states have notoriously poor human rights records. Saudi Arabia, Venezuela, Nigeria, Angola, Algeria, Libya, and Egypt all gained substantial wealth in terms of overall GDP after discovering oil. But they generally have very poor democratic institutions or sharing of the growth among their populations. The powerful get rich quick, but from a small segment of their economy, and one that doesn't rely on the work of much of its population, so those powers rarely feel any obligation to enfranchise them.

Saudi Arabia is anomalous; until recently it had not asked its citizens to pay much, if any, taxes. The country provides infrastructure and social programs for its people without taxing them, essentially paying the people to not raise a fuss. However, in 2018 the Kingdom imposed a 5% sales tax to cover a decrease in oil revenues. This worsened in 2020 due to the global pandemic, and the government decided to triple that tax. Imagine what will happen as oil cartels continue to increase the price of oil (desperately manipulating it), making renewables and electrification more attractive, and ironically expediting the decline of oil in the long term.

Not only do these desperate taxes underscore the lack of resiliency that comes from relying on a single sector to fund a country, but they change the people's relationship to the government. When people are taxed, they expect a say in how their tax money is spent and how the government they are funding treats them. The same is true for China—as people become richer, they demand more say in their political and economic lives. It's yet to be seen, but if China can transition peacefully to a more democratic or inclusive way of guiding and managing the country, that would be an immensely positive development for the Chinese government and for the rest of the world. The West's Magna Carta was passed after a rebellion against wars and taxes—forcing King John to make concessions to the people he claimed to represent and protect.[11] We can expect more societal conflict and instability in countries that don't develop in a way that is perceived as beneficial by and for their citizens—especially in the age of social media.

Conversely, those who develop their economies, build wealth for their populations, and implement transparent representative government are more likely to succeed and pull ahead in the coming years. Between renewables that are by nature distributed, startups that are creating new adaptations to a changing world, and the on-demand economy, there are plenty of opportunities to create shared value for any society around the globe that chooses to recognize them.

The Vital Relationship Between Crisis, Growth, and Innovation

Examples similar to the US and China abound, but on smaller scales. It inspires us to wonder whether these turnarounds were the result of good decisions by individuals at the time, or perhaps an instinctual human behavior pattern that arises when a large number of individuals face challenging conditions and need to adapt. But what's more important is how we can utilize it. When a research project led by Josef Taalbi at Lund University looked at innovation in Sweden, they sought to identify the causes and factors that lead to innovation and change by asking a few basic questions.[12] Is innovation:

- Simply driven by making investments in certain areas?

- A response to crises?

- A response to new technologies entering the market?

- Catalyzed by individuals who just happen to have the right idea?

The study looked at 3,377 different cases of innovation. They separated the innovation triggers into four categories:

- **MARKET OPPORTUNITIES,** in which an organization tried to capitalize on a consumer trend or changes in market prices, or to meet a new demand.

- **INSTITUTIONALIZED SEARCH,** where a company basically tried to throw money at innovation to create new opportunity for themselves.

- **TECHNOLOGICAL OPPORTUNITY,** when a new technology had become available to the market or became affordable enough to become part of a larger product or solution.

- **PROBLEM-DRIVEN SOLUTIONS,** where a crisis occurred, an obstacle came up, or a problem happened, and entrepreneurs, companies, or governments tried to address it through innovation.

Researchers studied Sweden's response to several triggers, including environmental problems, liberalization of the telecommunications industry, and an economic and energy crisis. They found that the two largest causes of innovation by far are *problem-driven* and *technological opportunities*, which can catalyze two to four times the amount of innovation that comes from institutionalized search or market opportunities.

In the oil crisis of the 1970s, shortages and elevated prices led to rationing in many countries, and large lines formed at gas stations in advanced countries around the world. At the same time there were increasing environmental problems from unsustainable industrial production, dirty fuels, and unregulated pollution. The air, water, and environment were becoming polluted. Workplace health problems were emerging due to new chemicals like asbestos, along with injuries from robots and machinery. Essentially, the industrial innovation that had led to an era of strong economic growth was destabilized by global political conflicts, and some of the technology that provided so many benefits began to cause many environmental and health problems at the local level.

Back in Sweden, the environmental problems were significant, but most critical to its success during this time of crisis was a communal mindset that focused on solving these problems. Residents were not only aware of the problems but also demanded sustainable innovations to combat them. Many innovations in renewable energy and emission reductions for vehicles followed. For example, catalytic converters were created and became a standard for cleaner emissions.

The remaining forests in Sweden were being ravaged and dwindling in size, but a combination of regulations and new technology allowed for better resource efficiency in forestry. Robotics and machinery were created to harvest trees more efficiently, use more of the wood and reduce waste. Forestry practices changed as well, moving from clear-cutting entire swaths of land to more selective harvesting that allowed the ecosystems to regrow and recover.

Sweden was early to liberalize telecommunications regulations, in 1993. This enabled a variety of innovations from Swedish telecom Ericsson, including the first Bluetooth product, as well as the first phone that could connect to the internet through wireless access protocol, and mobile phones that can communicate through Bluetooth and Multimedia Messaging Service (MMS), allowing users to send images and other media via messaging.[13] This was a part of a wave of innovation that happened after liberalization energized the telecom to explore new markets and partnerships to develop new technology.

By reviewing conditions like these, researchers found that waves of innovation seem to come in patterns. Innovation doesn't necessarily cause GDP growth, but there is an interplay between innovation and growth. Often a crisis occurs, innovation happens in response, then a society grows out of the crisis, and new technologies find more robust markets with new applications and uses. This, along with new ways of combining these technologies, paves the way for the scaling up that makes the new products and services more affordable and viable, creating new opportunities and even more innovations that play their part in catalyzing new growth.

Inevitably the next external or internal crises would occur, some of which (such as the environmental crisis) were caused by previous innovations, which instigated a new creative cycle. Overall, there's a virtuous cycle of innovation, growth, and crisis. In the Swedish study, new waves of innovation came about every forty years, following economic crises in the 1850s, 1890s, 1930s, and again in the 1970s. In the cases where innovation was most effective, it was directed at solving a problem or an obstacle. As the innovations matured, they became cost-effective enough to be commercially exploitable, able to be productized and included with other technologies for productized solutions. Much of this also depended on platform or infrastructure readiness, creating an *enabling platform* that powered the next wave of innovations. For example, if you have the connectivity infrastructure provided by telcos plus mobile phone availability, you can create and access apps not previously possible. These enabling platforms become the foundation that enables the new innovation. This allows new solutions to diffuse out into the economy, enabling adoption and complementary solutions in a self-reinforcing cycle.

What does this mean for us? The two elements that catalyze the most innovation are present in abundance today. Essentially, all the new technologies and new crises mean myriad opportunities to advance technology and create new solutions and new businesses to solve real problems. These examples show us that innovation is a societal response to change and that we can rise through crises by innovating and collaborating our way through them. But the solution can't be just technology. A holistic approach of technological, policy, and cultural innovation is the most effective mix for overcoming obstacles. Our current global challenge of climate change carries the added risk of destabilizing our societies and economic infrastructure (through rising seas, increasing natural disasters, and more pandemics) to the point where we cannot innovate our way out of it. Change may be so drastic that we might not be able to maintain our accustomed way of life—but we stand our best chance if we go about meeting this challenge together, deliberately and intelligently.

For the entrepreneur or an innovator, the historical combination of innovations and crises provides not only a meaningful problem to solve but a meaningful economic opportunity. In Chapter 3, I shared the ways that the world around us is changing and the directions in which tech and social trends are headed. A dizzying array of technological opportunities is arising, but many crises are also either arising or well underway. Today we live in a perfect time to create innovations to have a positive impact on the future of humanity and the world we live in; in fact, we can be very successful if we manage to solve these challenges. It's on us to rise to the challenge of this crisis.

Despite the difficulty crises bring, they seem to also bring important benefits. The Brookings Institution conducts in-depth research that leads to new ideas for solving problems facing society at the local, national, and global levels. After an extensive review of historical analysis, they see that crises continually bring unexpected benefits in the following ways.[14]

- **RAPID PROBLEM SOLVING AND INNOVATION:** A crisis can motivate innovative responses to what is seen as a clear and present danger.

- **INCREASED RESILIENCY FOR THE NEXT EVENT:** The impact of the disruption and the innovation it led to can galvanize support to prepare for the next crisis.

- **NEW LEVELS OF COOPERATION, EVEN AMONG RIVALS:** Problems that are bigger than individual interests of organizations or nations can necessitate cooperation and closer relationships, while opening an opportunity for more in the future.

- **SYSTEMIC CHANGE:** Crises can overturn old norms and overcome the existing power structures' resistance to change, sometimes even by destroying those structures and practices.

- **DRAMATIC POLICY SHIFTS:** Crises can motivate the public to demand change, or force leaders to make significant changes that, before the crisis, could have required immense courage or led to political suicide.

- **EMERGENCE OF TALENT**: When confronted with crises, people rise to the challenge and rally around projects or solutions that they can contribute to in order to better their world.

History teaches us that when we rise to a crisis, envision what could go right, and work together to create that vision, we can impact the future in positive and enduring ways. If we seize this moment, we can reach a level of abundance and sustainability that will enable us to keep moving forward, potentially indefinitely.

The Opportunities in Solving Big Problems

While the past saw times of stability, it has also seen wars and immense human tragedies that wasted the potential of millions if not billions of lives. For example, while the roaring 1920s were a great time for many, the surrounding years were highly volatile. With few financial or business regulations during an incredible proliferation of new technologies, there were giant booms followed by giant busts, with few supports for those harmed by these cycles. This includes the Great Depression, which sapped the energy, optimism, and potential of a generation. But from this suffering came determination to make a change for the better, and the larger trend of progress continued over time. Few would disagree that living in 1950 was way better than in 1915, and living in 2015 was way better than in 1950, even more so if you were a person of color or a woman, or had sexual preferences other than heterosexual. We still have business cycles, but they have been much less extreme, and at least some social protections are in place in many countries for people who lose their jobs, health, or homes or are the victims of crime. We still go through phases of chaos, uncertainty, and change, and they are hard and painful, but we seem to make continuous improvements over time. Now is the time to make the world even better.

Think back to the 3 Horizons model we discussed in Chapter 2. Right now we must address the conflict of ideas that we are confronting in our time; we must keep in mind that when we've gone through this process in the past, humanity has tended to come to a new synthesis of ideas that led to a newly stabilized world that was better than what came before. Will 2050 continue the trend and be better than 2015? If history is any guide, most likely it will, but there will be bumps and risks along the way, and adaptations we will need to make. How it turns out depends on what we do today and how we rise to our challenges.

Thankfully, conflicts today are generally less violent than they have been in the past. The average annual deaths from conflicts in the 1950s were 90% higher than in the first decades of the twenty-first century. Additionally, increases in healthcare availability and quality have prevented many of the indirect wartime deaths from starvation and disease that happened in past conflicts.[15] Hopefully this trend will continue, and times of conflict will become more growing pains of change, dialogue, and competition than the brutal slaughters of the past.

As we turn our sights back toward the future, we must set our vision on that more stable scenario where we do figure things out, come back together, unleash our creativity, and prepare to be more resilient in the face of whatever comes next. There'll inevitably be more natural disasters, conflicts, new pandemics, or other unforeseen consequences to what we're doing, and we'll have to react effectively and solve those problems. It can be daunting, but throughout history, even when things have seemed to be falling apart and going horribly in the short term, in the longer term they have been trending in a better direction. Situations might be painful, and it will always take work to continue pushing ourselves forward, but in the long view we can see we are just temporarily derailed or distracted from our better collective human destiny.

The COVID-19 pandemic offers a recent example. Increased frequency of pandemics is one consequence of globalization, with human settlements encroaching on wild areas, bringing humans into more contact with wildlife, along with regular global air travel. These are consequences of population growth, family separation so people can migrate to cities for work, and the need for long-distance transportation to explore the world or revisit our homes and communities. Consider the number of innovations from companies and people who rose to the challenge to limit the spread of COVID-19 and develop a vaccine in record time. Regardless of the smaller number of those who chose to ignore the virus and resist measures to control its spread, most people in most countries have responded by doing their part to help. As incremental improvements in small cycles add up within the larger meta cycle, we could see incredible leaps forward from this crisis. For example, this pandemic could lead to a healthcare technology and policy revolution that gives us more tools to keep ourselves healthier than ever before.

If you see crisis for the opportunity it is, then you—and the world you live in—will get through it more effectively and prepare for the next one with more creativity and resilience. If we wallow in the difficulty of it, or all the reasons why any solution might not work, then there's little chance to get started creating solutions that might work, to eventually find the one that will work. A mindset that embraces change, collaboration, and problem solving empowers you, and all of us, to innovate in ways that solve problems, ultimately leading to what could go right in our world.

Who knows what the future will bring? Something will happen that blows our minds, and we don't know what it will be, but history has shown that we can trust the fact that change and new paradigms will come along. Any of these could create new crises, and if we survive them, these crises will compel us to create new innovation cycles. The past essentially tells us to be ready for anything and to embrace change, because it's all an opportunity to create a better world. As Plato pointed out, necessity is the mother of all invention. I would add that crises are the labor contractions that tell us it's time to push for a change. A change that, much like a birth, is coming whether we are in pain or not, whether we're ready or not. When we join the effort to nurture that potential, we can affect the direction and outcomes of the changes that come our way, and in doing so, direct our future.

Part Two

A FUTURE WE CAN BUILD IS A FUTURE WE MUST FIRST ENVISION

THANKS FOR GETTING THROUGH ALL THE DOOM

and gloom. Now for the fun part! We will dive deeply into envisioning what could go right in the near future, for both people and the societies they live in. To do this, it's important to take a holistic and systems-thinking approach, which gives us an effective approach for envisioning what's possible. For all of us to thrive, each of us must be able to thrive. As luck would have it, we are part of a living world that demonstrates a framework for how to do this.

As living organisms, we enjoy an empowered experience that allows us to have an executive function and overarching control over the roughly thirty-seven trillion living cells that make up our body, although we have little control of each of them on their level or many of the organs they make up—that immense complexity all functions automatically.[1] We have some knowledge about how this all works, assembling physical, psychological, and emotional information into frameworks that attempt to capture the human experience and understand it better so we can help ourselves do things like eat more healthily, perform successful surgeries, and enhance therapy to make a lasting difference. But try as we might to understand them, living systems simultaneously bewilder us with their complexity and surprise us with their simple elegance, defying our efforts to duplicate or control outcomes to the degree that we wish.

Much of the problem lies in the fact that we often try to look at parts of systems in isolation, not seeing how they are connected to or influenced by the whole. We also face this challenge when working to create a better future. But seeing things more truthfully, as ever-moving systems that are parts of interacting systems, can help us in our efforts.

Consider the phenomenal complexity of the human brain. With one hundred billion neurons communicating in circuits of electricity and biochemical reactions, sharing information, and coordinating action, it is arguably the most complex network in existence.[2] It also somehow enables us to experience the most mysterious phenomena in the universe: consciousness. Despite what popular science magazines say, we have no idea *why* it works, and we've been able to explain only a pitifully small amount of *how* it works, despite immense amounts of research and progress in recent decades. Every time we create a more complex machine, we compare it to the brain. When we had switchboards, which operators plugged wires into so people could talk to each other on the telephone, we saw an analogy: The brain is an incredibly compact switchboard. Then we came out with punch-card computers to record data, save it, and plug it into another computer that could read it. So we described the brain as a series of punch-card computers. We did the same thing for computer processors, and now we're applying the same approach to quantum computers and the internet. Essentially, we make our understanding of the brain analogous to the most complicated technology we're aware of, and every time we create something more complex, we use it to describe the brain's role in the body.

It's likely no machine in our lifetimes will ever be as intricate or effective at doing all the things the brain does, because nature has a *four-billion-year head start* in the R&D process of evolution. But even the brain, with all its magnificent complexity, cannot survive on its own; it is just one system within a larger and even more complex system. That's why, to provide an analogous framework to our complex global civilization, we turn to the ultimate system of systems: the human body. It is a highly functioning, synchronized organism capable of responding to a variety of environments and situations. Each organ in the body does its job in an interconnected, relational, and interdependent way. The liver is not in competition with the brain or lungs; it depends on their ability to thrive so that it can survive and thrive itself. Each organ has an interest in the others' health and success, as a failure in one organ or part of the body—even a minor one—can have a detrimental impact on the entire system.

Our communities, cities, countries, and global society can each be viewed as an interrelated organic system in which sustaining a highly functioning whole depends on addressing the health of each part of the system. When we see every social structure as interconnected and interdependent, instead of in a siloed vacuum, we can approach its social, economic, and environmental issues from a more holistic and, therefore, more true perspective. Just as the human body requires information about the needs of its different organs to optimize the use of resources throughout the body, human societies depend on all segments and how they influence the health of each other and the whole, and they can do this better with accurate information and frameworks with which to understand themselves. Societies that can understand and act in service of this big picture can address the needs of their citizens and organizations so that every individual—and the society as a whole—can thrive.

I call this interconnected reality *omni-thriving*, in which thriving must take place in all parts for the whole to succeed. When the individual parts are thriving at their maximum level, allowing the overall system to thrive at its maximum level, omni-thriving occurs. This balance has been shown to be beneficial in our bodies (organs depending on each other), natural ecosystems (multitudes of species evolving symbiotic relationships and balance), businesses (when customers, workers, suppliers, and decision-makers are collaborating well, the business succeeds), and even society as a whole. In the next part of the book we'll apply an omni-thriving lens across sectors so we can see how, when all parts of a system are flourishing, the whole system flourishes to its fullest potential.

Chapter 6

A Societal Hierarchy of Needs

WHAT WOULD AN IDEAL, HEALTHY SOCIETY LOOK like? In answering this question, we can't assume that society is a machine. It is more like an organism, like a human body, with physical, mental, and emotional needs. It's made up of smaller organisms—all with nourishment requirements, weaknesses and sicknesses, enemies and allies, and ultracomplex networks and signals. The ancient Greek philosopher Democritus was the first to describe the individual as the "social atom" of society, but we can also consider a human being to be a smaller organism that's part of a larger superorganism. The emergent consciousness, or the emergent executive function that arises, is seemingly the result of the complexity of a connected network of smaller organisms living out their lives and working together, though they may neither know why nor see the bigger picture.

For example, just as antibodies attack viruses and die off along with the viruses, and mountain lion populations increase and decrease along with the deer population, human societies go through cycles tied to their resources and adapt to changes. Attacker-protector and predator-prey dynamics occur within and between societies, similar to how cycles oscillate within nature and our own bodies. But a society is not simply physical; it is also a psychological being. Similar to an individual, a society's personality is made up of myriad internal influences and diverse factors that make up its culture, which we can consider the psychology of the society.

Because these influences and factors that create culture are based on people, they heavily reflect the psychology of the people involved.

Societal Behavior Is Motivated by Societal Psychology

If we go back to Psychology 101, Abraham Maslow's hierarchy of needs gives us a simple framework to understand how critical basic needs are when it comes to supporting the progression of a person's physical, mental, and emotional health. The hierarchy depicts how, once our basic bodily and safety needs are met, we can focus on community, and once community needs are met, we are freed to explore self-actualization. Maslow described this as "The desire to become more and more what one is, to become everything that one is capable of becoming." But it's very difficult to reach any of the higher levels of the needs hierarchy when the lower levels are not satisfied.

If we haven't satisfied the physiological needs—like food, water, and shelter, or a psychological sense of safety and security—it's unlikely we'll be able to think about self-esteem, love, and belonging, let alone such an esoteric concept as self-actualization. But once we have our physiological needs met and our survival is not threatened, then we can start thinking about things like owning a home, saving for retirement, acting on our values, and being a resource for friends, family, and community. As each level is satisfied, it's easier to focus on, and reach for, the next level. We are innately and instinctually active, curious creatures who always want to expand and learn more, grow and do more. We rise in the social hierarchy to the point where we can acquire resources, social alliances, and the means to use our talents to bring our life's visions to life.

Each human being is the basis of a larger social organism: The social atom or, in our updated biological model, the social cell. It follows that this hierarchy of needs also relates to a society. When a nation is at war or fears for its survival, there is little focus on building long-term infrastructure or programs; instead, energy is focused on defeating an enemy or hoarding resources. The fear of annihilation does not allow for the widespread programs that support curiosity about our place among the stars, or programs that seek to better educate our children—instead we focus on how to feed ourselves and keep our children safe through the night. Once we move beyond thinking of society as a machine—particularly as an exclusively economic machine—we can instead regard it as a living organism, making the connection to Maslow's hierarchy more clear. Let's take a closer look at Maslow's hierarchy of needs, applied to society.

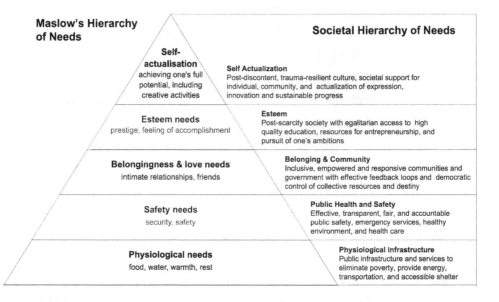

Maslow's Hierarchy of Needs provides a framework for human needs and their prioritization. Expanding this framework to account for similar needs of the society can help us envision the policies, initiatives, and businesses that can be developed to help advance our communities and societies to meet our collective needs.

PHYSIOLOGICAL NEEDS: Any society needs to first and foremost meet the physiological needs of its people. The birth of civilization is often linked to the discovery of agriculture, which created an abundance of food that allowed people to stay in one place and specialize in activities other than finding food. If an individual's physiological needs are not met, they will become desperate and go to extraordinary lengths to meet them in the name of survival. If a society doesn't meet physiological needs—say, water is polluted or not running, or food is scarce or too expensive—the safety and security of the community can be at risk. Violence, theft, and other crimes of desperation often ensue, and a fundamental breakdown occurs.

SAFETY AND SECURITY NEEDS: Once people have their physiological needs met, they are next concerned with the safety of their body, others in their immediate group, and property. Meeting these safety needs helps people relax and become more social and creative. If citizens feel their property isn't secure or their family is threatened, they're not going to be interested in making friends with the neighbors or building up their community, because they fear an attack or loss if they don't maintain a defensive position. A community in this stage is fragmented and disconnected at best, if not troubled by fights between factions at worst. In this environment, little to no progress can occur.

LOVE AND BELONGING NEEDS: Human beings are social animals by nature. We don't simply enjoy each other's company; we *need* it to maintain both physical and mental health.[1] In fact, research finds that loneliness is as dangerous to our health as obesity or smoking fifteen cigarettes per day.[2] If people have both their physiological and safety needs met but they don't have love and belonging, they're putting their health at risk—and they will be missing a fundamental sense of support. They'll have a hard time developing a strong sense of self-esteem, respect for others, confidence, or the desire to educate themselves or seek achievements in entrepreneurship or the arts.

This is damaging on a societal or civilizational level—for the economy, for health costs, and most importantly in the impact on human lives on a larger scale. Without intimacy and friendship, people may seek antisocial attention and notoriety or simply try to self-medicate with possessions. In modern consumer societies, how many products and services use advertising to exacerbate this social vulnerability or simply fill the void left by a lack of strong relationships? Much of our consumer economy is reliant on this strategy, making us feel insecure and in competition with others so we'll buy goods that offer temporary satisfaction and comfort—fleeting relief from the haunting pain of not belonging or feeling loved. The temporary satisfaction is just that—temporary. It does not lead to a society with sustained energetic gain, creativity, or the benefits of stability and interconnectedness that come with strong communities and widespread belonging. Societal belonging can come from strong families, neighborhoods, cities, states, and nations.

SELF-ESTEEM: People who are emotionally secure and possess a healthy sense of self-esteem are more likely to avoid abuse, assert their needs, and be more decisive, realistic in their expectations, and resilient.[3] Likewise, a society that is secure will be less likely to get embroiled in needless wars or conquests, or try to violently acquire or hoard resources, and will be able to move into the future with a more accurate picture of reality, undistorted by the lens of insecurity.

If people's fundamental needs are met but they don't feel the self-esteem that comes with feeling confident and competent, they won't feel like they can achieve much in life or feel motivated to try. Without self-esteem or self-respect, they'll remain in a fear mindset, worried about disruptions, losing their job or risking instability by taking a chance on an entrepreneurial dream. When this is the case, or when people feel humiliated, such as in post-WWI Germany or mid-1700s France, they are more likely to support war against their perceived competitors or to revolt against the system that they feel humiliates or oppresses them.[4] More recent populist movements globally can be correlated to a perceived loss of jobs, social stature, or a sense of "losing" to a competitor. This feeling can be very dangerous if it pervades a society widely enough, while societies that are economically secure, stable, and relatively equal (such as the Nordics) most often have very little appetite for war or revolt.

Once a person's needs for self-esteem, respect, and emotional security are met, they naturally open up, able to gain more insight from their experiences, become more creative, have a strong sense of moral duty, and focus their social energies not on beating others or winning at others' expense, but instead being kind to others and wanting to help them. This self-esteem at a societal level often comes from a strong educational system, meaningful careers, a psychologically healthy and supportive culture, emotional strength, livable wages, and an upward trend in people's expectations of the future.

SELF-ACTUALIZATION: When a society has all these elements, it reaches a point of openness to widespread creativity, kindness, and spontaneity—ingredients for innovation and economic dynamism. With more adaptability and resilience, a society can adapt and innovate its way through a crisis. When the urgency of a crisis is coupled with a society that is free to be creative, responsive, and spontaneous, it will embrace transitions so that it can adapt to changing circumstances quickly.

An example is Silicon Valley, which sprang from the creative and permissive culture of the 1960s. It encouraged people to feel safe to be themselves, allowed them to be weird, different and even visionary. This led to many new businesses, creative new products, and revolutionary services like a free and open internet, which are now fundamental engines of innovation for the world. These innovations have helped us adapt to a changing world and created incredible new ways of carrying out communication, learning, and commerce—inventing new ways for us to solve persistent challenges, while providing new jobs in technology that were impossible only decades ago. Contrast that with North Korea, which is not considered an innovative or advancing society, partially because people live in an overwhelming state of fear about standing out and being different. Any urge to do so is quickly crushed and the person is castigated as a betrayer of the state (assuming that person is not the Great Leader).

When an individual becomes ready for self-actualization, they are truly empowered to realize their life's potential. When a society reaches this stage, it doesn't just create the future (as any dystopian, yet powerful society can do); it is more likely to create a future that is truly great because it is created by open, secure, and caring people, to meet the multifaceted needs of its larger community.

This hierarchy is a progression that we each go through personally and also societally. A society or community can assess what needs aren't being met, build programs or solutions to ensure they will be met for everyone, and then progress from there. The goal is an omni-thriving economy in which people can meet their needs, express themselves, have mutual respect, and feel good about who they are and what they choose to do with their lives. This approach not only nurtures the physical and social infrastructure systems of society but also boosts the economy. Just as individuals thrive when they balance work, family, friendships, exercise, diet, and personal growth, so a society thrives when it nurtures all its facets: culture, relationships, environment, business, sustainability, innovation, economy, public programs, education, equal opportunity, and general quality of life for its people. Imagine what a day in your life would be, living in this society. How would you feel, knowing that all your needs in the pyramid can be met? And what would you do with your time?

We Can Be an Omni-Thriving Social Organism

Just as Maslow's hierarchy of needs is a powerful framework to invoke when envisioning what you can do to help things go right in the world, thinking of society as having all the complexity—and the fundamental systems—of an organism helps us better understand society's patterns, dynamics, and reactions. If you've ever lost a much-needed job, felt depressed, been lonely or isolated, gone through a major health crisis, or been stressed to the brink of burnout from too many commitments to fulfill, you quickly realized that when one aspect of your life isn't working, it can throw everything else into chaos. If you sacrifice too much time with friends to take up more and more of your waking hours with work, your relationships suffer. And if you shirk your work responsibilities to pursue recreation for too long, you may well lose your livelihood. Luckily, most of us get tired of doing only one thing anyway and thirst for balance. Without this natural tendency, the imbalance compounds and leaves you feeling unenergized and lacking the strength and resilience to get through challenges or unforeseen disruptions.

On the flip side, consider when you have been at your personal best: when you're in great physical shape, you're emotionally supported, you have close friends to spend time with, you're in love, or you feel inspired by the work you're doing. Having the fundamental bases covered enables you to be impressively productive, highly creative, a joy to be around, more confidently funny and playful. You become an all-around more capable and resilient person. If hardship comes your way, it's easy for you to either solve the problem or let it roll off your back.

This is what omni-thriving feels like on a personal level. Imagine what it could look like on a societal level.

Holistic Societal Transformation

Many cities and governments are seeking to thrive by becoming more sustainable, but also more humanistic. The notion of "smart cities" was nonexistent just twenty years ago, or only hinted at in the annals of sci-fi, but today many communities are making progress in becoming better places to live, using the new technology and data available to them, along with more humanistic approaches to governing. One example of what can happen when a holistic approach is taken with social, economic, and sustainability goals is Andhra Pradesh, the eighth largest state in India and home to approximately fifty-three million people. City planners, government officials, corporate entities, and other concerned stakeholders use multiple types of data analytics and advanced technology solutions to solve complex societal challenges. They have holistically applied innovation and data-driven approaches to resolve sustainable resource management, poverty, education, agricultural and public safety issues, and natural disaster response.

Under the umbrella of its Real Time Governance Center, the state provides ongoing monitoring and reporting across its entire ecosystem of thirty-three departments and provides more than 745 services. Andhra Pradesh is able to integrate massive amounts of data from IoT devices, security and traffic cameras, department databases, and citizen surveys to enable constructive, immediate, comprehensive governance. This integrated approach enables the state to track its progress in reaching its United Nations Sustainable Development Goals by tracking measures such as life expectancy, education, economic opportunity, and other factors that help improve the state's Happiness Index. This improves the lives of its citizens, provides an example of a model for holistic social transformation, and has resulted in exponential benefits.[5]

"But how will we pay for it?" This is a very important question and possibly the most common response to big-picture thinking and programs, especially for taxpayer-funded governments. However, it assumes a false choice: that social benefits are strictly cost centers that should produce financial returns, when in fact solving societal problems can not only impact human beings in a positive way but also reduce costs in related areas or create new indirect revenue streams. For example, when the city of Dallas looked at its homelessness issue, data showed that taking no direct action was costing taxpayers a combined $40,000 per year per homeless person, between jail time and emergency services costs. They shifted to a holistic approach, addressing complex factors that lead to persistent homelessness directly and including programs for housing, mental and physical health, drug addiction, and job training. These housing-first programs now cost the city just $13,000 per homeless person annually—a dramatic financial improvement thanks to actually addressing the problem directly.[6]

Whole-System Problem Solving

Societies often tend to attack each of their challenges in isolation— sometimes simply by "throwing money at the problem" without deeply understanding the issues in the context of other challenges and influences. To be fair, this way is much easier but also less effective and often more work in the long run. This approach also ignores the principles behind healthy organic systems. In our bodies, it doesn't work to have one organ, or one system, that is extremely healthy while any other part of the body is failing.

Anyone who's ever had a kidney stone knows that even something very small going wrong in one organ can require the entire body to cancel other plans and focus on nothing else. If you have the healthiest liver in the world but a decrepit heart, failing lungs, or severely damaged digestive track, your entire body will die. You can even lose your life if you experience too much inflammation in your appendix, a tiny element of your digestive system whose purpose and function we're only recently learning about.

Similarly, within the societal organism, we must recognize and value all levels of needs and the people who have them. If there is a lack in one part of society, it affects the whole; for example, extreme inequality leads to any number of interrelated ailments, including unequal educational or health outcomes, increased crime, terrorism, populism, and even global conflict. And if any aspect is not functioning, eventually it can collapse an entire social organism, much like a small tumor left unchecked. It could even be said that this is the grand challenge of our time: to develop societal models that fulfill the higher levels of needs and lay waste to the scourges of poverty, ignorance, insecurity, disease, desperation, and apathy—all while doing so sustainably.

Just as your pancreas is not in competition with your lungs for resources and your liver is not in competition with your stomach to outperform the other, societies need not see themselves as being engaged in antagonistic, territorial, or zero-sum competitions to fulfill a limited number of needs. Meaningful solutions for the whole can be developed when we address specific issues and opportunities for the parts. When we combine tools, technologies, and unified data with operational expertise, opportunities are boundless for solving difficult issues in critical areas such as infrastructure, sustainability, safety, education, transportation, and more. This is particularly meaningful with urban global populations projected to reach over six billion by 2045.[7] As cities grow, the best solutions can adapt and scale in an omni-thriving way.

Building an omni-thriving society should not start with what technology to use, but rather what its goals are. Much of Andhra Pradesh's success can be attributed to the way in which the state started with the objective of increasing happiness and reaching sustainable development goals. Only then did it envision how technology could be used to provide a higher-level, broader, interrelated view that delivers insight into every aspect of the state's social programs, distribution channels, and response methods, allowing for coordinated issue resolution and better performance of social services and coordination. Tools that I discussed in Chapter 3—such as data analytics, AI, 3D LiDAR sensing technology, and 5G networks—are reaching such a level of sophistication that they can be united to help assess and manage entire social systems and can do so transparently to the citizenry, while protecting people's privacy. The choice between privacy and insight has become a false one; powerful governments and corporations have no excuse not to protect our rights and civil liberties. Auditable solutions are widely available, with features that protect privacy while allowing for the capture of valuable information that can be used to improve the places where we live and work, as well as the public services we pay for. Whether the system is an enterprise, a city, or a country, these tools can support the resolution of complex issues in a holistic, balanced way that benefits us all socially, economically, and environmentally.

Embracing Cultural Innovation

Technology itself is only half of the equation—it must be combined with new ways of thinking and new ways of working toward our goals. It's critical to recognize that while fifty disconnected social projects acting independently might generate small changes in a few areas, they will fail to bring about the large-scale cultural change we need to transform our world for the better. To do this, we must think in terms of interacting and interrelated systems, ensuring that all parts of a social organism are not only functioning, but flourishing, so that the whole can thrive at its maximum potential. Only then will we reach self-actualization for humanity.

Rome was not built in a day, and neither will the future Rio de Janeiro be. No one is building a society all by themselves, a la the game *SimCity*. Just as your lung, bone, and stomach cells have very specific jobs to do to support the growth and operations of your whole body, we each have our own roles to play and our own work to do—to support, energize, and evolve the different systems in our society. By building a thriving foundation of people and communities, we can enable society to build itself up more dynamically, ethically, and sustainably, while unleashing our global creative potential to build a better future.

We are each working on our own part of this story, and to work toward something, we need a vision of what that something is. In the coming chapters, we will dive into what a thriving society could look like. We will design for ideal outcomes; in other words, by starting with what could go right. We'll see how this enables innovative visions to address society's toughest dilemmas, from the perspectives of a few of the different industries or sectors that comprise the social organism. We will keep ourselves within the realm of the possible, including only those technologies and solutions that are available or nearing commercialization today.

With that in mind, please consider these to be merely examples; I invite you to expand on them, add your own ideas, and seek examples that might help your community or even your career. It takes creative, passionate, energized people to build the future we need. What part of our future are you excited to envision and help create?

Chapter 7

Physiological Needs: The Energy to Power Everything We Do

ANYONE WHO'S EVER BEEN BACKCOUNTRY camping can appreciate experiencing the world as it was before electricity . . . for a few days. While the lack of thought-interrupting notifications and technology can be rejuvenating, most of us wouldn't be comfortable or even survive long if this were a permanent situation. However, as recently as 150 years ago, nearly anyone who lit their homes and businesses did so with oil lights or candles. Now the presence of electricity is so ubiquitous that we can fully appreciate it as the core physiological need it has become only by considering what would happen if we suddenly didn't have it. When extended electrical blackouts occur during forest fires, strong winds, or ice storms, think of how crippled our daily lives become. US defense experts have compared the effects of these storms to what might happen on a larger scale if a high-altitude electromagnetic pulse (HEMP) from a nuclear weapon took out the power grid nationwide, frying the circuitry of electronics in our homes, cars, stores, and infrastructure.[1]

Imagine the dystopian effects: no communication (TV, radios, cars, phones); no form of transportation (gas pumps down, traffic and streetlights out, mass transit inoperable, airlines grounded); no energy (even oil and gas delivery would grind to a halt). We would have no running water, and without stoves we'd be cooking and boiling water over open fires. Without refrigeration, food supplies would quickly spoil and become exhausted. Most stores wouldn't be able to rely on the supply chains they need to stay open. Much of our electronic banking and money systems would become inoperable, and the methods we use to transact, ship goods and resources, and communicate with each other would be unusable. People on dialysis and life support would not endure long as hospital generators ran out of fuel. Doctors would operate and deliver babies by flashlight or candlelight. Deaths from exposure, carbon dioxide poisoning, and house fires would increase. With no heat, ways to cook, or running water in our homes, we'd become refugees as we sought out supplies for our most basic needs. Our days would be spent scavenging or looting for food, water, and shelter. Essentially, we would return to pre-industrial conditions without the survival knowledge or skills that our ancestors had, or the infrastructure we depend on today. Rebuilding what we have constructed over decades or centuries would be aided by collaborative countries, but getting back to any semblance of normality would take very long indeed, and many would suffer or die in the process.

This fragility of the power grid makes our own lives fragile: As you read earlier, it's estimated that in the HEMP scenario, 66 to 90% of the US population would likely perish within one year from starvation, disease, and societal breakdown (as estimated by Peter Vincent Pry in his 2017 testimony before a congressional Homeland Security subcommittee). Electricity has indeed become a critical physiological necessity that enables modern society to survive.[2]

Design Objectives of the Past

As the US transitioned to electric power at the beginning of the twentieth century, the first eighty years saw a focus on safety, reliability, and cost. US regulators and utilities designed policy and infrastructure projects based on these objectives. Centralized generation was a desirable way to go, through facilities located away from end users that could be safely managed at scale and send power to customers through a network of high-voltage transmission lines. These facilities included fossil fuel–fired power plants, hydroelectric dams, and later nuclear power plants. As the needs of the new consumer society grew, so did the centralized networks. The New Deal extended the grid out to rural America. In the post-WWII era, with new electronics and products being invented, there was increasing need for more accessible and affordable electricity in our homes. This was all seen as a part of laying the foundation for a consumer society, focusing on how big these centralized power plants could get, how much energy they could create in a single place, and then how that could be pushed out to consumers.

In the 1970s, the oil crisis catalyzed thinking about energy conservation, independence, and sustainability. At the same time, there was growing awareness of the ways our energy production harms the environment through air pollutant emissions, water use and discharge, waste generation, and land use for facilities and transmission lines. This, combined with a growing recognition of the need for environmental sustainability, accelerated a movement to start designing more renewable energy technologies and systems. President Jimmy Carter even put solar panels on the White House to encourage the wave of environmentalism. But when Ronald Reagan became president, he removed them—signaling how politically charged the energy policy issue had become. The political divide continued: Alternative systems were essentially ignored by the public for two decades, even while innovations and incremental improvements were being made in the background.

Then in the new millennium, a resurgence of awareness about climate change and its potentially catastrophic effects arose, especially with the first generation that would see and suffer from the worst of the projected cataclysms. A wave of interest in and enthusiasm for clean energy arose, for renewables like solar, wind, hydro, tidal, geothermal, and biomass. This manifested in startups and large companies alike, leading to better engineered renewable systems, built economies of scale, and reduced costs, bringing us to where we are today: In many places, wind and solar are the cheapest sources of energy, surpassing "grid parity"—the cost at which renewables are no more expensive than the current grid.

This is a fantastic trend, but it brings new challenges. Due to the unpredictability of renewables caused by clouds passing over solar panels, or wind speeds varying throughout the day, managing the flow of energy is vastly more complicated on the face of it than a coal plant that runs at capacity 24/7. Renewable energy is created on its own schedule, not in accordance with peak demand times: Generally the sun is going down when commuters get home from work and start using lights, stoves, and entertainment devices, and wind speeds tend to be highest at night when we are sleeping. So storage and transportation are a challenge. There are emerging solutions, which we will be covering later.

Despite the complexity of renewables, they are more important than ever. Unfortunately, many predictions about climate change are being proven correct even earlier than expected. The rate of global sea level rise between 2006 and 2016 was 2.5 times faster than for almost all of the twentieth century.[3] The number of annual weather-related disasters that cause over $1 billion in damage has doubled since 1980.[4] The UN estimates that climate-related deaths will increase to an average of 250,000 per year between 2030 and 2050—and sadly, many of these will be children.[5] Whether it's a hurricane that can knock out power even for a community the size of New York City or wildfires that engulf hundreds of thousands of acres, climate disasters are happening more often, and with higher intensity, urgently showing us that we need to reconceive our energy system. Currently, many energy grids can go down with single points of failure—a tree branch falling on an important wire can knock out power for many parts of the US Northeastern Seaboard. This is what happens with centralized generation and distribution, especially when not built on principles of resiliency. It's high time for something new.

Setting Ideal Design Objectives for the Future of Energy

So how might we think beyond how things are now to design an ideal system that can reliably meet our needs? I talked with an expert on regulated energy systems, Ted Ko, to sketch out an ideal energy future. He is an MIT graduate who has been a leader in clean energy and energy policy for more than a decade. Ted was vice president of policy and regulatory affairs at Stem Inc., and he works to advance policy-based market development toward a global clean energy future. According to their website, "Stem's solutions help enterprise customers benefit from a clean, adaptive energy infrastructure and achieve a wide variety of goals, including expense reduction, resilience, sustainability, environmental and corporate responsibility and innovation."

Ted talked about how essential it is to design for the ideal, even if it is rarely done. Most roadmaps to achieve an alternative energy system don't have a destination. Instead, they offer a technology or general ideas on overcoming barriers that don't consider what we ultimately need nor how to achieve it. In our conversations, Ted emphasized that "We need to create a long-term roadmap to a fully decarbonized energy system, by first defining that ideal future state and then detailing the policy steps to get there. Most of the technologies and business models that could dramatically improve the sustainability, reliability, and resilience of our energy systems are available today. However, as a highly regulated industry, what's lacking are the policy structures that create and sustain the energy markets of this ideal future."

Ideal Design Objective 1: Resilient

We have long and rightfully prioritized energy security and safety to protect something that, if brought down, would cause a national catastrophe. That means defending against attacks, making sure hacks don't happen, and putting up physical barriers to keep people out of dangerous areas. But if we were to think beyond safety and security, we could start to consider a system that's not only safe but also *resilient*. We must ask: What type of power grid could restart quickly, recover from disruptions, and still provide the energy that's needed? Resilience would make us less vulnerable to the increasing storms and natural disasters from climate change, attack, or unpredictable incidents.

Ideal Design Objective 2: Sustainable

About 27% of greenhouse gas emissions in the US stem from electrical generation; the only sector that produces more is transportation.[6] Plus, when you push electrons through wires or any conductor, energy is lost as heat in the material. In the US, the energy loss to distribution and transmission averages 5%.[7] More energy gets lost the farther we transmit it, as it moves from high voltage to the lower voltages that houses and personal electronics can use. Depending on the state, the loss can vary between 2 and 13%. In countries like India, it was as high as 30% in 2000; since 2014 it has been at about 20%. As of this writing, the world average loss is around 8.3%.[8] This is one cost of having centralized power plants that push electricity many miles to where it's actually used. Clean energy can have a big impact on reducing climate change, as it doesn't create as many—or any—emissions and is often generated much closer to the point of consumption, such as the rooftop of the house consuming the electricity, which reduces the transmission waste. In an ideal energy system that seeks to reduce its contribution to climate change, it's essential to design for sustainability.

Ideal Design Objective 3: Capable and Reliable

Clearly, any power grid system needs to be designed to be capable of providing enough energy to the right places, at the right time, in the form in which it needs to be used. Consumers shouldn't have to worry about blackouts, brownouts, or other disruptions.

Essentially, it should just work, which unfortunately is not a given for many people around the world.

Ideal Design Objective 4: Accessible

We all need power to function in the modern world. Electricity should be both affordable and available wherever it's needed. Accessibility provides economic empowerment, because the cheaper and more available this fundamental necessity is, the more people can count on it to support the things they need to do. Whether it means having light for children to study in the evenings, or being able to charge a smartphone so work calls aren't missed on the go, to having access to banking and emergency medical services, accessible electricity is a key physiological necessity of our modern world.

Designing the Ideal Energy System

If we were to imagine we lived in the *SimCity* video game, and to design an energy system from scratch, what would it look like? Ted and I kept ourselves within the realm of the possible, considering only the technology we already have, which is fully capable of achieving an ideal state that generates and manages energy according to the principles already laid out here. The gap is not technological; what we're missing is a wholistic vision and the collaboration to get us there.

Renewable Energy Already Comes to You

There are more ways than ever to generate renewable energy, from wind to wave power to geothermal plants deep in the ground. Which one of these is right for you depends on several factors, not least of which is where you live. But let's take the example of solar. It seems to be the best way of achieving local renewable generation because sunlight comes to you at some point of the day or season anywhere on Earth's surface. This local generation meets our design objectives, especially because it can be managed by intelligent microgrids with many power-generation sites rather than a single, centralized one. Above all, this omnipresence makes it *capable*.

More Locally Managed Sources Create More Stability

Microgrids operate on a small scale, within neighborhoods or even city blocks. Energy is generated and transmitted locally and connected to other microgrids throughout the system. But because it's decentralized, it is more able to cope with disruptions to the system. At local, regional, and national levels these microgrids intelligently or automatically shift energy from where it is abundant to where it is needed. There is no single point of failure, so a tree branch falling on an important wire can no longer cut power for millions of people. The system is therefore more *resilient*.

Sourcing Energy Locally Is Cleaner and Cheaper

Generating energy locally from renewable resources dramatically reduces or eliminates the toxins released into the environment. Harvesting energy from the sun that already shines onto roof panels can provide plenty of clean energy for a household. No need for so many acres for centralized power plants, or safety buffers around generation plants, water coolants, cutting through forests for power lines, or even skylines cluttered with poles and wires. Solar panels are also mostly recyclable due to their large proportion of highly recyclable glass, and the degree to which they can be recycled is improving quickly.[9] It is therefore much more *sustainable.*

Because of ever lower costs combined with increasing power per module, we can now access solar energy easily and affordably in more places and situations than ever. Solar systems can be purchased or financed by companies that also install them. This then becomes your power source, and you pay back the solar company— rather than the utility—through your monthly energy bill, until you own the system. This approach is being deployed everywhere from the commercial to the village scale, helping to bring solar to every corner of the world.[10] Because of the plummeting prices and many financial options, solar has become *accessible,* and other renewables are quickly becoming the same.

The Emergence of Energy Marketplaces

When we have a surplus of collected energy at our homes, we can sell that energy back to the grid and our local communities. We can actually make a profit on this, because renewables are essentially a zero marginal cost form of energy: You pay for the panels or wind turbines, and because no fuel is needed, there's little to no cost to produce energy, aside from occasional cleaning or maintenance. You're getting energy for free from the sun—the same source that plants and the living ecosystems they're part of have been successfully and sustainably powering their natural economies on for eons.

With an energy marketplace, we have a new way not just to save money but also to make money off the generation taking place on our roofs. This transforms us into prosumers: We don't just consume energy from the system; we also contribute it. Let's explore what the energy marketplace might look like for prosumers and its potential for bringing our society to a place of greater abundance, equality, and economic freedom.

The Problem: Volatility in Renewables

There's a big issue with renewables: They are very unpredictable and volatile, and they come from many different places. This is a nightmare scenario for a lot of grid operators who are used to stable generation from coal power plants, which take a very long time to ramp up but then operate on their own for long periods of time. A system that relies on this kind of timeline makes it difficult to manage the volatility of renewable energy.

Renewables can generate too much energy when it's not needed, or not enough at peak hours. However, a slew of solutions have been created to tackle these new challenges, from AI-driven power management to energy storage innovations that range from smart batteries to pumping water up a hill when energy is cheap and letting it flow back down over a turbine when energy is expensive. These innovations lay the groundwork for renewables to power everything we do, and the sooner we can utilize them at scale, the better.

A Solution: Energy Storage and the Energy Market

Energy storage and batteries are becoming cheaper, more effective, and more recyclable. Plus, we now have intelligent software that can manage the flow of energy into the batteries and back out to the grid. And the meteoric rise in electric vehicle adoption presents an opportunity: Batteries are everywhere, and they often sit unused most of the time. This energy can be used by vehicle-to-grid (V2G) or building-to-grid (B2G) solutions. Basically, anything with a battery can now plug into the grid and even interact with it to help power and manage the local microgrid. That means you can store energy when it's abundant and then deploy the stored energy when it's scarce. This not only helps to better manage the energy flowing throughout the grid but also helps users economically, so they can buy energy when it's cheap and sell it when it's expensive.

Now this process needs to be intelligent, because we don't want to spend our days at home staring at a screen, figuring out when to buy or sell energy like some kind of stock day trader. The autonomous economic agents we covered in Chapter 3 are basically AI software that can go out into the digital world and find me the best deals with buying or selling at certain times. These same types of agents can be used to manage energy at an independent individual battery level, a home level, or a community level. These agents can be used to understand the market of energy, what the prices are, use data to predict what prices are going to be, and then store and feed energy back into the grid at the appropriate (most profitable) times.

A Day in the Life of a Prosumer in the Energy Market

What might the energy market look like on a personal level? You come home, you plug in your car, and let's say you're at 70% capacity. Maybe your smart home will look at your calendar and wait to charge your car until the evening, unless you have something scheduled. If not, why not feed energy into the grid during peak hours and generate income? While you are at home cooking or watching TV, your car will be selling energy for you and making you money. The batteries that were charged during the day by the solar panels on your house can do the same. Ahh, true energy independence.

Tesla is one well-known visionary in the electric vehicles and renewable energy industries. Tesla came out initially as a car company, but really they're becoming a vertically integrated collection of startup companies building solutions for the future. Today these products and solutions benefit their core product (cars), but they can be developed to serve other markets once mature. These solutions range from electric drivetrains, batteries, and AI for autonomous driving and the semiconductor chip it runs on to home solar and batteries, and more.[11] Most notably for our discussion here, Tesla has created battery innovations, the solar roof, and the power wall for homes. This company and others deliver all the parts necessary today to build the foundation of the future vision just described. By using intelligent software, you will be able to activate this type of prosumer ecosystem whereby your home, your community, and your car interact with the energy economy and generate money for you. You've now got an asset that's generating value for the system while bringing you income. Now imagine when your self-driving car can be sent out to drive as a taxi while you don't need to go anywhere—another new revenue stream from the combination of intelligent software running valuable hardware and interacting with a market. This prosumer market will touch much more of our economy as we progress.

It's not just cars that will be making people money. Soon, fleets of school buses, freight trucks, and delivery vehicles will go electric, and when they're plugged in, they'll be helping to stabilize the grid. Then when drivers are about to pick up kids or packages and drop them off, they'll have the energy they need, when they need it. Often these types of fleets have predictable routes, so they know how much energy they'll need to make the trip each day, and how much they can supply back to the grid.

I love beautiful architecture, and our built environment is amazing. But most buildings today don't make use of the innovations and opportunities available to them. We have a historic opportunity to make our buildings work smarter and play a greater role in our energy ecosystem. New smart spaces technologies and analytics can help buildings become safer and more sustainable, and provide better support and functionality for their tenants. Buildings can even trade energy or other resources, creating new income streams for a company or family.

This doesn't only benefit the world as a whole; it also benefits the self-interest of building owners and operators. If you run a grocery store, manufacturing facility, shopping mall, or office park, you can use renewable energy storage systems and smart services as both a new revenue source and a way to cut your costs. That boosts your bottom line, providing more financial flexibility that allows you to take more risks, invest in innovations, and spend more money on services for your employees, family, customers, and others. For example, entrepreneurs could make that office park a great place to work and attract the best companies, or a shopping mall could provide new services and experiences. Making our existing assets more productive and generating more value from them is a sustainable choice that is good for business.

But how do we get there? We need more than tech; we need policy, businesses, and new solutions to enable and accelerate the transition to renewable energy and energy efficiency. This ranges from simple actions like caulking and insulating windows to installing solar panels and more complex undertakings like designing and building electric vehicles and power walls, along with software and AI to better operate and manage the system and enable new business models. Every point along this value chain represents an opportunity to contribute to sustainable energy independence, efficiency, and empowerment.

Chapter 8

Safety and Security: Complex Problems Need Holistic Solutions

CRIME DAMAGES TWO LIVES: THE VICTIM'S AND the offender's. It not only damages the life or property of the victim and their families but also reduces the potential of the perpetrator's life. This person could have been prevented from harming others and lived a better life, brought more joy to their community, and contributed more to society. Every person we lose to violent crime is a wasted life that could have been saved if we knew how to prevent the conditions and choices that led to the crime.

Let me put it this way: Somewhere there is a three-year-old, laughing and playing and pestering his (because it's most likely to be a he) parents as all children do. Within twenty years, that beautiful child will murder someone. Not because of who they are, but because of who they will become, largely due to the experiences they will have between now and then. What can we do to ensure that this adorable child has experiences in his life that don't lead to him robbing someone at gunpoint or slaying a fellow member of their community for drug territory? Some inevitably will turn to crime and will need to be kept away from society, but many developed countries don't have these problems to the degree that the US and some other more violent countries do. We can do better. We owe it to this child, his family, the family of his victims, and ourselves.

Today most conversations about public safety revolve around police responses to crimes and emergencies. This is one very important aspect, and it is critical to ensure that those who serve us in uniform have the equipment, technology, and training to do their jobs effectively and get home safely to their families. But ensuring the public safety is not only about responding and reacting to crime. It is also about the factors that lead to crime and violence: poverty, instability, and fear; perceptions of injustice and corruption; and lack of confidence in the government and institutions to work effectively and efficiently for the people they govern. If we are to envision an ideal future and work to build it, we need to think about safety holistically, in ways that address the root issues, with a broader definition that goes beyond safety of body and property. We need to include the *feeling* of safety a population has and the accuracy of their perceptions.

Safety sets a foundation for people to reach their full potential, for society to flourish, and for business to thrive. It's not just about preventing the bad—it's about enabling and unleashing the good. People tend to hold back creativity and openness in times of danger. In fact, fear actually shrinks our brain—making it less creative.[1] To meet the needs of our time in a world that is evolving rapidly and facing new challenges, creativity, openness, and new ideas are going to be critical. Without public safety, we have little chance of adapting our society to the degree that we need. So let's dig into what this strong foundation could look like.

Crime in Today's World

In polls, generally people overestimate levels of crime, and most are surprised to learn that crime rates have actually been decreasing over the long term. With news and internet clickbait highlighting sensational stories in their ever more sophisticated hunt for views, the world can easily seem like a very dangerous place that is getting worse by the day. What does this sort of false conditioning do to a society's psyche? First, it causes fear; second, it desensitizes us to violence in general; and third, it can normalize crime, which leads some to believe it's acceptable to commit crimes, and others to expect crime to happen to them.

As we noted earlier, since peaking in the 1980s and 1990s, violent crime has been declining steadily by 50% or more in most Western countries. When you look back even further, the situation appears even better. One study estimated homicide rates in Europe dating back as far as 1300 and found a dramatic decline, from between 20 and 70 murders (depending on the country) per 100,000 people to around 1 in 100,000 today.[2]

If you ask a hundred people why crime has decreased so dramatically, you'll likely get a hundred different answers. *We've put more people in jail, so criminals are off the streets. Technology has made it harder to steal or to get away with a crime. The advent of social media and phones gives people more distractions to keep them busy. There's more educational material available and perhaps more economic opportunity.* But the fact that crime is decreasing on average doesn't mean that violent crime isn't an issue—in fact, its distribution is extremely unequal, based on factors like country, neighborhood, race, and socioeconomic status.

For many people today, especially for the disenfranchised and disempowered, the world *is* still a dangerous place. In fact, 83% of violent deaths occur today outside of conflict areas (war zones). Brazil had more violent deaths than Syria in 2015, and in the period between 2007 and 2014 there were more violent deaths in Mexico than Afghanistan and Iraq.[3] In an ideal world—that future that we've been talking about creating—everyone is safe from a violent death, regardless of socioeconomic status, the location they were born, or their race or gender.

Uncovering the Causes of Crime

Some key causes for crime include desperation from poverty, real or perceived corruption, organized crime, inequality and tensions between groups, lack of trust in authority, cultural or learned behaviors, and disenfranchisement. Research finds that crime happens most often in destabilized and unpredictable environments where people feel forced to do something illegal to either gain the resources they need to survive, defeat the forces that threaten them, right the wrongs and injustices they perceive, prove their worth to their fellow gang members who have become their only support network, or just feel significant in a world that seems to overlook them.[4]

Much of our common understanding of crime today comes from the classical theory of utilitarianism developed by Jeremy Bentham, who lived from 1748 to 1832. According to this theory, we all undertake a cost-benefit analysis when making decisions, whether they are about committing a crime or making an economic choice. Basically, people are simple rational machines, cost-benefit calculators, who will do what gives them the most pleasure (or value) for the lowest price or does them the least damage. This way of thinking has been carried over to criminal justice theories. If criminals perceive crime as bringing them more benefit than harm, they will do it. Therefore, the best response to prevent crime is to swiftly make the pain of committing crime much higher than the benefit. In other words, make sure crime doesn't pay.[5]

Other theories have ranged from classical approaches that simply call for revenge, to genetic determinism that assumes behavior is deterministic and passed on from generation to generation (causing much discrimination along the way), to phrenology, which asserted that the shape of the skull correlates to the areas of brain development (or lack of it) and therefore could reveal people with criminal tendencies. Another theory, atavism, popularized by Cesare Lombroso (1835–1909), asserted that born criminals could be identified by attributes like crooked noses, long arms, ears with smaller lobes, and above-average amounts of body hair. As ridiculous as these theories seem today, they actually came with very real consequences: depictions of criminals that still show up in our culture today, and policies and punishments that affect the life chances of the descendants of people who were discriminated against in the past.

Today we take a more scientific and nuanced approach, but we are far from having a theory of everything to comprehensively explain the causes of crime. We know that crime is influenced by a combination of social, psychological, cultural, family, and situational factors, as well as environmental pollutants and an individual's hormonal and biochemical levels. Research also finds common threads that include corruption or perception of corruption, distrust that those in authority will value and protect people, unequal and unstable societies, and increasing tensions between groups, whether economical, ideological, or political. In short, we're not the rational calculators we imagined ourselves to be; rather, we're emotional animals that commit crime for a variety of reasons.

Maybe crime helps one person feel like they belong. Another person may commit a crime because they are desperate. Or maybe they've been trained to do it by their family or mentors, so they feel it's a trade or skill. There are also crimes that are widely accepted or unequally enforced, such as cocaine use in the affluent homes of Beverly Hills, California, versus the nearby chronically impoverished and heavily policed streets of Compton. In short, we are complex and multifaceted individuals with an equally complex variety of reasons why we commit crimes. Therefore, to solve this problem we must address the entire person and their needs, perceptions, and environment.

Unfortunately, because of recently growing and widespread distrust in institutions, economic disparity, and cultural tensions, we could be seeing the conditions for another large uptick in crime. And the means to harm people these days are much more sophisticated and more readily available. We are approaching a very dangerous time if we don't get this right. Not only are weapons readily available, but tribal tensions are being stoked by political leaders and their internet megaphones to gain from those tensions. The US is a recent example, as are Brazil and some European countries. We could be facing an oncoming explosion in crime because of these tensions. But we also have more knowledge than ever about what to do about it—to continue our trend toward a safer, more peaceful planet.

If given widespread peace and safety, people could feel truly free, creating an environment in which creativity and innovation can flourish. People would feel not only physically safe but also to be free to be diverse, live differently, or have different opinions. This feeling of safety comes from mutual respect and the ability to express oneself, to be able to be different by birth, race, ethnicity, or just the clothes you wear or what you do. Allowing that freedom ends up making people safer not only physically but also emotionally and mentally. It defuses the misunderstandings that can lead to alienation, loneliness, and adversarial thinking, which threaten the safety of us all. Embracing diversity and freedom enables us to communicate with each other more easily and about more things—laying the foundation for a safe society.

Setting Ideal Design Objectives for Crime and Public Safety

Unfortunately, with a punishment-centric mindset, we often cut off the potential for rehabilitation and helping people build a life that doesn't rely on crime in the first place. Especially if after the offense a person cannot find a job, is discriminated against, financially crippled, or institutionalized to the point where they don't know how to survive outside of prison, they are likely to simply return to what they know. Yet everyone is a valuable human being, and our goal is to help make their lives better regardless of who they are. So how can we shift from a public safety focus solely on getting the "bad guys" and protecting the "good guys" to nurturing and enabling the good guys within everyone?

Ideal Design Objective 1:
A Government Worthy of Trust

When people can't trust their government to protect and serve them, or they fear that organized crime is more powerful than the government, they support whatever organization has the upper hand or offers protection or opportunity. Colombia was once one of the world's most dangerous countries. Kidnappings and shootings in the streets were commonplace. Bogota had a homicide rate of 81 per 100,000 in 1993, compared to the US nationwide average of 5 per 100,000.[6] That's almost sixteen murders every day, mostly driven by the drug trade and organized crime. But by 2018 it had become one of the world's top tourist destinations, with much safer streets and crime rates that rival those of many US cities, at 12.7 per 100,000. It's not perfect, but it's pretty peaceful, especially compared to the recent past. People now come from all over the world to enjoy Colombian cities, beautiful beaches, and distinctive culture.

What changed? They were able to build more trust in institutions, police, and other people in authority. They focused on disbanding organized crime, a major destabilizer in their communities. Previously, people didn't believe that the government or the community was able to protect them. People had to choose between trusting the organized crime rings or the government to protect them, and many simply looked the other way in the face of threats and uncertainty. Once organized crime was dismantled, communities were better able to prevent crime. The same is true for other societies—when institutions are trusted and communities are not afraid of organized crime, they are mostly able to police themselves and ask for help when they need it.

Another example comes from the American West after the Civil War, where states, local law enforcement, and governance were initially weak and violence was common. But crime began to fall rapidly after the establishment of strong states. Meanwhile, in the American South, as the states grew stronger, violence increased. What made the difference? In the South, violent groups like the Ku Klux Klan were allowed to operate by former Confederate politicians who used the culture of fear to hold power and crush opposition. In 1892, this corrupt and untrustworthy political approach created such a permissively violent environment that every three days there was a lynching.[7] Similar examples exist around the world, pointing to a universal truth: Where violent organized crime is allowed to operate and intermingle with politics, few of the citizenry are truly safe.

Ideal Design Objective 2: Preventive Public Safety

When crime does happen, we need to ensure that it's responded to effectively, to save life and property. Risks must be mitigated, and the police officers or emergency first responders must have the tools and technology they need to do their jobs effectively, then come home safely to their families at the end of their shift. Of course, we need to respond to crimes, but we want our ideal approach to be able to prevent crime and violence beforehand, instead of just arriving after the fact to clean up the mess.

As anyone who has been saved from a dangerous situation by a police officer knows, many officers are heroes in their communities. But since the widespread adoption of smartphones and body cameras, we also have proof that there are problems within police departments that need to be addressed. Anyone who wasn't yet aware of the amount of racism present in some US police forces was made painfully aware of it in the summer of 2020. We've seen that even good officers can and often do look the other way when it means protecting a fellow officer.

It has also become apparent that police officers are often forced to play an astonishing number of different roles. They are expected to be everything from a family therapist and a drug treatment expert, to a mental health counselor, domestic violence mitigator, soldier, and action hero. The overwhelming variety of demands we put on police officers can put them, as well as the communities they serve in unpredictable situations that can have deadly consequences. All these different roles go far beyond their training to protect people from immediate threats of violence or crime. This not only takes up the officer's scarce time, but it can also be more dangerous for the people they're interacting with. Of all police killings between 2017 and 2020, less than half were in response to a call for a violent crime, crime against another person, or a person with a weapon. More than half were traffic stops, mental health or welfare checks, domestic disturbances, or other nonviolent offenses.[8]

However, examples of how to solve this challenge are emerging, with some communities deploying resources to help cover the tasks that police officers either aren't well trained for or don't have the bandwidth to address effectively. The city of Denver, for example, launched a program that dispatches mental health professionals, mediators, or paramedics to respond to some nonemergency and emergency calls instead of police. Between June 2020 and February 2021, the program responded to 748 such incidents, and none required police backup, arrests, or jail time. The clear benefit is that this program frees up police to focus their training, time, and resources on fighting crime and responding to dangerous incidents that require a police presence to keep people safe.[9]

This raises the question: How do we train officers today? We teach police to first and foremost gain control of a situation. We traumatize them and train them to live in fear that around every corner someone might be lying in ambush. They are shown very graphic videos and told stories of extremely violent encounters as a cautionary reminder to remain vigilant. Simulations teach them how to draw their guns quickly enough to have a better chance at surviving a violent encounter. Given the incredibly difficult situations police officers find themselves in, this is not necessarily a bad thing, but after we put them through this training, we send them out to tackle many nonviolent situations that call more for understanding and de-escalation than domination or an effective shootout. While today there are more de-escalation trainings, meditation, and mindfulness exercises, police still spend an average of sixty training hours on firearm skills compared to only eight hours on community policing strategies, mediation, and conflict management.[10]

On the streets, however, police are overburdened with responsibility for mediation and conflict management and expected to handle many of the situations for which we've cut other resources. Police should be expected to do what they're trained to do, which is respond to and investigate violence and some property crimes—to get those situations under control, save lives, minimize any damage or injuries, and ultimately help keep our communities safe.

Unfortunately, in many countries, including the US, we've slowly defunded the rest of society over the last few decades. We've defunded education, public services, homeless programs, mental health support, and welfare systems. We've been pulling money out of our communities and societal foundations for decades, and now we're facing the consequences. Lo and behold, as we've put all of these expectations on police officers' backs, they have become overburdened with responding to situations they are not properly trained to handle. There have been many calls recently to defund the police. Instead of simply defunding the police, let's refund society to holistically prevent crime and improve public safety over the long term. Let's refund the programs that handle (best of all, serve to prevent) the social problems on our streets so police officers can focus on what they're trained to do.

Let's prevent crime by offering other sources of social support, which can help society function better for people so their life choices are better. In this world police aren't burdened with more than their fair share, and our communities have the highly trained support they need.

Ideal Design Objective 3:
Transparency and Accountability

When the public has access to information, police-community interactions improve. Body cams and opening data in communities can shed light on what's working or not. Body cams have been an essential first step in making police work more transparent and are the only surveillance systems supported by the ACLU.[11] A study by Cambridge University found that using body cameras resulted in a decline in complaints against officers by 88%, and a reduction in use of force by officers of 60%.[12] Combined with ubiquitous smartphone cameras in the hands of citizens, this can at the very least shed light on police abuses. In the past these would've been he-said-she-said situations where the courts trust the officers every time. The widespread protests we've seen in response to abuses captured on bodycams and smartphones isn't an indicator of more police violence, but more likely the outrage of finally having proof of how much abuse is occurring at the hands of the officers we pay to protect all of us, and how brutal, even deadly, it can be. In fact, killings of civilians by police have actually been decreasing slightly over the last decade in urban areas, with killings of Black Americans dropping 10% from 2014 to 2019.[13]

Despite this slight progress, we have a long way to go. Police officers walk our streets with the authorization to kill, yet thirty-eight US states either restrict or keep confidential police records of misconduct. Officers generally have discretion to turn off their body cameras whenever they feel it necessary, but sometimes this discretion is abused. In 2021, after the George Floyd protests, the city of Minneapolis mandated that officers leave their cameras on for the entirety of their shift.[14] Although some decry these measures as anti-cop, they can protect the good officers as much as punish the bad by empowering the public and investigators with objective data.

In a better world of our design, there would be not only video data but also feedback loops like customer service rating models whereby the people interacting with the officer could easily add their side of the story. This would be combined with the recorded video and a transparent rating system tied to the police officer's badge number. Reports on interactions that didn't include personal information could be publicly available, and the officer could include their perspective as well.

Using this method, police officers who are doing wrong would receive a bad review, impacting their beat, compensation, and duties (all of which should be viewed in context). This kind of system helps bring more light to public interactions with police and empowers the public to share their experiences. Contrast this with today's opaque and disempowering approach, which causes frustration and undermines the trust we seek to build. Instead of the police being expected to self-police themselves as they are today, which can be seen as a betrayal by fellow partners and officers, a community rating system could help bring awareness to and discourage poor police conduct.

If we were able to have public transparency and consistently shed light on the behaviors of police in our communities, then those police officers who were working together and have developed strong family-like bonds would not be protected from consequences by loyal teammates. What is today a cultural problem within police departments can be partially addressed by an external feedback system. Accountability improves when officers and the people they police are held to similar standards of conduct, with similar and fair punishments for all, and feedback loops help communities regulate police behavior. This makes us all safer—both communities and the cops who serve them.

Ideal Design Objective 4:
Opportunity for Offenders to Rebuild

When people who have been punished for running afoul of the law are later able to support themselves legally, they reoffend at much lower rates and find better outlets for their energy. Too often today offenders are simply punished or removed from their environment for a short time, then released back into the same conditions, often after more trauma in the justice system, then expected to change their behavior. Unfortunately but predictably, this is often ineffective.

A 2019 study of US prisoners found that within one year of release, 45% had been arrested again. Within nine years after release that rate was up to 83%, showing a dismal failure in our approach to rehabilitation.[15] And this is not for lack of resources. According to the US Bureau of Justice, we spend $80 billion per year to incarcerate 2.3 million people, roughly $35,000 per person, per year.[16] Policing costs our society an additional $100 billion per year, often to arrest the same people.[17] Perhaps some of this combined total of $78,000 per prisoner per year could be better spent?

One great example of the results of giving people economic opportunity is a project called Last Mile at San Quentin prison in California. Last Mile trains prisoners to code and become software engineers, then connects them to nearby Silicon Valley tech companies such as Google, Facebook, and Slack. The overall recidivism rate in San Quentin is around 70%, but for everyone who went through Last Mile's program, the recidivism rate was 0%. Helping people to gain competitive skills, get jobs, become self-sufficient, and restore their dignity works to reduce crime and enfranchises people to help improve their lives. At the same time, this makes their communities safer.[18]

We need to ask how we can actually help people change—how we can give them the tools to help them to rejoin society and support themselves. We need ways to find out what is at the root of their behavior and solve that problem to help them make better choices down the road. This will not be a one-size-fits-all solution; we'll need to address different needs for different people—whether they be economic, psychological, emotional, environmental, or something else—to separate them from bad influences and incentivize them to do better and more constructive things with their precious lives.

Ideal Design Objective 5:
Compassion and Community Support

If people feel that their community or society cares about their life and has their back, they are more willing to want to be a part of the community and resist gangs or criminal networks. Racial discrimination in policing, which has been reported for decades, is now clear to the public, thanks to a sadly overwhelming amount of footage. The Black Lives Matter protests of 2020 after the killings of George Floyd, Breonna Taylor, Eric Garner, and too many more to name here brought a long-standing issue to the forefront of the American and global consciousness, leading to calls for reform. The murder conviction of Derek Chauvin was an immense sigh of relief to a country that had grown understandably jaded and distrustful of the justice system after seeing so many police officers being exonerated or receiving light sentences after obvious assaults or murders of innocent people of color.

We all know the gist of the statistics: Black Americans make up 31% of police killing victims, despite being just 13% of the population. In police killings of unarmed Americans, FBI data shows that Black people were 3.5 times more likely to be shot than white people, especially in counties with high inequality. A common retort is that crime is higher in Black neighborhoods, but the same study of police killings of Black people found no relationship to crime rates, only a relationship to race.[19] This is worth repeating and should be more widely known: Police were just as likely to shoot and kill unarmed Black people in low-crime neighborhoods as they were in high-crime neighborhoods.

By creating the right conditions in our society, we can discourage people from committing crimes in the first place. This means convincing people from a cost-benefit basis that committing a crime is not their best option. We can also address cultural perspectives that could be encouraging crime in our society today. So often, especially in gangs, committing crimes is about finding community and belonging, about showing that you are a worthy member of that community. Only a holistic approach will help people feel worthy and choose communities that don't require them to commit violence in order to belong.

If people had more support from their society—if they felt less financial desperation and had more people to talk to in their family or community, and if more mechanisms existed to care for and nurture and support people through hard times, crime would be less of a temptation and police would have less work to do. People would not see crime as their only option to make ends meet or gain the respect they seek. In a society that helps individuals and communities reach their full potential, crime and violence not only don't pay, but the emotional pressure of social and economic pain and anxiety is less pronounced and less likely to push people over the edge.

A New Outlook for Policing

When crimes happen, we should be able to address them and prevent further harm from happening. In the public debate around public safety, there's a narrative that changing our approach to policing in any way (especially budgeting) will lead us to a place where police are completely impotent and unable to respond to dangerous people, so they'll need to just let crime happen.

Of course, no one wants police to be ineffective when responding to dangerous crimes or dangerous people. We also don't want police to be unfairly or asymmetrically targeting Black people or other minorities. The distrust that racial discrimination has created in the community actually stifles the police's ability to fight crime because people don't think they can trust that the police are there to protect them. Although it is not an easy task, a very important step is to repair relationships between police and people in our communities, and especially communities of color. To repair the perceptions and relationships between minority communities and the police, actions need to support the right perceptions. We've focused a lot already on fighting corruption and bias within the police ranks. But if we solve the transparency problem, what about helping them with their main job of actually policing and fighting crime while keeping themselves safe? There are a wealth of new data-driven technologies to assist the police in responding more effectively to crimes and emergencies. The police should have these tools available to work smarter, not harder, so they can do more with the resources they have.

Examples include predictive crime analytics, whereby AI analyzes crime data to help police predict where and when crimes will happen. They can then patrol these places ahead of time to prevent the crime from happening in the first place. Other examples are AI solutions that analyze emergency calls to speed up dispatch and determine the right types of expertise needed, gunshot detectors that triangulate location from microphones throughout the city, and video analytics on traffic cameras that detect accidents. Automated workflow engines then use that data and their own software to automatically create incidents with associated tasks for each team member that needs to respond.

These technologies and tools, with the right oversight, can be extremely helpful force multipliers to help police and emergency responders keep our communities safer and save lives. This doesn't just mean we need more militarization or weaponry; rather, it's about working smarter and protecting police so they can do their jobs the right way and be the heroes we so desperately need them to be.

A Fresh Take for Offenders

As discussed earlier, it's important to understand the causes of crime. There's a small percentage of offenders who are simply mentally unhealthy and have lost control of their violent impulses, and they account for a small minority of the crimes that are committed. There are people who simply need to be taken away from society and kept apart in order to keep others safe. But is this true for the millions of incarcerated people today? Highly unlikely. Sometimes crimes appear to be the best options for meeting basic needs, and we need to change that calculus. Many countries are very safe places to live—far safer than the US—and perhaps we can learn from them.

They begin by addressing the whole person. Offenders need opportunities to stand on their own two feet and feel the dignity and responsibility that come along with it so that they're less likely to slip into a life of crime. We need to give offenders the emotional and community support to resist the urge to join gangs or commit crimes, giving them a second chance. With our simple punishment approach, many offenders require a third chance, or a fourth—but we can't simply toss someone back into the same situation and expect a different outcome.

Today we have the witness relocation program. But what if we had a felon relocation program? Instead of paying $35,000 a year to keep someone in a cage, why not spend $10,000 to provide retraining, get them to a new city—especially one where they may have relatives, cover their first month or two of rent, and find them a job so that they can truly start over again? Recidivism rates are 20% lower for prisoners with stable employment, and those who are arrested again go longer without rearrest. Occupational training and licensing have also been shown to reduce recidivism 9.4%.[20]

When people can find good jobs and are able to reestablish their lives outside of prison, they are less likely to turn to a life of crime.

The Netherlands has reduced its prison population by half within a decade to achieve a rate of only 61 prisoners per 100,000 population—the lowest percentage of prisoners among any country in Europe. The United States, by comparison, has roughly 655 prisoners per 100,000 people—over ten times the Dutch rate. How is the Netherlands accomplishing this feat?

According to a 2016 government study, they have focused on implementing shorter prison sentences and examining how crime impacts society. Dutch criminology researchers have concluded from various studies that longer prison sentences do not actually lead to lower crime rates, as prison can often reaffirm someone's criminal identity and damage their ability to keep or find employment, a home, and social relationships. Offenders who wear ankle bracelets and are confined to their homes are less likely to reoffend than those who are serving prison sentences. Taking this research into account, judges in the Netherlands engage in a lengthy, careful, case-by-case consideration to determine whether a prison sentence would be helpful or harmful for that individual. Similar to San Quentin, the Dutch prisons have intervention and training programs that pair prisoners with a mentor and also invite employers to visit the inmates. As their release dates approach, the prisoners are allowed to work outside the prison and return in the evenings to complete lower-skill chores with the other inmates. Thanks to their change in approach and decreasing crime rates, the Dutch have closed or repurposed twenty-four prisons over the last decade.[21] Their refreshing new prison crisis consists of figuring out which prisons to close next and what else the buildings can be used for.[22]

A Move Toward a Crime-Free Society Is a Move Toward Equality

When people feel disconnected from and unsupported by their communities, government, or society, they feel disenfranchised. As a result, they may feel no responsibility to that society or the people in it. This is a very big, complex problem to solve, but it starts with enfranchisement and tackling inequality. In an international study across countries, strong correlations were found between inequality and crime, with a moderate correlation between unemployment and crime; a weaker correlation was found between poverty and crime.[23] This means that the strongest factors in predicting crime are not poverty in and of itself, but unequal wealth, unfairness, and inability to support oneself.

Let's look at an example of how this plays out. San Francisco is a beautiful, iconic city with a booming tech economy, one of the world's richest cities. But it is also one of the most unequal cities in America. The Tenderloin is a small neighborhood very close to the touristy downtown Union Square. It's classically been a high-crime district, known for gambling, strip clubs, prostitution, and Prohibition-era speakeasy bars. Today it's notoriously a place of open-air drug dealing, petty crime, and violence. Having lived in and visited quite a few cities in the US and internationally, I've never seen people openly smoking crack or injecting heroin on the sidewalk like I have seen in the Tenderloin. If you don't watch your step, you can easily step in human feces. Many people live in tents or just sleep outside. Many have mental health issues, and it's a common sight to see them pacing back and forth or even screaming at imaginary foes. It's a very, very sad place.

It's not unusual when driving through the Tenderloin to see people walk out in front of traffic, angry at the world and the drivers who honk at them. The feeling is clear: *You're mad about me making you wait an extra five seconds to get through the street, but you wouldn't stop to help me and you don't care whether I live or die on this street.* That's an understandable attitude from someone who feels like they've been just tossed aside by society and left to die. The widespread drug use and mental health problems don't help either. In fact, a 2015 study found that 55% of people experiencing chronic homelessness in San Francisco had emotional or psychiatric issues. In 1967, then Governor Reagan passed the Lanterman-Petris-Short Act, ending institutionalization of mentally ill people. The same year, the mentally ill population in San Mateo prisons doubled. In 1981, as president, Reagan repealed the Mental Health Systems Act that had been signed into law by President Carter, thereby pushing responsibility for mental health onto states (which already had inadequate funding) and reducing federal spending on the issue.[24] Yes, we need enforcement of the law. But in places lacking holistic support or capacity, that enforcement goes to waste—as it does in the Tenderloin when offenders are quickly released back onto the streets because of the lack of resources to address their mental health needs, or even enough space to keep criminals in jail for any amount of time.

If our society were to act more like a community that takes care of its people, we would see less despair, distrust, and antagonism toward that society. This would begin to ensure that the bright-eyed, impressionable three-year-old and his family that we mentioned earlier had proper support so he didn't turn to violent crime. We must extend this support to the millions of existing homeless, left behind, or disenfranchised people in the world. What works are relationship-building activities that make people feel like they're part of their community, elimination of organized crime, reinvestment in and development of education to meet the needs of our society today, and support for people whose family or community has failed them.

When we talk about public safety, rooting out corruption, or enfranchising people, it's not just about preventing a local shoplifter from stealing groceries. These fundamental problems of lack of opportunity, corruption, and cultures built on disenfranchisement and frustration can cascade into broader crime, destabilization of society, and even terrorism. There's a deep truth here: If we enfranchise people and create a system in which people can meet their needs or interests through the proper channels and structures, they won't be forced to go outside of the system to meet their needs in whatever way they can.

A common response to crime is a demand that people take personal responsibility. We talk about the personal responsibility of those identified as criminals, but we need to also start talking about the responsibility of citizens, along with civic and business leaders. These leaders have a responsibility to their society. The businesses and organizations they manage and build will be more successful if the society they operate in is successful. Abuse of power can lead not only to political violence and civil wars, but also a physical and emotional lack of safety for people within and even outside of their borders. This constrains the economy and the people who work to support it.

We must design a humane way to maintain personal and societal safety. A society that is free from corruption and empowers social mobility is one that helps people reach their full potential, uplifts the economy, and enables society to reach its full potential as well—all part of the journey to social self-actualization.

Chapter 9

Community and Belonging Within Government and Politics

AHH, THE GOVERNMENT. ALMOST AS MUCH A crowd favorite for the butt of a good joke as lawyers. But do we need to be cynical about our shared institutions? What would an effective, helpful government look like? Would it be possible to trust a government, knowing that it's competent and that your larger community has your back?

The majority of the political systems we see today are based on a long legacy of ideas and cultures built over hundreds or even thousands of years. We must be grateful for all that our ancestors have accomplished and passed down. But with a global society that is changing very rapidly, enabled by all of the new technologies that have become available, we have new options to consider. Of course, governments by nature are meant to think long-term and bring stability and reliability to our lives. But we're living in a time when there are many new ways of organizing ourselves, to get things done, build community, and advance our society. This leads us to the initial and most important question: What is a government for, and how can it help?

Governments are not there just to enforce parking limits or give us conflicting political tribes to shake our heads at. Governments are meant to be a representative of the citizenry, setting rules for economic and business arenas, regulating rules of conduct, and issuing punishments that restrict harmful behaviors. They were meant to represent all of us, to be a voice for less powerful people or stand up to those with power, to help stabilize our society and make it fairer for all of us. An important role of government is to leverage the collective power of the people throughout a society to protect them from warlords, feudal lords, financial lords, charlatans, and more.

Whoever is able to gain concentrated power through the various means and mechanisms of an economy and society must be balanced by some force that represents, protects, and nurtures both the majority and the minority of underrepresented people, so a society stays stable and social mobility is possible. When societies are extremely unequal or just allow highly concentrated power with no counterbalance, this can lead to injustice and corruption. These imbalances are usually overthrown through revolutions or other ways that people fight back against that power structure. Society eventually tends to rebalance and return to a more stable structure, but there can be violence and destruction in the meantime. In this cycle of class or power conflict, precious lives are lost, resources are wasted, and progress can be stifled for anywhere from a few years to generations.

Setting Ideal Design Objectives for Government and Politics

Ideally, we want to have a system of governing ourselves, setting rules for ourselves, and distributing resources in ways that help us develop our society along a positive path and build for the long term. We can take new technologies, knowledge, and examples into account to help us imagine a fresh approach, so we can design for the ideal and then create it.

Ideal Design Objective 1: Humanistic

An ideal government's purpose should be to serve people and help make their lives better; therefore it is humanistic. It should protect our collective organism from other large organisms that may pose a danger to it. It should also represent the people's interests. Although large groups or organizations can intimidate and take advantage of individuals, they cannot so easily take advantage of individuals who have the support of their collective whole. An ideal government would help nurture people physically, economically, psychologically, and even in their emotional development or protection from abuse. A government shouldn't just be restrained from doing harm; it should focus on doing and multiplying good, wherever appropriate.

Ideal Design Objective 2: Empowered

Next, we want our government to be empowered. We want a government that can actually do the work we need done. This is one of the biggest criticisms of many governments today: They are seen as ineffective and incapable of actually executing on goals and governing. In the US, for example, there seem to be endless filibusters and theatrical debates, using the checks and balances against the system to make it impotent and ineffective. Legislative service seems to be more about winning a political game, preserving one's job, maintaining funding, or serving donors and special interests. We want our government to be capable of proposing, refining, passing, carrying out, and enforcing policy.

Ideal Design Objective 3: Informed and Wise

We want our government to be informed and wise. Informed, meaning to have effective methods of sense-making. A strong foundation of any effective government is a population that can effectively engage in nuanced sense-making and accurately understand the world in all its complexity. This foundation is essential to support a functioning democracy, especially in an era of extreme volumes and diversity of information, all of which can be distorted by misinformation and disinformation. The problem is that disinformation can change the way people think, and that in turn affects the direction and rhetoric of its government. We could even say that our government in the United States might actually work just fine, but people's wants and needs are being manipulated by disinformation and misinformation, which results in the divided system we see today. Many people believe intensely in their divided world views, seeing the other side as the enemy. If we were to consider ourselves all seekers of truth, bringing different perspectives and experiences to the search (unpolluted with disinformation), we could do a better job not only of getting along with each other but also of governing and directing our society in a positive way.

Being wise is also about long-term thinking—the protection and transparent allocation of resources so that people are not prioritizing short-term gains over the health of society and future generations, or pillaging the resources of the future. But we also need to enable people in the present so we can live good lives ourselves. When we think about what work is, what companies do, what organizations do, it's really about using the time, energy, and work of human beings to build something, create something, or provide services to each other. If our government can help to steer the time, energy, and work of human beings in a direction that is creating a better future while maximizing the life potential of its people today, then we will all be in good shape, and so will our future society.

Ideal Design Objective 4: Restricted

A government has immense power and a monopoly on the legitimate (perceived or otherwise) use of violence. This comes with an awesome responsibility to be ethical and wise in the use of this power. A government shouldn't be just one more powerful, independent, self-serving organization in a society of many; it should be restricted from absolute power, while guided in the use of that power to do good where ethics, markets, or short-term thinking fail. The "horseshoe" model of organizational power argues that an all-powerful corporation or oligopoly of corporations is very similar to an all-powerful government, especially when it starts controlling things like media, information, and opinion. In this model the opposite ends of the political-economic spectrum, unbridled capitalism and unrestrained dictatorial communism are actually very similar:

controlled by one incredibly powerful institution or a small group of them that do as they please, often at the cost of the health, safety, and livelihoods of the many. No one wants either of these.

Ideal Design Objective 5: Adaptive

We also want a government that is adaptive. We've established that the world is changing rapidly. Our many new technologies come with many new implications. We have new ways of mass distributed communications and coordination through social media and an ever-growing variety of software tools. We need governments that can adapt quickly enough to keep up with the exponential pace of change.

An example is self-driving cars. The technology is advancing rapidly, but policy is struggling to keep pace with the availability of this amazing but potentially dangerous technology. Before regulators could draft rules and regulations, these cars were being tested on city streets, which could have been very dangerous. On-street testing led to the death of a woman who was struck by an Uber in 2018, and several other accidents have been blamed on autonomous vehicle (AV) software glitches, despite their being safer than human drivers, on average.[1] There are a few areas that allow autonomous vehicles to drive freely, like the innovation district in Las Vegas. In fact, the state of Nevada probably has some of the most forward-thinking AV policies in the US, where both safety and innovation are factored into the approach for testing AVs "in the wild."

Looking further out, we have urban air mobility (otherwise known as flying cars) on the horizon. Many companies, like Lilium and Joby Aviation, are making strong progress, and the actual engineering is getting close to becoming feasible. And while the technology may be nearly ready to fly, regulatory guidelines and approvals may take decades. This space is ripe for new businesses that are building up the physical and digital infrastructure to serve this new mode of transportation, from providing the flight ports on top of buildings to booking, advertising, and logistics software. With vertical takeoff and landing, flight providers will lease the space on top of buildings for new ports. Despite the exciting potential, the liability of a vehicle falling from the sky in a dense city, or even the noise produced by the engines will create issues that need to be considered.

But the regulatory mechanism isn't yet adaptable enough to provide guidelines fast enough to enable these new businesses, jobs, or technologies to reach their full potential. Not that we should simply open up a libertarian haven where anyone can do anything; there are real near- and long-term risks and impacts to be considered. We just need to be able to run this process faster, to enable innovation that helps us tackle climate change and other challenges, while also enabling a future that works for all of us.

Ideal Design Objective 6: Ethical and Benevolent

Ethics and benevolence are similar to humanistic values but resistant to corruption and other negative effects of using power unwisely. If you did a sentiment analysis of the word "Congress" on the internet, you'd probably find some pretty negative posts, regardless of the year. In fact, congressional approval ratings sank to just 27% in 2021.[2] Many people think their government doesn't represent them or behaves unethically. According to Pew Research, just 20% of Americans trust their government to "do the right thing" most of the time.

The French Revolution has become a popular trope of reference over the last couple of decades, likely because people are feeling a similar way: that the people who are supposed to represent them have become out of touch. Common attitudes state that our representatives are not responsive to the people's needs, no matter which side of the political aisle you sit on. The sentiment is that they're not getting done what we sent them there to do. They're not using our money in ways that help us. Listening to and helping the people should be their whole purpose, but instead, people feel unheard and unhelped. The January 6, 2021, attacks on Congress, while fueled by political conflict and disinformation, were to some degree channeling this broader frustration in part of the population. Both the political right and left feel frustration that the system just isn't working.[3] In designing the ideal government, we need it to right these wrongs and operate as an ethical, benevolent force for public good.

Ways Government Can Focus on a Better World

Let's explore some solutions for an ideal government. In this chapter we won't exclusively focus on revolutionary approaches of remaking government or dive deep into an exhaustive list of potential policies and organizational structures (you're welcome).

Instead, much of this approach is about tangible ideas to improve the inputs and feedback loops of the *existing* system of government.

Sense-Making Systems

Sense-making is how we determine and agree on what is real. It helps us shape our worldviews, values, and priorities. Good sense-making is the foundation of a healthy democracy; it enables freedoms of the people who determine their own fate. Generally, people with different information will take different actions. We've seen the power of disinformation and misinformation to influence people's perceptions of world events and who they consider to be heroes or enemies. This powerful influence can erode a democracy's ability to understand the world it operates in and render it ineffective at responding to disruptions or changes.

We find ourselves in new circumstances with the proliferation of internet news and social media. *Anyone can say anything to everyone*, often without needing to provide sources, fact checks, or context. This leads to a world without nuance, which makes it even easier to dismiss a group with different beliefs; it can lead to such high levels of division as to catalyze conflict, social breakdown, and even war. To combat this disinformation and even sort through the abundance of information available to us, we need better solutions and systems of sense-making.

One aspect of sense-making is designing news with context. Instead of simply trusting that our chosen news source is delivering us accurate, unbiased, and comprehensive information, we need systems that take all information into account, cluster the narratives, fact-check them, and deliver us more digestible information that is demonstrably true and fairly presented. With this ability to sense-make, we can not only better understand the world, we can better communicate with each other and debate potential actions, instead of fighting based on tribal loyalties.

Some harmful news reports may actually offer factual information, but selectively to support an untrue narrative. The far-right *Breitbart News*, for example, overreports on sexual assaults in immigrant communities, especially Somali communities in Minnesota. They also take special care to call out the race of the offenders as Black Somali immigrants, and especially the race of the victims when they are white women. Now, this is not to say that these horrible crimes shouldn't be reported—of course they should, and the perpetrators should be punished, and we should seek to prevent these terrible attacks from ever happening, regardless of the race or background of the attackers or victims. But Breitbart makes an obvious effort to reinforce and exacerbate classic racist tropes of Black men attacking white women, disrespecting the victims by using their tragedies as political tools to attack liberal values like diversity, multiculturalism, and compassionate immigration policies. They do this without actually engaging in a debate about these issues based on fair information and argumentation. In short, they are weaponizing information. I'm singling out Breitbart here, but the problem is not just the far right weaponizing information and using logical fallacies to push political agendas—the left and right are both guilty of this approach, albeit on different topics and using different communication styles.

One solution could be to leverage technology to help us better process the information out there and seek to better understand the world in all its nuance. I've personally worked on a project to try and tackle this weaponization of disinformation with a website called SpectrumReport.com. Others, like Ground News and AllSides, take similar approaches. The goals are to

1. Break down echo chambers by giving people information from across the political spectrum, left to right.

2. Identify the narratives that are being displayed by one side or the other.

3. Fact-check those narratives.

4. Provide sentiment analysis (showing positive, neutral, or negative language) of the types of emotion being ingested, to reduce the onslaught of language focused on disgust or anger, which can encourage people to caricaturize one another and lose the patience for the communication we so desperately need.

These types of solutions, further empowered by natural language processing (NLP) AI, can help us sort through massive amounts of information, identify patterns in language that point out when we're being manipulated, and show us the narratives being targeted at us, all so we can make better sense of the world. With tools like these, we'll be more empowered to focus on the problems that are truly problems and the effective solutions. We can also empower distributed management of politics, public services, and policies, so that power is less concentrated in a few hands that might corrupt and more widely distributed among many minds that can make transparent, informed decisions.

Voting Systems Based on Issues and Knowledge

In a democracy, we have the freedom to determine our own fate, but we have the responsibility to vote in an informed way and elect representatives that will carry out informed governance and policy for us. We also need voting systems to be transparent and trust-worthy so we know that our votes are counting toward the future we hope to build together.

Science fiction often provides interesting explorations and classifications of futuristic forms of government or political systems. In some stories, our political system could be based on the human mind. "Syntellect" is the idea that a unified civilizational mind could integrate all individual minds through informational networks for shared sense-making and decision-making. Similarly, the internet allows us to share ideas and information around the world today. Once AI and brain-computer interfaces become sophisticated enough, people could set up a singleton: a single decision-making entity based on the ideas and inputs of the entire population. However, this should be approached with full awareness and caution: The outcome could range from utopian collaboration to terrifyingly dystopian surveillance and control.[4]

Imagine an ideal world, where everyone's vote or opinion is connected through the internet (as is becoming more possible every day), or technology like that being developed by Neuralink, the brain-computer interface company cofounded by Elon Musk. In this world everyone is connected to the internet, and assisted by AI, we could all see and process all of the information available to humanity. In this world, a sense-making system like Spectrum Report would help us understand what is true, using the tools and techniques described earlier. Then everyone would be able to coordinate and decide what needs to be done, because they would be interpreting actual reality using a shared base of information, even though perspectives will differ. In this ideal, sci-fi world—keep in mind we're visioning; no need to explain how it would actually work—we wouldn't need representatives, because we could more easily decide collectively what we want to do, and we'd have the information available to make those decisions responsibly.

Until we get to a point (if we ever do) where people's brains are connected and super-powered by AI and the internet, we need to be informed voters who elect representatives that are informed about their areas of decision-making. Today, most representatives are generalists who get their information from the same compromised news sources we do or in the form of corporate marketing, lobbying groups, and think-tank research organizations that have an interest in influencing their decisions, and therefore usually do.

Issue-based democracy is another option, which includes a concept called liquid democracy. Liquid democracy is meant to be a balance between direct democracy (where everyone gets a vote regardless of their knowledge of a subject, leading to a "tyranny of the majority") and representative democracy (where an elected person makes decisions for us but may not have specific knowledge about a topic they are deciding on). The idea is to voluntarily delegate your vote about an issue to someone who is an expert in a given subject. For example, your cousin may be passionate about our energy future but not follow policy herself. If she knew someone who's a specialist in energy policy, she could transfer her vote to that expert and let them make the decision. In this way those who study an area would have more weight in influencing its future.

A risk of this system is that it could become a market where votes are sold to the highest bidder, and we end up in the same conundrum of money running politics. A regulated system could manage these transfers and make selling or buying of votes illegal. This balance between majority rules and generalist representatives could work more effectively to give scientists and other experts a greater say in running the specific areas they cover. These "virtual departments" could open up governance to new troves of expert guidance and specialists that would make highly informed decisions.

Localized Government Structures

As we are becoming a more globalized society, platforms like Shopify, Amazon, and eBay make international trade accessible to even the smallest of local entrepreneurs. In this new world the borders between countries have become less relevant than they were in a world of isolated and competing nation-states. In this historical context, the city-state is reemerging as a natural government and organizing entity.

This may be a good thing. Mayors, for example, are locally accountable and locally powerful. Compared to a president, congressperson, or senator, they are more directly accountable to their constituents and work on more visible and tangible local projects. They get reelected or rejected based on their performance locally. It's also much easier to audit their performance based on how they manage local outcomes and get projects done.

For these reasons, mayors are emerging as a powerful force in political systems around the world, especially in a globally connected society where cities trade directly with other cities and make a lot of their own rules throughout the world. Thanks to trade agreements, entrepreneurs in Los Angeles can easily trade with businesspeople in Shanghai without having to go through Washington DC or Beijing. More payment transfers are being established that are much easier to do without national interference through systems like cryptocurrency. As shipping and communication systems are increasingly being managed by distributed networks, the centralized power structures of the world get subverted in the short term and lose some relevance in the long term.

It's not only localized governments that are becoming more powerful; distributed digital communities are as well. These entities aren't geographically local, but local in a digital space, which can enable intense collaboration and coordination. The coordinated pumping of GameStop's stock in 2021 by a subreddit called WallStreetBets was a powerful example of how a group of motivated people could launch a financial attack on traditional hedge funds while beating them at their own game. Communities like this give more power to previously disconnected groups of people and are right in line with the "distributed everything" trend that we highlighted earlier. These distributed groups of connected communities are becoming increasingly powerful and capable of doing much more in the future. The Metaverse—a virtual reality space where people can meet, hold concerts, and even purchase virtual land—is quickly becoming mainstream and bringing together people separated by distance. How should we govern to ensure that these spaces and activities are free but not destructive?

These distributed but coordinated groups in digital space are affecting everything from our economy and financial markets to our politics and social dynamics. We saw this with social media platforms, trying to figure out how to govern themselves and find rules we can all live with. Do they simply try to fact-check politicians and pundits who spread disinformation or entirely shut them down? Do they allow a mob to "cancel" anyone who has said something offensive or simply had their statements taken out of context? Who do they allow on the platforms? Who do they keep out of the platforms? How do they detect and deter the use of these platforms for coordinated disinformation attacks that seek to fray the social fabric of entire countries? We seem to be in a stage of these networks being pressure tested and having to come up with worst-case-scenario procedures and practices to defend the societies they serve—and, ideally, all of humanity.

Another important aspect to localized structures is that different cities offer very different life and cultural options. This is important because it allows people to test out different models of living. You may be able to go to Houston, Texas, and have a larger house and lower income tax than you would in California. You may love the conservative political climate, the industry opportunities, the access to Mexico and the Gulf. If you like having the governmental support, liberal cultural climate, coastal scenery, protected forests, and vibrant, diverse neighborhoods that San Francisco, California, has to offer, and you can handle the cost of living, then you can choose to live there. With more people shifting to remote work, the ability to test out new communities to live and work in is freeing many people to find and live the lifestyles they choose.

This is becoming even more true globally. We might get to a point where cities hyper-specialize even more than they do today, testing out different models of living, working, designing public space, and regulating themselves. This is happening to some extent already. Remote work visas are being offered by more and more countries, seeking to attract tech workers and their buying power. Cities like Dubai, Hong Kong, and Incheon, South Korea, for example, are testing out systems with few economic rules and regulations. Some are even free of taxes, hoping to stimulate investment and trade. Cities of the future may look to specialize even further in order to attract or build the communities they seek. Think of all the Silicon Valley derivatives out there today, hoping to build an entrepreneurial, productive culture that will create start-ups that may grow into the biggest companies (and employers) of the future: Silicon Beach (Los Angeles), Silicon Alley (New York), Silicon Desert (Phoenix), Silicon Hills (Austin), and my personal favorite, Silicon Peach (Atlanta). This trend continues across the globe, with Silicon Lakes (Stockholm), Silicon Wadi (Israel), Silicon Docks (Dublin), Silicon Valley of the Desert (NEOM, Saudi Arabia), Silicon Valley of Hardware (Shenzhen), and many more. Although these cities are all striving for something similar, they are seeking to bring their own local flavor to their economies. This nurturing of their preferred flavor of culture or lifestyle will diversify with more specialization and local empowerment.

Returning to the US gives us an interesting example of the tension this local empowerment of cities can create with state or national leadership. The legalization of marijuana—and more recently, decriminalization of psychedelic mushrooms—is continuing to gain traction in more cities, despite still being illegal at the federal level. Because the substances are decriminalized, or made the lowest priority of law enforcement, their sales and use are essentially not enforced at the municipal or state level. This creates tension between the cities that are asserting their power and the federal government. It also provides a feedback loop from the voters indirectly to federal representatives to help them prioritize issues.

A Ministry of the Future?

If a government should be considering the long term, does it need a designated function to represent our future citizens and their interests? The concept of intergenerational theft is gaining traction in the public consciousness, especially as the potential impacts of climate change and ecosystem destruction threaten the livelihoods and lives of our future generations. The effort to address intergenerational theft asks: What makes the lives and experiences of citizens who are alive today more important than the citizens who will be alive in ten, fifty, or one hundred years?[5]

If we all existed at the same time, we would agree that our rights are equal—even the rights of those who will outlive or succeed us. Maybe a bill of rights for the future could be the next step in civil rights, encompassing more of the human race than before, helping us to consider longer-term impacts of our decisions and policies. We've made some progress on inclusion of all races, genders, and sexual orientations, but what if we also included people from different times? If you're taking away the potential livelihood of someone who's going to live fifty years from now, should that be allowed just because you don't know exactly who will be affected and how, even if it's sure to be negative? We hope that technology and innovation will help us and our descendants, but perhaps we could deliberately seek to do so through intentional and empowered organizations, tasked with including our future in our considerations. This would be a wise government.

We already aim to protect future generations to some degree with our current financial system. We consider how borrowing from future generations will burden them with debt and affect their lives. Maybe we need to shift our thinking to encompass additional types of debt that we are saddling our future selves and children with. A parent's love is one of the strongest and most basic instincts that we have, so surely we ought to protect our future children's and grandchildren's interests on a societal level.

So why aren't we including these intergenerational issues today? Maybe we want easier lives or higher social status. Maybe we want mating rights. Maybe we want more creature comforts, whatever they happen to be. Our current system encourages us to have unlimited wants that we can never satisfy. Why are we choosing to satisfy these wants at the expense of our grandchildren's basic rights of clean air and water, availability of food, and stable social systems not oppressed by tyrants, civil war, and so on? These social breakdowns can be expected to manifest as natural resources dwindle or change happens too fast or becomes too much for change-weary populations to adapt to. Although it may sound daunting, we need to include these risks to our future generations when designing policy and governmental systems.

Theoretically, business activity involves putting work into something that provides value. Whether it's a product or service, it should somehow solve a problem in someone's life, job, or the world. But there are some problems that businesses are not incentivized to solve, or even worse, problems that businesses can be incentivized to create. On the other side, the tragedy of the commons is a failure of public ownership. The commons refers to resources owned by everyone, so no one has the incentive or responsibility to maintain or protect them. People get to internalize the benefits, but they have every incentive to externalize the costs. Car rental companies and auto leasing contracts solve this with individual charges for individual damages. One of the core functions and purposes of government is to correct market failures and create punishments, policies, fines, or taxes to encourage people and businesses to do the right thing when economics incentivizes them to do the wrong thing. This could mean setting up incentives to take actions of value for the common good and disincentivizing actions that are harmful or destructive when markets and private enterprises fail to solve the problem.

As a humanistic entity, the ideal government should be helping us to correct market failures when they occur, to help make whatever future form of market economy more viable and humane. We have addressed some market failures in the past, such as when companies could more easily dispose of waste in a river than at a treatment facility and had no incentives to do otherwise. We've created regulations with financial and criminal punishments to make the cost of polluting more expensive than disposing of toxic chemicals responsibly. This is but one precedent of many. The government exists in order to give collective power to people to solve the collective problems we face. Carbon credit policies, using "vice taxes" on harmful goods to subsidize healthier alternatives, and early-stage investments in technologies that can help society (but aren't commercially viable yet) are just a few ways we can help solve market failures. We simply need to apply more of these where we need them.

Perhaps a ministry of the future could focus on where free markets are failing to align the interests of current and future societies, and rectify them in order to achieve a free economy that also ensures the basic needs of people are met. This could help direct us toward the positive future that we all want to live in and would be proud to bequeath our children. That may be the most important future of all to envision and create.

Chapter 10

Self-Esteem: Funding Humanity to Unleash Our Full Potential

WHEN THE WU-TANG CLAN DECLARED "CASH Rules Everything Around Me," they were right, to a degree. Money is energy, stored and made transferable. It is the fuel that we use to move along a modern economy and society. The closest analogy we have for money in the natural world is the energy and nutrients that are exchanged throughout nature's ecosystems, reaching all of the organisms in some way or another. In an ecological process, free energy from the sun enters our atmosphere and is transformed into fuel—sugars and nutrients—that are used by plants to grow and later by the animals who eat them. That energy is then transferred into waste products and exchanged with the bacteria and fungal mycelium in the soil, which proceed to break down and convert them into the nutrients that the trees and plants need. Once they die, these are eaten by animals or microbes in a repeating cycle of exchange.

Despite our efforts to convince ourselves that we are independent from this system, we are in fact just another part of it. All human activity is made possible thanks to the free energy of the sun heating the atmosphere, moving the winds, and providing life with the fuel it needs to participate in the ecosystem. With the convergence of technological and business innovations comes an opportunity for us to rethink how we use money in our world, and how it can serve us better, instead of the other way around.

In 1930s Austria, a small town named Wörgl took this concept to heart. It was in the midst of the Great Depression, suffering from economic gridlock. Fear had led the exchange of money to basically dry up overnight, and there wasn't enough to go around. Banks were afraid to lend money, and businesses were afraid to spend it. Production became stagnant; businesses were shutting down and collapsing. Income from taxes plummeted sharply, and the town's debt grew. Unemployment soared and brought great human suffering with it.

But the same people were still there to do the work, and they still required the same products and services as before. The same businesses existed to provide them, but no one had the money to pay each other.

The town then started to consider the unconventional ideas of an economist named Silvio Gesell. Silvio had lived in Argentina and had seen the human suffering brought on by continuous inflation and deflation and the lack of reliable money to exchange. In his book *The Natural Economic Order* he proposed a theory of "free money" to increase the availability and circulation of money and therefore economic activity. Back in Wörgl, the mayor attributed their economic breakdown to stagnation in the flow of money. Because money was not being circulated, production had decreased, causing unemployment to increase. When the mayor learned of Silvio Gesell's idea of "free money," he decided to try it.

Wörgl started a "free money" system by printing labor certificates, which could be used as money only in Wörgl. The certificates decreased in value over time, so workers were incentivized to spend it at local businesses, which increased production, and therefore needed more workers, who now had more money to spend at local businesses. Repeat, ad infinitum. The new local currency provided a kickstart that dramatically increased economic activity and helped pull Wörgl out of the recession. Similar programs were then implemented in other countries around the world, including back in the US in struggling communities in Iowa and California to achieve similar results.[1] This small town gives us an example of how we can rethink our assumptions about currency and economic systems to redesign them in a way that creates abundance for everyone involved, and does so sustainably.

Some goods, such as buildings and construction materials, become physically scarce at some point, but thanks to the growing economic tension between the old-guard scarcity thinking and the new paradigm of zero marginal cost goods created by software and automation, much of our economies function according to new and different rules. Even food, a foundational necessity for living things, is no longer scarce, thanks to our technological advances; it is scarce only for the people who do not have the money to pay for it, or in local areas where the distribution mechanisms have broken down. That starvation is still allowed to happen in a world rich with food—solely to preserve a paradigm of scarcity—is an obvious failure and tragedy based on lazy thinking. We can and must do better.

I would argue that today's world is a little like Wörgl. Our problems are not only about the velocity of money; they also stem from the availability (or lack) of money—for entrepreneurs, workers, and businesses who have ideas for solutions to our problems. We have plenty of smart minds, passion, and resources available to tackle our grand challenges and build an incredible future, but the money system and the mechanisms we have constructed to defend our paradigm of scarcity (back when it really was necessary) are constraining us from doing so. More of the things we need in our world are already abundant and zero marginal cost, from education and communication on the internet to the tools we can use to collaborate and funnel resources into projects that need them. The latent human energy and ingenuity standing ready to be unleashed by the free flow of capital are immense, and cracks are emerging in the walls holding them back.

Setting Ideal Design Objectives for Money and Economic Systems

Thinking about the overall purpose of money in an economic system helps us to consider our ideal design principles. The following principles can help serve as a guiding foundation for overhauling our money system and help all people live in a world of abundance.

Ideal Design Objective 1: Reliable, Stable, Safe

One of the first coins we know about was called the Shekel, which meant "weighing" in Hebrew. We can trace it back to around 3000 BCE, in what is modern-day Turkey and the Middle East, where it was used as a commonly agreed upon measure for the trade of wheat and other goods.[2] Money was developed as a store of value so that a person's expended energy could be returned to them in a different form that they needed, when they needed it. Money should also have predictable value over time. People originally minted coins or had blocks of stone or wood that they used as currency, and a ledger system was developed to serve as a record of the work they had done. This currency ledger system could be kept and stored after one person provided value to the community. It would then be exchanged with someone else who provided value in return. So individuals didn't have to master all the different skills needed to, say, fix a chariot, grow beans or harvest wheat, or build a much-needed couch to relax on at the end of a long day; they could pay someone else who had the needed skill. And with currency serving as the store of people's energy, it has to be as safe as possible from extreme losses or fluctuations like the ones Gesell saw in Argentina.

Ideal Design Objective 2: Abundant, Free-Flowing, and Fungible

A foundational principle of money is that it's fungible, which means it can be freely exchanged for anything legal. If all I have is chickens to trade for your furniture repair services, but you don't eat chicken, we're in a pickle. We need some money to be easily tradable for any goods and services we might want to exchange. And like the energy from the sun that powers our planet, money should be accessible to all who are providing value, and not constrained by a few to hold power over the many. Sure, there is competition, but if someone is willing and able to provide a needed value in an economic system, they should be able to be compensated for that value, and not expected to provide it for free.

Today, someone who wants to provide value and be paid for it needs to find someone who has an abundance of money to pay them to do it. The worker already has the value to provide, and the entrepreneur has the ideas and energy to create. In our current system someone may still choose to provide value for free until they eventually find someone to pay them for it, but meanwhile the rent is still due and food costs money. And while access to funding is improving through crowdfunding, and the ability to connect remotely is easier than ever, the biggest deciding factor in someone's ability to succeed is still whether they either have enough resources to get a business off the ground or know someone who will give them the money they need to do so. This entrenches higher socioeconomic levels and privilege, while discouraging creative risk-taking by all but the most wealthy people in a society. Reducing the barriers to finding funding or payment for value not recognized by the system today will unleash the latent potential of the under-resourced around the world and accelerate human innovation toward realizing our true potential.

But isn't the money we use today based on something of equal value? The money itself is created through a treasury and distributed through the Federal Reserve Banks. Regular banks purchase this currency and are allowed to lend out much more than the initial deposits, creating more "money" as they loan out the majority of it, collect interest on it, and keep the initial money on their books in a system called *fractional reserve banking*. This approach could be (and is) the subject of many books in itself, but in short, money is created out of thin air thanks to credit lending and accounting. The banks become the arbiters of money and where it initially flows. People can exchange it, but for those who need loans to pay for basics like housing, education, and transportation, once it is gone, it simply becomes a liability. For entrepreneurs and well-off people, it can be invested and create more money, in addition to ownership of money-generating assets. Due to social dynamics, the majority of this money and the wealth ownership it enables generally stay in the hands of fairly well-off groups and communities who decide what to do with it, which may include paying lower-wage workers to perform tasks. But significant amounts of money don't usually trickle down to where value is being provided, and trickle down of ownership almost never happens. There are exceptions: Silicon Valley startups often pay some workers in both salary and stock options, giving them ownership in the company they are helping to build. Since ownership, inheritance, and investments are how most wealthy people became that way, increasing these for more people would do humanity a lot of good—and increase wealth for the struggling and wealthy alike.

Ideal Design Objective 3: Accurate in Our Economy

Prices help us make choices. It's the job of prices to accurately compensate for the value being provided and the costs of providing that value. A big problem today is that a lot of those costs are externalized to the surrounding environment or society and not baked into the price paid by the consumer. An economic system should accurately price products and services so the costs are truly recognized.

Oil, for example, is extremely useful because it gets us around, is the basis of many materials in our products, and is used to generate energy. Oil is involved in basically everything we consume. We could say the last two centuries of human success and growth have really been a giant oil party, leading to cheap transportation, energy, and materials. This was a major innovation to kick off the technological development of modern human civilization, but today the costs of using that oil are becoming extremely high. The emissions and pollution from oil acquisition, processing, and use are destroying ecosystems and raising the earth's temperature, which contributes to more severe natural disasters and sea level rise. This could result in complete flooding of coastal cities and extensive destruction. These longer-term and more widespread costs are not captured in the price of oil or goods made from it, despite the high prices at the pump today. Much of the fossil fuel industry is in fact highly subsidized by government money.

So if pricing doesn't account for the collective costs of the damages from things like wars, climate change, or social upheavals that could be caused by the impacts of that climate change or widespread job loss from automation, it's not accurately helping us make choices. For a recent example, if Twitter and Facebook allow widespread harmful disinformation on their platforms through targeted campaigns from adversarial countries, they could inadvertently be used to destabilize an entire country (think of the efforts we've seen in recent elections and in spreading disinformation about COVID-19). While the companies would still be gaining click revenue, this could lead to social destabilization or even war, leading to a longer-term negative business outlook, which would impact the platforms themselves eventually. But there are few short-term feedback loops that would get them to internalize the costs or stop externalizing them (except, ironically, activism campaigns on social media). Luckily, some of the executives at these companies have recently started taking disinformation seriously and have started to remove or filter information that is likely to be disinformation or is intentionally politically inflammatory. But who's to say that the founders who are designing the next wave of social media companies for the people who are now de-platformed from traditional social media like Facebook or Twitter won't do the same? Terms and conditions on Donald Trump's TRUTH Social, for example, which says it was created to stand up to big tech censorship, gives the social media company the right to censor speech that criticizes the site or its management.[3]

In addition to our current approach of governmental regulations, complementary currencies and reputational systems can help us provide feedback loops that can assist in the regulation of economic or political actors. These systems, combined with accurate sense-making solutions, would be democratic and provide the faster feedback we need to be adaptable enough to recognize the true costs of the rapid changes we are experiencing today—and will continue to experience in the coming decades.

Ideal Design Objective 4: Valuable and Given for Value

This one may seem obvious, but money not only needs to account for, store, and be tradable for other valuable goods and services, but also should not be scarce for anyone providing personal or societal value (arguably everyone). There are not only externalized costs but externalized benefits that aren't captured by pricing or payments. Parents having children and raising them is arguably one of, if not *the* most valuable job on the planet. However, if you base the value of parenthood on our current economic reward or pricing mechanisms, it would appear to be completely worthless. There is no measured financial value to a parent having a child and raising it; in fact, there is a significant cost. In economic terms, at most there is value in creating a new consumer. But hopefully when reading these statements, you have cringed as much as I did in writing them. They may seem cold and out of touch, but they are accurate in stating how we represent ourselves through the lenses of our current economic rewards and paradigm. As human beings, we all know that mothers, fathers, friends, and communities have immense value, but we don't structure our economic systems to reflect that. This would be fine if our survival didn't depend on economic recognition. While this paradigm is a social construct, the very real consequences of poverty and inequality are reducing life span, quality of life, and opportunity for families around the world.

A family member doing household work isn't reflected in the financial assessment of value. People who are helping a neighbor, helping the proverbial or literal old lady cross the street, cleaning up the community are all doing volunteer work, which doesn't garner the income needed to sustain a person. Yet your being a good person and being liked in your community makes other people feel happy and improves their quality of life and productivity. This also reduces the risks of depression and suicide and is tremendously valuable in a number of other ways. At the same time people often report they want to do jobs that help the world, give them meaning and engage them, but only 15% of workers worldwide report that they are engaged at their jobs today.[4] This means 85% of people are disengaged, partially because they feel a mismatch between what they want to do versus what they are doing. How much latent potential is locked up in all the people working at jobs they don't care about simply to pay the bills and survive? Meanwhile, automation of many jobs is becoming more feasible by the day. This is a perfect storm just waiting for a great opportunity to shift people to better jobs and do away with boring work. But we need to plan how to ensure that people can realize their potential, provide value to the world, and build real wealth, rather than paying the price of poverty or even starvation.

Ideal Design Objective 5:
Responsible and Sustainable

We have reached a point where the question of economic production is no longer simply "How much can we produce?" but rather "What and how much *should* we produce?" Thanks to industrial processes and automation, we have the ability to create an abundant world for all of humanity. But we still live on a planet with finite air, water, land, and ecological resources, so we must make choices about what we produce and consume. Any money or economic system we design should take these limits into account. Investing in recycling capacity and technology, and building a circular economy both can help to extend our limits, but infinite growth is simply not possible.

Money also shouldn't be used to create harm or manipulate people into doing unethical things. One part of this is ensuring that people are not so desperate for money that they commit crimes to get it, but money shouldn't be manipulated by political interests either. We don't want to get into an Orwellian situation where all activities are controlled by a government, nor one where money can be freely used to sponsor terrorism, for example. Some transparent and democratic controls must be in place. Imagine a crowdfunded startup run by an extremist militia with the sole purpose of using money for bombs and weapons, and running campaigns to kill members of a civilian group. Obviously, such a horrific scenario should never be allowed. As we create a more abundant world, we will need feedback loops to steer growth in a positive direction and prevent that abundance from being used for destruction.

Achieving True Wealth

So what is money in practical terms? Money is the means by which we incentivize ourselves to create value and wealth in the world. But what is wealth? Wealth is sometimes what money can buy, but often it's what we get through other means—a healthy environment to live in, a healthy community to interact with, a comfortable place to call home, and the tools and freedom to go out into the world, discover who you are, and reach your goals. These are in addition to having products and services available to you in the economic marketplace. In short, money is the means by which we gain some types of wealth, but *not the wealth itself*, despite the two often being confused. Let's take a look at a few solutions and ideal innovations for our money and economic systems that can help us all to achieve true wealth.

Complementary Currencies

Money serves many purposes, but some forms of money serve specific niches. Airline miles, credit card points, and loyalty cards are actually a form of complementary currency that we've already gotten used to. These reward us for loyalty and other behaviors (incentives!). But we can create others that reward different types of work or value, such as community building, innovation, or even taking time for one's mental health. However, these complementary forms of currency won't always need to be backed by a government to have value.

For example, reward systems that use blockchain-based cryptocurrencies like Bitcoin, Ethereum, and others can be created or used to incentivize people to interact with new systems in new ways and even create new businesses. ICOs (initial coin offerings) are similar to the better-known IPOs (initial public offerings) in which companies become publicly listed on the stock market, or private fundraising from investors in order to build or grow a company. However, with an ICO a company offers a set number of coins (minted on the blockchain) to the public in order to fund the launch of their company, similar to stock but also a fungible currency. Because it's vastly easier to launch an ICO than to take a company public from a regulatory and paperwork perspective, this method of creating complementary currency, in addition to crowd-funding, makes access to startup capital much more accessible. But these coins are also used to reward use of services from a system or network of people.

Community Coin is one example of an idea for a complementary currency designed to help compensate and motivate people to do good. I worked on this idea with a community of people for a Financial Empowerment Challenge put forth by IDEO, a top design thinking and consulting firm. The purpose of Community Coin is to empower people who don't have an abundance of money to share; to create money where the value is created and/or traded where value is provided. In this system, a person with a smartphone could take the initiative to clean up a park, help a neighbor, tutor children, or cook for a family who's strapped for time. The value exchange would be confirmed by both parties, and coins would be delivered to the person providing value. No intermediary like a corporation or bank would be needed to fund the transaction. Instead, the coins would come from the distributed community. As an intermediary step, these coins could be either cryptocurrency or more mainstream points of various kinds from participating organizations, such as credit card points, air miles, and the like.

If you improve people's access to money, then people can be compensated for the value they're providing, even if members of a community don't have traditional currencies to pay with. For example, if you do something great for me but I don't have money to give you, then I can't compensate you unless you prefer bartering or working for free. That's fine if you enjoy it, but otherwise it doesn't scale in the economic system we live in today.

New forms of money may combine with social media to become closer to memes in the future, as we've seen with Dogecoin, Shiba Inu, and other meme coins and tokens. Complementary currencies can represent different markets and interests, or reward different types of contributions to a community. They could also simply pick up on a trend and run away in value. While fun, this can lead to abuse, in which "pump and dump" schemes can cost people hard-earned money or destabilize the reliability that money needs to have.

Overcoming Pitfalls of Monetary Policy and Business Cycles

Building a world of abundance would start with ensuring that everyone has access to at least enough money for life's necessities, educational resources to learn how to bring their value to the world, and access to funding to try out their ideas. By doing this, we eliminate the desperation that leads to a high portion of crime. It is important to be able to provide money more freely to people, especially for projects that provide human value.

With all the rising prices beginning in the economic resurgence of 2022 and the supply chain shortages, you may hear a voice screaming inside your head: *But what about inflation!?* Of course, inflation can and does occur, but this example is due to economic disruptions. This chain of events is a singular example that included a pandemic;

worker and material shortages and disruptions across production, assembly, delivery, in addition to a war in Europe, and more; dramatically reduced bandwidth at ports; immense new money printing; spikes in online shopping by populations forced into lockdown, and so on. The current inflation should be *transitory*, meaning that once things get up and running again and normalize, production will catch back up with demand and prices should restabilize. The global economy could've recovered from a pandemic, the war in Ukraine, climate disasters, food shortages, or an increase in money supply. But, not all at once or in rapid succession, which we should expect more of in the future without a transition to a sustainable and resilient economy. We're experiencing how continued disruptions without strong resiliency measures can throw the whole system out of whack, and lead to continued delays, shortages, and price inflation. If we don't prepare for and mitigate disruptions that we know are coming, like climate change-related disasters, new pandemics, and geopolitical conflicts, leveraging technology to reduce costs and improve sustainability and resiliency, we will face impacts similar to or even worse than those we saw following COVID-19.

So why wouldn't increasing the financial wealth of people cause more inflation? If we revisit Economics 101 for a moment, you may remember something called the *production possibility frontier*, which lays out the concept of how much one economy can produce. It also points out that all production is a choice—we need to choose to create one good over another because resources are limited. The classic example is butter versus guns. You can focus your entire economy on creating guns or creating butter (side note: this economy would be absurdly unhealthy and/or violent in this simplified example). However, the assumption we often make is that our economy is already producing at 100% (at the production possibility frontier), so when you introduce more money, you have more money chasing the same number of goods, so the prices go up. It's this classic demand and supply example.

There are two problems with that model today. One is that we're not producing to our full capacity, even though with the proliferation of automation and intelligent software, we can produce far more by the day—unlike in days past, when supply capacity and flexibility were much more limited. Instead, we struggle with stagnant demand or managing the up-ramping and down-ramping of production to meet changes in demand, which companies are getting better and better at by the day, thanks to sensors and predictive analytics. Big enough disruptions and crises can cripple the system, however, as we've seen in recent years. We've also seen how quickly demand rises once people have more cash in their hands— as when stimulus checks arrived during the pandemic, spurring a sharp uptick in demand and temporary shortages of things like toilet paper and masks. In areas like high technology, however, we do see more prolonged shortages based on raw materials or components like semiconductors. We see this for luxury goods, Teslas, or lithium for batteries, for example. But in the mid-to-long term we have the capacity to scale production up and down to meet all our basic needs and to manage production intelligently with the help of technology. To meet demand today and curb longer-term or structural inflation is much less of a risk than in the past, especially in advanced nations. Add sharing models for scarce goods and system-wide recycling, and there are plenty of resources to go around. Companies enjoying high profit margins may take some time (and competition) to decide to reduce prices again, however. The bigger, long-term question here is how to make supply chains sustainable and resilient and achieve a circular economy where waste is infinitely recycled so we don't overshoot the carrying capacity of Earth. Without sustainability and resiliency, our global production machine will quickly spin out of control and transform our Eden-like paradise of Earth into a hellish landscape of waste and toxic junk. Creating a circular economy to prevent this is an enormous business opportunity.

So much of the economic malaise we experience today is mainly about people having enough money to provide the demand for the goods we could be producing, and to produce them sustainably. If there were more money in that system, there would be more demand, more customers; businesses would have more demand to supply to, and thus more money coming in. Evidence of this can be seen in how much time and money is spent creating demand through marketing and advertising, some of which is emotionally manipulative and damaging. We may also want to consider whether we truly need much of what the economy produces, especially if we have to try so hard to convince ourselves that we need it.

Digital Economy to the Rescue?

Consider, too, that an increasing portion of goods and services are now digital. These goods can essentially be infinitely created and provided to anyone with a foundational device and connectivity to access them with. If a significant portion of your goods and services are digital, that means they can be provided to a million people almost as easily as you can provide them to one person. Where does that leave us with a production possibility frontier and inflation? If this digital economy is based on renewable and resilient sources of energy, it becomes nearly limitless, accelerating our shift to the zero marginal cost society. Add widespread automation, a circular and sustainable economy, and distributed/shared ownership, and altogether we have a recipe for accessible abundance.

E-books and digital music are good examples of this transition. We saw a similar wave of this with Napster and torrent files, which freely shared digital copies of music and movies in the 1990s. Artists decried the collapse of their industry and feared that no artist would ever make money again. The perception was that people were committing theft and should just purchase music the old way. However, the market was telling the industry that there was an enormous opportunity arising to deliver music and movies to people in a way they had already demonstrated that they preferred. Eventually, after storming dorm rooms and arresting college kids for stealing music proved ineffective, the industry realized that this whole digital entertainment thing might have legs. While the entrenched players sued listeners, innovators built Spotify, Pandora, and Netflix, and laggards like Blockbuster and CD stores quickly died out. Now, with the streaming wars, everyone from movie studios to marketplaces like Amazon are competing to sell digital entertainment directly to their customers. Some are even eating traditional Hollywood's lunch, vertically integrating with their own production studios.

This shift didn't happen because enough consumers gave up on digital music or movies, but because the providers finally recognized the opportunity and delivered entertainment to their customers in the way they wanted. Huge growth and revenues are their rewards. Economically, the production of that song is the initial fixed cost, but then the distribution (not counting marketing) of it is nearly free to each additional listener—unlike records or CDs, which cost money to produce more of every time. Digital media is simply electrons running through a computer, which is extremely cheap and getting cheaper by the day.

So we've established that people pay for digital entertainment. In reality, all of it could be distributed for free to everyone. But to be fair, it costs money to write a book, take the time to write and perfect a song, employ actors and actresses, or do special effects for a movie. Building and operating reliable digital platforms is also not easy or cheap. When Disney puts out a movie exclusively on Disney+, they're recouping some of those costs, and that's good for keeping their business going and delivering the family entertainment we all love. However, if someone takes time to produce a fantastic YouTube or TikTok video, should they also be paid for it? Some platforms are sharing more of the ad revenue with "prosumers"—people who produce as well as consume—but in an ideal system, anyone providing value would be paid for it to some degree. This could be accomplished via cryptocurrency without ads, or just regular old payments from an intermediary. But new models will emerge to solve this challenge. Some may leverage a small portion of a user's processing power to mine cryptocurrency; others would pay in network coins, which increase in value as more content is consumed.

Without delving into copyright law, if a digital file is essentially free to deliver, should it be free to consume? That's a legal, philosophical question, but let's stretch our thinking a bit. The cost is basically free. It should drive down costs the more people see it. Once a movie is a bit older, the rental price is lower and people pay less and less for it, whereas if it's brand new, fresh on the digital shelves, it's more expensive on a marginal basis. Unlike our simplified supply-and-demand cost model, the truth is sellers try to get the most money out of us that we are willing to pay. Economists call this *capturing consumer surplus*, and personalized pricing that matches not only ability but willingness to pay is likely to grow rapidly for these types of goods and services, while expanding content access to more people and revenues to more prosumers.

Sustainability: An Imperative in a World of Abundance

We all want an abundant world. The first part of achieving it is ensuring everyone has their basic needs provided for in a way that is sustainable for themselves and the planet. We're already over carrying capacity on the earth by about a magnitude of four, meaning that if all the world lived like Americans, we would need about four and a half Earths to sustain us. We can debate the numbers, but whether it's two or ten Earths, we don't have enough. While it'll take time for our overconsumption to catch up with us through ecosystem collapse, global warming, and the resulting loss of ecosystem services, we're already in overshoot, according to most people who are doing the research. We're basically living on ecological credit cards and not paying them back. To live in an abundant world, we need a truly sustainable, resilient, regenerative, and circular economy, one in which all goods are recycled, repurposed, and reconstituted, and we don't need to pull any more nonrenewable resources out of the earth, unless we're able to regrow or replace them.

Many startups and companies are working on different aspects of this, but there are still incredible opportunities to convert waste streams into raw materials or components for new goods. We can take carbon and pollutants out of the air from the production of our goods and put them back into trees or ecosystems that need them to grow, creating raw materials for us to consume again. By achieving this circular economy at scale, we'll enable the abundant world we seek. The good news for entrepreneurs and companies is that there is a huge opportunity in developing ways to help everyone meet their basic needs in a sustainable way.

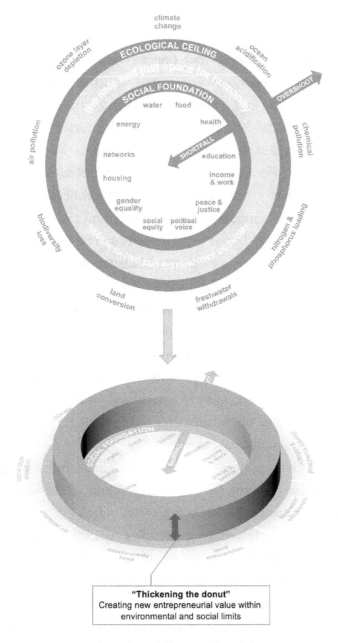

"Thickening the donut"
Creating new entrepreneurial value within
environmental and social limits

Donut Economics seeks to shift economic activity to operate
within the limits of the social foundation and ecological ceiling.
The job for entrepreneurs, business, and innovators is to create more
value within these limits, essentially "thickening" the donut.

Donut economics is a term coined by economist Kate Raworth to describe an economy that operates within ecological limits. It visualizes the economy as a donut, in which the inside limits are human needs and living with enough resources to have dignity (what she calls social foundation). The outside limits are the ecological limits of the surrounding ecosystems that our economy relies on (called ecological ceiling).[5] This framework has emerged in an attempt to corral economic production between the inner limits of ethical support for human lives and the outer limits of ecological capacity. Donut economics is a great starting point for the effort to ensure that we don't unbalance the stability of social and environmental systems upon which we depend. But I'd argue that the task of entrepreneurs and leaders in our generation is to expand the richness, or thickness of the donut portion itself, between the inner and outer limits. This means new innovations, services, and products that provide new value but do so sustainably, using circular economy materials and inputs. As we innovate, we can create more abundance for people, while respecting or even expanding the ecological capacity.

An abundant economy should give people the freedom to create at will because they now have the means for survival and the money they need to create. A system with frictionless but vetted crowdfunding and complementary currencies could fund new products and solutions. Startup capital would infuse the system with the resources to catalyze innovation, adaptability, and empowerment. Systems to track and measure the value added would also be an improvement over today's basic pricing system. This could be accomplished with reputation systems, like we have for both drivers and riders on Uber, to encourage good service and treatment of each other, as well as sensors and automated measurement. This also helps make sure the money in the community is used for the intended purpose. It's transparent, it's traceable, and it incentivizes responsible use. These mechanisms would ensure that money isn't being used to create harm or manipulate people into doing unethical things that put their society and themselves at dangerous levels of risk. Imagine a world where people could follow their passions and not have the temptation to sell out their dreams for unethical companies or work for toxic bosses, because they have the freedom of financial stability and abundance.

Free-Flowing Money

We've covered how money can come in different forms and reward what we value, like creation, innovation, and people providing value of some kind to others. Money can also incentivize spending when economies are depressed, and saving when stability is needed. We are not talking about big brother programs for control—people should be free to do what they please, as long as they're not hurting themselves or others—but we can use money to incentivize what our society needs. We already do this through interest rates, reserve requirements for banks, fines, loyalty rewards, credit scores, insurance requirements, and the like. The difference is that we have an opportunity, through all the new forms of money, to encourage applying these to what our communities and society need.

To get a sense of how money could help us shape our society, let's return to the small Austrian town of Wörgl and the efforts of Silvio Gesell. This again provides us with a great example of how money can be used to free up economic gridlock. Recall that the town decided to create free money by implementing a new local currency. But in this case the town wanted to increase the flow or velocity of money. In addition to increasing the amount of money available to people, they essentially decreased the value of money over time through a process called *demerge*. This is similar to controlled inflation and done only with the new stimulus money. This incentivized workers to spend the money soon after they received it, stimulating demand for products and services from local businesses and unlocking the seized local economy.

A parallel approach in the modern world is an economic stimulus package, especially when actually focused on putting money in the hands of people who are impoverished or working class. These groups of people are more likely to spend the money quickly than wealthy people because they are in need of immediate supplies of food, clothing, rent payments, services, and so on. Someone who already has an abundance of money is usually more likely to save this money during times of uncertainty, so the stimulus effect is delayed. Often it is said that these people are the employers, and therefore will create more jobs, which is true in some cases but not in others. But by funneling money to the customers who will create demand, we give producers and employers a more direct, immediate boost and a reason to hire.

In a more focused approach during nonemergency times, some forms of compensation could be designed to lose value over time, to stimulate spending and demand. Others could gain value over time, such as stock market compensation and deflationary cryptocurrency, which could incentivize people to save when savings rates are dangerously low—a situation that can exacerbate the impact of the downside of a recession. Ideally we would have both inflating and deflating money available, creating tools for abundance of demand for businesses, and resources for people, leaving our ideal economy with no one impoverished. In distressed, impoverished areas, people lack the money to be customers. But when people have the ability to build locally owned businesses that thrive in their neighborhoods, it stimulates the creation and exchange of value while increasing local wealth.

Basic income has long been a concept for creating an income floor for people, especially in an economy like the one we find ourselves in today, with immense income inequality, change, and automation of jobs across sectors. The immediate questions are often who pays, how much, and whether people would lose all motivation to work. Nothing is a silver bullet, including basic income, but it does appear to significantly improve well-being and a sense of buy-in for people who otherwise feel left out or dismissed by society.[6] Today we fear the automation of jobs and the social upheaval or malaise this may lead to. But with some form of basic income, we could support people through this transition, and even speed it along so we can build our better future faster, and benefit more people in the process.

The "labor shortage" of 2021 after COVID-19 stimulus payments would seem to support the assertion that if given financial support, people will work less. But this was also in the middle of a pandemic, when people were being asked to either stay home (working from home does not work for many livelihoods) or put their health at risk. The stimulus checks also amounted to only a few thousand dollars over the course of a couple of years. Let's not forget that corporate profits have been steadily rising while worker wages have stagnated for decades.[7] Economics 101 teaches that if wages are too low, workers will refuse to work, but in the recent economy, workers have had little power to actually say no, taking whatever they could get, carrying out tasks that could be automated, and often working multiple jobs to make ends meet.[8] It's no wonder people are burned out and feel adversarial toward their employers. No wonder people are taking this time to question whether they really want to continue doing the work they've been doing. With some basic income support, they have the power to reject poverty wages and push back on toxic workplaces. Will blue-collar industries actually have to compete for workers for the first time in decades? If this raises wages and benefits, it could result in lower poverty, better health outcomes, lower crime, and a more vibrant economy, ripe with demand and entrepreneurship.

Having the Economic Freedom to Make a Difference

We are moving from a world of centralized power to decentralized power, to the extent that "freedom" is gaining new meaning for how we apply our labor. When we have economic freedom, we can design careers so our work goes into efforts we believe in. This change can empower your own vision as you earn money by doing personally meaningful work.

An analogy from history can be helpful here. Not very long ago, you had a choice of only a few television networks to tune in to, and a production company in Hollywood generated entertainment for you. They tried to figure out what people wanted, through surveys, focus groups, and interviews, but they also used this information to influence people to want what they had to sell. On the arguably positive side, this created a world with lots of social cohesion and shared culture, because everyone watched the same shows and people saw the world through a similar framework. They saw characters on the television as shared community, with the most successful shows being syndicated from London to Los Angeles, Delhi to Sydney. That's a good aspect of centralization, in that it creates a shared experience and cohesion, but it also can create a monolithic or homogenous culture.

Contrast this to our current reality, where platforms like YouTube, TikTok, Instagram, and Facebook enable anybody who's creative or just has a ridiculous cat to generate entertainment. Or the deep thinkers among us can create open philosophical discussions into the nature of ourselves or our reality in the universe. Unlike that recent history in which we needed to tune in to a show at the time and channel of the network's choosing, now we can find nearly anything at any time, but we can also produce our own content and share that with the world. We still have the option to consume from a central provider, but now we can also consume a variety of content from around the world, and produce from our own home, vehicle, or neighborhood. We can produce content for free, sell it, or monetize it indirectly through ads. This becomes a distributed system where all members within that system are not only consuming information and content from the network but also actively engaged in providing material for the network. This is a microcosm of how life will be across many areas of our distributed world. However, we will still have to tackle the problem we already see today: the "superstar effect," whereby only a few people make significant money from these platforms. And so basic income in some form looks inevitable if a stable society is to continue.

This transition, far from being new for humanity, harkens back to our more egalitarian history, where everyone in a village provided some work for the village, and all members of society were cared for, in addition to providing help for the community to thrive.

While individual and clan dramas often unfolded as they do today, in the aggregate everybody was looking out for everybody, and everybody was producing for each other at the same time. That actually led to a lot of leisure time for people in a hunter-gatherer society. Leisure time to build stronger relationships, develop a variety of skills and knowledge, try new things that lead to innovation and play—all of which foster stronger mental, emotional and physical health. With so many of our modern illnesses resulting from stress, a transition to a more egalitarian and connected world, combined with the technological conveniences and protections from the dangers of the natural world, can result in a better world than humans have yet experienced.

Economic freedom is still a pretty rare experience for most human beings, but the trends seem to point to a fundamental change in this dynamic. If I'm bought into the system as a prosumer, I'm involved in the entrepreneurship, production, and risks of it. I now have a stake in it, I have something to say, and most important, I have power and another source of self-esteem.

In the ideal design for our future world, there is a true experience of freedom; you're self-sufficient and connected to your neighbors and you all contribute and rely on each other. This is actually true today, in that we do all contribute to and rely on each other—but it's all largely mediated through large third-party organizations that mask our interdependence. Our ideal design provides economic freedom, in that you can generate revenue or income from a system like this, based on the assets you or your community owns, builds, or produces.

Right now, most people participate in a wage system in which they have become workers for others who own something and generate a profit. The trends show that we have an opportunity to evolve toward a system in which people enjoy a mix of income from wage labor and from being prosumers. In that world, you have more flexibility and confidence to do what you think is right, without putting your livelihood at risk. You can better meet your basic physiological, safety, and security needs, without worry that you'll die of starvation or homelessness because you lost a job or fell ill through no fault of your own. As traditional wage labor dries up, and distributed sharing economy work and prosumer opportunities ramp up, we see yet another need for basic income in some form. We could think about this as a dividend from our society. Why should we receive a dividend? Because our society is becoming rapidly more productive thanks to automation and the solutions we are outlining in this book, but less in need of traditional forms of work.

Still, some ask why we should get free money just for being alive. Well, the sun is free, oxygen is free, and water is free, but you and I, like the animals around us, need some way to obtain food. Today the territorial construct of private property provides protection of homes and businesses. This positive development has reached such obsessive levels of reverence in some Western societies that community assets and services are somehow seen at odds with individual liberty. In reality, communities that support their people have greater physical safety, lower property crime, and higher levels of entrepreneurship.[9] Necessities that are free are castigated as handouts for the unproductive in society, but in reality we all rely on free energy, natural resources, and ecosystem services to live and do anything within our economic sphere.

As we empower people to participate more in all the different types of economies that are being advanced, distributed, and built, we all become a bit of an entrepreneur or owner ourselves. This leads to self-reliance. You are no longer driven to work by fear of destitution and poverty. You can have the freedom to do what you want to do. And when you do what you want, you will be consistently more engaged, skilled, and productive.

To introduce a system like the one we've just discussed, we need to answer the other questions: Who pays for it, and what is the motivational drive for workers? If not out of fear and desperation (do we really want our economy running on this anyway, when there's plenty to go around?), what would people work for? As we can see with people who have abundant resources, we naturally begin seeking work that is more creative or meaningful to us, with teammates we like working with. Add to this the ability for people to access capital more easily for testing new ideas, starting businesses, and providing new services, and we can revitalize neighborhoods while helping people live more satisfying and engaged lives.

This new system can catalyze the latent potential of many people for whom it is very difficult to contribute today, whether because they can't find a job or they are stuck in a dead-end job simply to earn money while their potential languishes. In this world, basic needs would be met, people would be able to take risks because of the safety net, and they'd have access to seed capital to try out their best ideas.

What would you do in a world full of abundance? If your time were freed up and you had the resources available to you, what would you do? Imagine living several hundred years from now, in a world similar to what we see on *Star Trek*. With replicators that could 3D print any food, device, or material wealth that you wanted or needed. There would be no money to earn, just wealth available to you to create or reach your potential. What would you do with your time? How would you contribute to humanity or your community with the lifetime you have available to you?

Now imagine a combination of this abundance and radical life extension, whereby you have a much longer life, or even as long as you want. On the lighter, self-indulgent side, you could try all different forms of entertainment, travel everywhere, drive any luxury car, and so on. And then what? What would you do after you've tried the temporary pleasures that appeal to you, but feel unfulfilled in the long run? (Neuroscience confirms this pattern of dissatisfaction.) What would really make your life feel as meaningful and fulfilling as possible? To have a sense of contributing to your own creative, intellectual, scientific, or artistic potential, and that of your fellow human beings, animals, the environment?

These are important questions for us to ask, not simply as thought experiments but because, as we've seen from the convergence of technological and societal trends, combined with our ability to build the ideal world we seek, many people alive today may have to answer these questions, and not just hypothetically. The bottom line is that innovation is giving us an opportunity to rethink what money is and how we use it, in order to direct it in the service of building a better world. Reality may confront us to the point that we have the privilege to live this dream. We would be wise to be prepared for that day, because the quality of our future world depends on our answers.

Chapter 11

Whole-Person Education to Advance Societal Self-Esteem

OUR WORLD HAS CHANGED RADICALLY OVER the past two hundred years. Our education system has not. The foundation for our current Western education system was designed for a very different time and society, one adapting to the nascent Industrial Revolution and moving from an agricultural society, with most people working on farms, to a factory-based economy, with employment clustered in urban areas. To find employment, people moved into denser cities and started working for a wage, instead of producing what they needed themselves. A similar shift has happened in China and other developing countries over the last few decades, only at a much faster rate, resulting in the rapid growth of the modern Chinese cities we see today. The goal was to educate people in standardized ways, for standardized jobs, with more specializations to help them play their part in growing and maintaining the industrial machine.

Today we find ourselves in a dramatically different world, with new resources but also new challenges. Climate change is looming over all of us, beginning to wreak destruction and soon will reshape our coastlines. Macro and microeconomics are in flux for people around the world. Most people now have access to almost limitless knowledge at the click of a button, with smartphone penetration rates surpassing 83% globally in 2021, although strong disparities still exist in the developing world.[1] Pakistan for example has a smartphone penetration rate of just over 20%, and these types of digital divides will become more important to address as the digital world becomes a more critical aspect of the global economy.[2] AI and other technologies are reshaping the ways that we learn, collaborate, and work. Automation is dramatically reducing production costs and making more and more products affordable and abundant. This also means the type of work we need to advance to the next step of our social evolution has changed dramatically.

Despite the dramatic changes in our society, our educational systems have largely remained static. School tends to be organized around a unidirectional transfer of knowledge from teacher to student. Beyond the elementary grades, there are separate classrooms for each discrete subject. Instruction is often designed with a one-size-fits-all approach, and students are almost uniformly grouped based only on age, despite different ways of learning, different skill levels, and different educational needs.

An Education System Designed for Mass Production

In the industrial age, education was designed to help train people for the jobs of the time. Whether that meant forging steel, building machines and parts for railroads on an assembly line, or constructing infrastructure, workers needed to do the repetitive tasks that made mass production possible. The introduction of assembly lines, prefabrication of parts, and systematic approaches to construction dramatically increased productivity and reduced costs. To meet this challenge, people needed to be trained on how to be good workers—to be reliable, communicate with common ideas regardless of where they were from, and follow the regimentation required for this new work structure.

Step-by-Step Instruction and Following the Rules

Employers and policymakers wanted to ensure that people were obedient and followed the rules of their employers for three main reasons:

- It's just easier to manage obedient people, especially when you need to manage large groups collaborating on complex tasks and projects.

- Steel plants and industrial factories were very unsafe. Today the fatality rate for workers in the US averages around 3.5 per 100,000. But fatality rates in common jobs such as mining and railroad work in 1889 ranged from 100 to 800 deaths per 100,000 workers—over a hundred-fold more than today.[3] Given the unsafe conditions, following the rules was one key way to avoid major workplace accidents or even deaths.

- There was a massive drive toward efficient labor. Scientific management involved scrutinizing films of people's movements as they worked and finding ways of cutting out unnecessary movements. The goal was to find the most efficient way of carrying or moving equipment or material, so that workers could do more work in the same amount of time (and for the same amount of pay). New rules and training were crucial to ensure that efficient practices were followed.

Some people needed to have specific knowledge about how to work machines, or how to manage a project, but most just needed to know how to follow the rules and be physically fit enough to work long hours—and in some lucky cases, have enough knowledge to manage an operation.

The Banking Concept of Education

Education was very regimented and process oriented. People needed to learn how to carry out specific processes effectively, because that was the world they were training for. The system of education was based on a hierarchy of expertise and an approach called the *banking concept of education*, in which a teacher has the knowledge and deposits it into the students' heads. The students could then use that knowledge to work competently. Much like money deposited into a bank, this knowledge was meant to accrue interest as students worked and advanced on the job. They would be all set to work at the same job for decades or even a lifetime, an experience that is extremely rare today.

Centralized, Top-Down Learning

The banking concept works in a static environment, where the knowledge that students absorb will remain relevant and accurate for long periods of time. It also works well for military and industrial training, where veering away from the training or disobeying orders could present a danger to trainees or their peers. These fields often require centralized and top-down approaches where people need to follow orders, repeat discrete tasks, or play a defined and relatively predictable role on a team.

At that time in our societal development, human beings were trying to figure out how to organize and collaborate in larger and larger groups. Going from working in small groups to thousands of people working on thousands of parts in factories located in different locations required incredible amounts of precision, management, regimentation, and coordination from above. The top-down manager sees the whole project and manages people like cogs in a machine, which is how people in these systems reported feeling.

We saw that feeling in many of the narratives in stories and movies of the time. *Metropolis* is a great example. A silent film released in 1927, it portrayed exactly that experience of workers of the Industrial Revolution. People felt like parts of the machine. Life was nonstop repetition. They went to the factory and worked their days away while risking life and limb for a paycheck. The people with the knowledge and power lived at the top of the tower (naturally), looking out over the city and workers they sought to control. Android hijinks, revolutions, and liberation abound in this film, but the stark dynamic between the workers and powerful owner was made clear.

Like all great art, this cynical portrayal of the relationship between labor and management held truth to power, showing the perception of workers as disposable, malleable, and powerless. Apologists may point out that it's incredibly difficult to manage such large projects if you don't have distributed ways of helping people manage themselves. During the Industrial Revolution this top-down approach to management may have been needed. But the world we live in today is undeniably quite different, especially the one emerging before our eyes.

The New World We Find Ourselves In

Fast forward to today, where we find ourselves in a dramatically different world. The entirety of human knowledge is available to almost every person on the planet at the touch of a button, and there is a wealth of apps designed to help groups plan and collaborate. The structure and type of work are changing, from reliable and well-paid, full-time factory jobs to work structures that are more remote, temporary, and knowledge based. Instead of someone repetitively making a component for a widget in a factory, they are bringing their knowledge and creativity to help that factory make just the right thing. It could be the right thing for their customers, or just the right design to catch people's attention, or just the right message on social media that gets people's attention—or just what the world needs.

The economy has changed in so many different ways, automating or making obsolete much of the repetitive, regimented work that employed masses of people in the past—and this trend is accelerating. This is not to say that trade schools won't be important in the medium term to help people build skills that the world needs. But more repetitive and process-oriented jobs are being automated by AI software or robotics—and this is a good thing (if we can figure out a more humane economic philosophy that adapts to our modern age). By eliminating these tasks, we empower human beings to be more, well, human.[4] It's not that AI will do everything for us, but it will become a great ally to humanity, just like any other tool—made better by our skillful and humanitarian use of it.

Our economy is shifting to one that needs people who are more creative, entrepreneurial, empathetic, and collaborative—people who can define and create the solutions that will help us overcome our grand challenges as a species and bring us closer together. With a world full of challenges, education must prepare people to solve them. The challenges and opportunities are different from those of the past in type and in scale. Let's take a look:

- Climate change is going to wreak ever more havoc on our lives if we don't slow or reverse it. Even if we do, drastic adaptation will most likely be needed within the next few decades and definitely before the end of the century.

- Because of the social changes happening in reaction to change, we will need to be able to process knowledge and sense-make better than people ever have in the past.

- We will also need to collaborate better, make decisions across distances, and self-govern ourselves and our communities. Especially as boundaries begin to dissolve, thanks to more powerful tools for worldwide collaboration that become widespread and abundant. That requires a decentralized and democratic shift for us to be better able to manage ourselves.

- Economic approaches are in flux as we try to figure out new ways of adapting our human society to be more sustainable and resilient, both environmentally and socially.

- With limitless new ways to work and to make a living, we're becoming newly empowered professionally. An abundance of free platforms that we can jump on instantly enables us to create everything from entertainment and instructional classes to providing services like graphic design or deliveries. If you're a photographer, massage therapist, or drone pilot, you can offer your services easily. Or if arbitrage is your game, eBay, Amazon, or an e-commerce site have never been easier to sell on. However, you also now face competitors from around the globe.

These are not trivial challenges, and unfortunately the current education systems in most countries are inadequate to empower the children of today to meet the needs of tomorrow. We need non-trivial updates to our education system that can help people solve those problems, adapt to a rapidly changing future, and create their way into a happy, fulfilling world that brings sustainable peace and prosperity to all. No pressure!

However, the current education system is not just inadequate to meet the challenges of tomorrow; it is failing students today. Few people or students feel adequately prepared for life getting out of school. According to one study, only 42% of high school graduates felt prepared for a career—after twelve years of "successful" schooling![5] According to another Gallup survey in the US, only 5% of respondents considered high school graduates very well prepared for work.[6] This only improves to 13% for college graduates.[7] The most common shortcomings mentioned center on collaboration between employers and educators, to provide real-world project experience from internships and apprenticeships, work on long-term projects, build relationships, and gain mentorship from staff and faculty. This has led to 25% of college graduates failing to thrive later in their lives and careers.[8]

This is a sad state of affairs for our future leaders, workers, family members, and friends—not to mention our communities and civilization. One thing is clear: We need to redesign how we go about educating our people, young and old, to attain better well-being, success, and resiliency—as individuals and as a society.

To better understand what the ideal future of education might look like, I spoke with Kristina Ishmael, an education leader and consultant who has worked with local and state public schools, the education think tank New America, and the US Department of Education. She focuses on education equity, innovation, and inclusivity. According to Kristina:

In order to design for the ideal education system, we need to take a holistic look at not only students, but the context within which they live and are being educated. The history of American education was rooted in the Industrial Revolution, when the goals of education were much more around regimentation and training for factory work. It also has perpetuated deep inequities in our society (sometimes intentionally and other times unintentionally) that cannot be ignored when we seek to redesign for the ideal. There are incredible new technologies being introduced to help educators, but this is only a piece of the puzzle—we must consider the whole human being, the society they live in, the curriculum they are taught, and the history they are a part of in order to give each student equal opportunity and make real progress in education.

Setting Ideal Design Objectives for the Future of Education

Let's start with the basics. What is education? Why have education? If we were to redesign anew, what would we be trying to achieve? The Dalai Lama has an interesting take: "The aim of education should be to train happy individuals who make up a peaceful society. It requires warm-heartedness and taking a broad-minded, holistic and far-sighted approach that enables people to cope, whatever happens. It entails focusing on the good of the community."[9] This reframes what education is for, from the older goal of training people for employment to a new understanding that education is for nurturing and growing fulfilled, resilient, and compassionate individuals. Of course, part of this is gaining real-world skills to be able to contribute to society and work with others effectively, but this is a means to the broader end of the peaceful society put forth by the Dalai Lama. This vision describes peace not just as the absence of violence, but as the presence of compassion and happiness.

Another important aspect to consider is how we can leverage all the tools and knowledge at our disposal to make education more effective. Our current educational system rarely uses all the technology available today. Most schools in developed countries now have computers and internet access, which helps provide the basics, but the students actually have better tools on their smartphones—and those games, apps, and connections are designed to be highly sophisticated at competing for students' attention. Further, AI and analytics are used in manufacturing, social media, HR, and medicine but are not being used for one of the most important industries— education. If we were to approach educating and enabling people holistically, and with the same level of sophistication as the Facebook or Twitter algorithms that hook our attention on their platforms, imagine what we could achieve.

So with all this in mind, what might we design for in an ideal education system?

Ideal Design Objective 1: Being Humanistic and Holistic

The first objective is being humanistic and holistic. We should design an education system that helps people to be fulfilled and happy in their lives, not just as a worker but as a complete person. That includes a career, it includes being able to carry out tasks, but it also includes many other softer skills. We want to address the entire person and help them to be happy, fulfilled, and successful— and know what that means to them. An effective education should start with helping the student answer some important questions— from the most basic to the most practical:

- Who are you?

- What do you get energized by doing, and what are your talents? How can you get paid to do these things?

- How do you socialize with others in a way that helps you build fulfilling relationships?

- How can you develop disciplined habits that help you be effective, avoid distractions, and concentrate on work or tasks when you need to?

- How can you deeply reset and relax to a degree that you're not only more productive but also can think more clearly, understand your next step, and understand your life strategy or your life journey?

- How do you fail fast, learn from your mistakes, and not feel ashamed of them?

- How do you navigate your emotional world and respond effectively so that you have healthy reactions to your work and communicate effectively with your teammates?

- How do you learn to become good at new things?

If we address those fundamental questions and emotional issues within education, future generations will look for work and relationships that are secure, nurturing, and fulfilling. They will seek adventures that make the heart beat faster but don't put anyone at unnecessary risk. Maybe for one student that involves racing cars, for another it involves international travel, for another it may be athletic challenges, and for yet another it may come through artistic expression. They will be doing these things because it makes them love their lives, not because they want others to recognize them, or to quiet the persistent pain of a trauma from long ago or last week. All of these are aspects of an education system that is more holistic and humanistic.

Ideal Design Objective 2:
Personalizing Education

Education needs to address specific individuals' needs and dynamics. When a class is in session, roughly half the students are at least somewhat bored, half are somewhat lost, and some small fraction of them are getting the education they want at the level they need. That's a tragedy for everyone involved. How do we better personalize education to serve the needs of *everyone* in the class?

One way might be to learn from the activities that are already engaging people very effectively: social media and games. Artificially intelligent games, interactions, and assignments could learn and adapt to each student's own pace, track their progress, understand how they respond and learn, and then fine-tune the learning process to give students a continual challenge at the right level. We don't want the work of education to be so challenging that students feel discouraged or give up, but we also don't want it so easy that they feel bored or disengaged.

The good news is that we already have a good understanding of many of the technical, user experience, and interaction design approaches. They're being used by Facebook, Google, and other advertising firms, continually optimizing to keep us engaged and keep us clicking. What if we could use this type of apparatus and intelligence to help people learn better, and to help people advance their own capacity to learn, grow, and be more fulfilled and effective in the world? We've nailed that for marketing and advertising, with both positive and negative side effects. So why not nail that for education and use these advancements for the betterment of mankind?

What happens in a world with AI, engaging educational games, and radically personalized education? The most obvious aspects of education that could be automated are memorization and focused, non-group work. These could be the basics of math, foundational science, reading, writing, or history. Time both outside of class or in-classroom focus time could be spent highly engaged in these types of learning. In-classroom time can also be spent on collaboration, discussion and critical thinking, learning rhetoric, socialization, and communication.

Where does the teacher play a role in this techno-enhanced world of education? This is similar to other industries, but in education I think it gets to the heart of the AI and automation issue. AI is very, very good at engaging people's attention or helping them learn certain kinds of skills, but it's terrible at helping a person understand who they are and what they want to do with their lives, or how to become more emotionally intelligent.

In this world where technology takes some of the weight off of teachers, human beings can take the lead in doing what human beings are good at, which is not regurgitating facts or repetitive education. Humans are good at collaborating and communicating—helping each other understand themselves and their world, and figuring out what they want to do in life. Human beings can handle the humanistic side of education, and continually learning AI can adjust learning activities to make many of the repetitive assignments that bore students today much more engaging.

We can't talk about personalization without mentioning the vastly different experiences that students have in and out of school, and how these affect their education and prospects. Many students of color, in particular, go through school without seeing a teacher or professor who either looks like them or understands their experience. Economically disadvantaged students can also have a sense of imposter syndrome in schools where they feel that they don't belong or are not represented. This can follow them through their careers and hamstring their potential if it isn't confronted and worked through. An important aspect of education is inclusion—making sure everyone is given equal opportunities to succeed in a world that claims to be meritocratic. Let's make that claim a reality.

Ideal Design Objective 3: Collaborating with the Real World

What makes us a successful species? Is it our opposable thumbs, our advanced voice boxes, our frontal lobes? All of these are very helpful, but our species would not be nearly as successful without collaboration. We humans are a social and industrious species that has survived, advanced, and persevered because we have each other, and because we work together. Regardless of our technological advancement, people need to understand how to work together in groups to be successful. What do we do when we get out of school? For the most part, we go to work on teams and group projects. In the modern world of more distributed teams and collaboration to solve ever more problems, the ability to initiate and manage these projects is becoming more important. A small portion of students will work on their own, but even in this case project-based learning is a core part of being able to succeed in and contribute to society.

We need to better prepare our students with project-based education, while ideally putting their work into projects that have real-world impact. What if we made an education system where students had the safety to try new things and learn from failure but also built a portfolio for themselves by working on projects that would continue past graduation or contribute to the world?

Consider this: Instead of working exclusively on projects that are solely for in-class credit, what if students worked on solving real problems, so that when they get out of high school, they have work experience and the option to continue working on what they've built? School could be more of a ramp-up internship or transition into the world of adult independence rather than coming to an abrupt end without a real connection to what comes next. If they choose to, students could launch a startup, service, or new product that gets built while they're in high school, with the help of teachers and the surrounding business community, and transition into the life that follows school by continuing to build the project. Suddenly that barrier between school and adult life begins to fade away, and we not only bring school into the rest of the world but also bring that world into school.

Of course, not everyone is going to be an artist, a founder, or a manager—no one should feel compelled to pursue any livelihood based on others' expectations—but through working on projects with other people, students can figure out which roles they'd like to play, which roles they wouldn't, and how to communicate more effectively. Learning effective communication and collaboration on projects as early as possible is a game changer for many students—whether they work in construction or corporate strategy.

Ideal Design Objective 4:
Fostering Adaptability

An education needs to prepare children and adults to be adaptable and have the tools, confidence, and habits that help them succeed in whatever world we're going to live in five, ten, or a hundred years from now. Of course, we can't predict the future, but we know it will be different from our present, and by being adaptable we can be ready for it. The right kind of education helps the learner be more confident in both the present and their readiness for the future. So an educational system that succeeds in helping learners develop the basic self-esteem needs of Maslow's hierarchy will be crucial for enabling current and upcoming generations to solve the world's challenges.

The education system itself can't evolve at the pace at which it's been evolving for the last century, because the world is evolving much faster, and people are being left behind. The way we educate people needs to be rapidly updated for adaptability to changing technological, business, and economic dynamics. We can get there by enabling technological infrastructure but also by bringing in employers and innovators from the community to provide the most recent updates and understandings of the challenges they face. In addition to working on "real-life" projects, this will shape education to be more applicable to what students will encounter outside of school.

Ideal Design Objective 5: Moving from Administrative to Collaborative

The role of teaching is changing from authority figure to facilitator. Teachers are setting the rules of the game and assisting students as they work through challenges and projects. Teachers no longer need to have all the answers. Instead, they need to ask the right questions and help people use the right approach to find the right answers. They are also human beings in a system dedicated to human beings, and this uniquely qualifies them to balance out the ever more ubiquitous technology to help make education more humanistic, holistic, and inspiring. Well-rounded teachers building relationships with students over time will dramatically improve student outcomes.

Ideal Design Objective 6: Understanding Information Interweaving Technology

Part of today's education is about helping students understand how to gather and interpret information. Whether using an old-school library ISBN sorting system or the latest mobile apps, an ideal education system helps students understand the tools they can use to find answers and relevant information. Thanks to the internet, the challenge has moved from remembering facts and doing routine tasks to being able to find, interpret, and present information in an engaging way. Knowing the times tables is a useful life skill, but a calculator can run more complex calculations in an instant. This will become increasingly true across the board, so the broader goal may become to prepare students to know which tool to use for which task.

A personal experience helped me understand this transition. A friend had overestimated my technical capabilities and asked me how to solve an issue on his computer. Instead of pulling from my nonexistent programming knowledge, I just googled the issue with the name of the software and found the solution. We both paused, and he said to me, "Wow, this is the best thing that I've learned, not the answer to a specific problem—but knowing that the information is out there and how I can solve the problem myself." Indeed, many IT experts today simply get answers by knowing what to google. Worry not, tech support, we will still need your help on many things, first and foremost making sure our device is plugged in, but many of our specific issues can be solved by simply knowing how to use Google.

Here's a disturbing example of the importance of asking the right question. In China, a test program was rolled out that requires students to wear a headband that senses their brain activity. The headband can tell whether they're concentrating, distracted, or tired. It lights up a different color for each, and the teacher can see when someone is distracted and call them out or offer assistance. In other test programs, video analytics can monitor student emotions, noting how often students check their phones or yawn during classes. These technologies can generate analytics for the teachers and parents to see how their student is performing in class, and can track progress over time. Today we still generally measure progress from homework and exams, but in the future we might analyze brain analytics instead.[10]

I dare say this is interesting and innovative (yet unproven) technology, but poorly applied. It assumes that achieving mental concentration is the goal of education and that the banking concept of education is best for the students: They should be sitting still, listening attentively to a teacher, who, of course, has all the knowledge. Concentration is a good ability to have and hone, but in our current world, we also need students who can bring a diversity of brain activity to work, to increase creativity, collaboration, and play, and reduce stress for the team. This is not to say there can't be some benefit of these technologies, but we need to apply them in humanistic ways, not automatically leaning on the ways of the industrializing past.

If we applied technologies like this in more humanistic ways, it would help students understand and direct themselves—to be able to be focused and concentrated at the right times, and more intuitive and creative thinking at other times. Some of the most valuable thinking that we need today and for the near future is creative thinking that connects concepts and learnings from multiple disciplines and perspectives and then uses that creative thinking to solve complex problems. That often fails to happen through linear-focused thinking and approaches. Creatively solving problems happens when different types of people come together and find different applications for existing tools or entirely new approaches to solving a problem. Diversity of thought and collaboration across cultures and individual experiences and inclusion of unconventional ideas have played a key role in getting us to where we are today—and it will play an even greater one in getting us to the future we want.

There is no clear technology or business-only solution. Policy is essential to making education not only effective but equitable. An uncontrolled, techno-enhanced, and highly educated population could unintentionally exacerbate the inequality we see today. To prevent these potential harms, from resource inequality to full-blown techno-feudalism or techno-fascism, policymakers must act to ensure that guidelines and resources are available to educational organizations for all segments of society.

Finland is widely recognized as a leader in this area, with a focus on equity as well as excellence, a higher collaboration-to-lecture ratio, focus on collaboration, real-world training, and dedicated time for teachers to advance their own studies.[11] Finland also happens to be the happiest country in the world—perhaps this is related to good education. Despite the fact that Finland has no standardized tests, teachers don't assign much homework compared to Western peers, and students spend only twenty hours a week in school on average, most Finnish children graduate with command of two languages and score above average in math, science, and reading, and their socioeconomic status has a lower impact than average on overall performance.[12] Maybe there is more we can learn from their society to become a happier society ourselves.[13] If we want to have a happier future, we need to update education to meet both our collective needs and the needs of each individual. Now that we live in a world of sophisticated technology that can influence how we think and who we are, perhaps we should be asking ourselves "Who do we want to be?" Instead of our previous view of ourselves as "cogs in a machine," this holistic approach to education will help us lay the foundation for nurturing self-actualized people, and therefore a self-actualized society.

Chapter 12

Self-Actualization for All

FINALLY, WE ARRIVE AT THE TOP OF THE PYRAMID of needs. What would it really look like and feel like to be self-actualized and live in a self-actualized society? Perhaps a take from the man himself, Abraham Maslow, would help:

> Musicians must make music, artists must paint, poets must write if they are to be ultimately at peace with themselves. What human beings can be, they must be. They must be true to their own nature. This need we call self-actualization.[1]

Just as self-actualization is not possible for an individual without first satisfying the other needs of Maslow's hierarchy, a society that is dealing with needs lower on the pyramid cannot fully reach self-actualization. Traumatic events like war, food scarcity, or disease can bring a society back down the pyramid, and if a significant portion of the population is struggling, the society will largely be pulled back to survival, safety, or community needs, at best seeking status and social mobility. This has been the state of most of humanity throughout our history of civilization, with the majority of people focused on day-to-day survival, and a privileged few working on themselves, or their artistic or scientific endeavors. That all has the potential to change in this century.

Gathering food and supporting our basic needs used to take up a significant amount of our time, even when we were hunter-gatherers. However, there were diverse cultures, with some clans having more abundant territories than others and enjoying more egalitarianism and leisure time. But threats were abundant, infant mortality was high, and survival was never guaranteed. Once we developed agricultural technology, surpluses led to food abundance. This created an enormous shift in how we human beings spent our days, freeing up time for leisure, art, invention, and services. The Industrial Revolution provided a similar shift, reducing the amount of work devoted to farming through machinery and innovation. This meant more time and wealth to create products at industrial scale, and a proliferation of the types of jobs people could do.

Now, our society expends only about 5% of its labor on agriculture, and there's a whole world of other things to do.[2] As automation, AI, and software take over for much of our mental work, just as tractors and combines took over for our muscles, it's likely that we will reach even higher levels of abundance. This will present new ways to spend our time and energy, just as unimaginable to us as IT and tech jobs would have been to our Stone Age ancestors.

As the tasks of survival and achieving status through resource accumulation dwindle from a majority of our time to a minority of our time, thanks to the abundant world we are in the process of creating, there's going to be a whole new world of challenges, discoveries, and activities to spend our time on. We are innately a very curious and active species, so it's unlikely we will simply turn to actual couch potatoes, although as we can see with today's widely available entertainment, some will inevitably choose that path. More likely, life is going to be much more about scientific exploration or pushing the limits of knowledge, creativity and the arts, and enjoying sports and physical challenges, all while enjoying more leisure time with each other. It could also mean more caring for our planet, spending time in nature, and many things that we consider recreational today but actually greatly improve the quality of our lives.

As we enter this new age, we will, of course, be empowered by our technology. This can help us achieve great heights but also enable us to commit unspeakable horrors if we are not emotionally mature enough, individually and as a society, to handle the responsibility of our creations. So, ironically, we are at the climax of a long journey to reach the liberation of self-actualization, which we desperately need to achieve to prevent ourselves from threatening our basic survival.

Setting Ideal Design Objectives for Self-Actualization

Success in building a self-actualized society and supporting the actualization of the people who compose it comes down to design principles based on the experience of self-actualization and what this enables us to do. We must not consider being self-actualized as a destination, however, but more of an experience, of a lifelong approach to our journey and relationships.

Ideal Design Objective 1: A Post-Trauma Society

It has been said that "hurt people hurt people." People who have not yet healed from trauma will perpetuate trauma in others by reenacting traumatic experiences with them—either out of a desire to protect themselves or the person they are traumatizing from a world they view as inherently unsafe, or simply as revenge on the world at large. People who have healed from their trauma, however, are much more compassionate and interested in helping others to heal and succeed in their lives.[3]

This first objective is to free people from trauma and/or manipulation by others. Of course, people will suffer from time to time; traumatic and difficult things will happen to all of us. But people need to be able to cope with and overcome the effects of trauma. Furthermore, we all want to be free from the emotional overrides and triggers that manipulate us into doing things that we wouldn't want to do otherwise. We can all relate to this. This is a therapeutic aspect of self-actualization: to overcome the bad experiences or impulses we have within. It could be argued that simply helping people be resilient in the face of trauma—and liberated from basing their behaviors on it—could heal many of the social ills we face today.

Ideal Design Objective 2: Accuracy and Sense-Making

Accuracy in how we see and interpret our world, a process I described earlier in the book as sense-making, is essential to self-actualization. How can we develop better systems and approaches to processing information to get a better sense of what is true in the world? The information people receive drives the way they interpret world events and societal problems and shapes their judgments and actions. This has become amply apparent in the increasingly divisive political narratives of recent years. Echo chambers and tribalism threaten our ability to discuss ideas, disagree with the purpose of finding the truth, and therefore collaborate and build our future together. This is especially relevant in a world where anyone can say anything about anything to everyone, on social media, blogs, dubious and opaquely controlled "news" sites, and anywhere else on the internet where people get their information.

This world is very different from that of previous generations, where institutions were trusted and monolithic, offering a single point of view that unified cultures and societies. But there were disadvantages, especially if some institutions couldn't be trusted. Our new world has the potential to give us a more accurate and comprehensive understanding of the world, as long as we can implement systems that help us avoid the risk of weaponized information, which leads to a fractured, divisive, and highly manipulatable public psyche.

Ideal Design Objective 3: An Inspired and Engaged Society

What good is an accurate and enlightened worldview if one cannot act upon it? We must ask how a society can activate the energy and inspiration of its people to go out and make positive changes in the world. In our ideal world we would have a clear path, from being at peace by healing trauma, to accurately viewing the world and how it works, to becoming energized to help our ideal world develop into its next phase. When we speak of self-actualization, most people probably think of becoming enlightened. But it's not just about sitting in meditation; it's also about walking, acting, and creating your vision in the world with that enlightenment (whatever that means to you). This isn't simply about accomplishment or reaching a higher status level; it's about deeply knowing who you are and why you want to do what you want to do, and being able to do it effectively.

Ideal Design Objective 4: Effective People in an Effective Society

All of these design principles lead us to the fourth, which is having the tools, knowledge, and relationships to be effective at actually creating the future. No matter how enlightened or inspired you are, if you aren't able to get buy-in from others, collaborate with them well, or have the discipline to execute on a project, the fruit of your intellectual and emotional actualization is likely to wither on the vine. In an ideal world, people will be actively and enthusiastically building the future together and sharing in the fruits of each other's work.

In a World That Thrives, People Thrive

At this point, any rational person might well ask "How on Earth are we going to accomplish such an ambitious undertaking? What does a society with these design objectives actually look like? How do we get to this place? And what does it mean for ourselves and the rest of society?"

When we establish as our goal the abundant, post-scarcity, and zero marginal cost society that we have talked about earlier in this book, we set the conditions for human beings to thrive. As we've discussed, most people today spend most of their time trying to survive, trying to make rent, or at best trying to advance their careers. A lot of our precious lifetime is spent on survival or achieving status—the latter often at the behest of advertisers. While it is obviously essential to survive physically, and some degree of social status is important to that survival for a social animal like ourselves, we have so much more potential that we could realize if these thirsts were quenched and we could focus on more meaningful pursuits. Our time in history is ripe to enable us to reach that potential. What might our internal world look like when most of our outer world is nearly free from these distractions—when we have material and informational abundance; when we're living in a post-scarcity society?

A Post-Scarcity versus a Post-Discontent Society

Some people are already living in a post-scarcity world. In our modern era, in the developed nations wealthy people can have nearly everything they want and most people can afford the basic necessities. But we don't have a *post-discontent* society, in which people are fully satisfied with their lives and able to overcome the aftereffects of trauma. Just having what we want doesn't necessarily make us happy or satisfied or help us find meaning in our lives or relationships.

In fact, some people or communities with less material security or wealth (not speaking of the desperately poor) actually report higher levels of happiness, often because their dependence on each other helps them form stronger bonds and relationships.[4] This finding takes us back to the rest of the pyramid and underscores the fact that all of our needs are important, regardless of how high up the pyramid we've climbed. Once people have material wealth, what do they do with their lives? Faced with the restlessness of having no more critical survival challenges to solve, what do they do to grow, find meaning, and avoid becoming destructive? No generation to date has faced this challenge as much as we do, so we're unsure how they might have responded.

When life loses purpose in a post-scarcity society, one might see boredom as the biggest danger. And while we should not be so naïve as to think that we will run out of problems to solve anytime soon, we should be aware that as the challenges we face change, some people will lose sight of their sense of purpose, stability, or worldview, and this could ironically create the biggest collective problem of them all: a "perfect" society full of people with nothing left to do—or, perhaps, even to live for.

Technology of Consciousness, Information, and Discovery

When a child is shown something new, their curiosity goes through the roof. They (sometimes obsessively) study everything they can about it and test out their new knowledge with creative play. Over the years as we learn and grow, we also learn to curb our enthusiasm, but this instinct lives on in all of us—providing a potential source of curiosity, discovery, and energy. With the tools of self-understanding, therapeutic techniques, and applied collective knowledge, we may be able to maintain and nurture these high levels of curiosity, engagement, and energy throughout our lives. Add to this all of the tools of collaboration and creation, data-driven insights, and community connections available at our fingertips today, and a limitless world of opportunity opens up to us. This could allow us to act on our curiosity and create incredible things while living rich lives of passion, community, and meaning.

Getting there includes, as we have discussed, making education that's as close to phenomenal as possible available to all including self-healing and discovery. As people move from survival or status needs to better education and self-esteem, and from an emotional state of fear and scarcity to one of openness and curiosity, scientific and personal discovery become of higher interest. People find a lot of meaning in scientific or athletic pursuits, but also in their inner exploration. There is a lot of knowledge available to us about how the world works, but much knowledge remains undiscovered, especially when it comes to consciousness and the nature of reality. Some of these mysteries will outlive us, so for that which is unexplainable by science today (or potentially for the rest of our lifetimes), people often turn to some flavor of what we generally call *spirituality*. But science and spirituality can not only coexist; they are actually complementary. We can have both rigorously vetted scientific discoveries and a general culture of curiosity, discovering new phenomena and questions for us to apply the scientific method to. Importantly, though, we need to be able to bifurcate the two into what is proven and what is being explored. If people don't have to spend their days trying to survive, and unending entertainment doesn't grab most of their attention in the long term, it's likely that people would turn to science, art, creative innovation, and discovery while also exploring their own inner world of experience and consciousness.

With this new freedom and unleashed curiosity, we can discover more of the secrets of ourselves, our world, and our universe. Research doesn't have to come from scientists at Harvard or MIT, as long as the scientific method is used. With proper education and more abundant tools and better sense-making methods available, anyone can contribute to the world with their true passion, whether that's an artistic endeavor, scientific discovery, athletic achievements, social relationships, and the list goes on.

The internal science of self-actualization and the technology to assist in it is still in its infancy. As brain and consciousness technology improves, we can not only understand how our brain works but also interact with it and direct it in new ways. There's a lot of new technology emerging in this area. Some are electronic, such as transcranial current stimulation for enhanced learning (which showed 250% learning improvement in one army study), and influence brainwaves for better focus.[5], [6], [7] Others are chemical, such as nootropics for everything from creativity to attention, and psychedelic therapy for treating addiction, persistent depression, or PTSD.[8] Psychedelic-assisted therapy has become popularized recently and even achieved breakthrough status with the US FDA, leading cities and states to propose and pass sweeping decriminalization measures. Oregon is the first state in the US to decriminalize psilocybin (otherwise known as magic mushrooms) for use in clinical studies as well as therapy for depression and end-of-life anxiety for terminally ill patients. In addition to psilocybin, MDMA and other substances like ayahuasca and mescaline are being shown to improve emotional and mental health outcomes when used in a supervised setting as part of a therapeutic treatment regimen.[9] If we can think about this in terms of consciousness technology, the responsible and professionally guided use of these substances and technologies will one day help us not only heal our traumas but also discover and fulfill our true callings and potentials. They could also help us have higher-quality relationships with others.

Between targeted electronic brain measurement and stimulation and the world of psychedelic-assisted therapy, serious research institutions like Johns Hopkins, NYU, and others are having success solving addictions to alcohol and opiates, persistent depression, and PTSD, which could have profound effects on everyone from soldiers who return from war emotionally traumatized, to adults still suffering the effects of family-related childhood trauma. Despite limited progress for years, these new types of consciousness technologies are finally helping us make progress in ways that are not just incremental, but profound. With so much research and development going on in this area, public awareness of these technologies and the potential benefits is rising. Adoption could grow rapidly, similar to more familiar consciousness technologies like meditation apps and gamified learning. The profound effect that widespread use of these technologies could have on a society should not be understated. However, we need to ensure that they are available to people across the socioeconomic spectrum, to prevent further disparities in wealth or ability, exacerbated by the advantages of access to these types of technologies.

Reenvisioning the Four Types of Civilization

In 1964, Soviet astronomer Nicolai Kardashev pondered the advancement of civilizations and came up with a phased framework of three stages. In his thinking, a type one civilization can use all of the energy available on their planet. A type two civilization can use all of the energy coming from their star system. And a type three civilization is able to use all of the energy from their entire galaxy. This is a common framework in science fiction to describe advancements of civilizations, but (forgive me, fellow sci-fi fans) it's shortsighted and stuck in simple linear, expansionist thinking.

The Kardashev scale highlights the problem of projection when trying to predict the future: We are tempted to take what we have today and extrapolate it into the future, whether that's tens or tens of thousands of years down the line. This approach ignores checks and balances and exponential change, and it leaves no room for how new technologies and techniques could fundamentally change how we go about using and organizing our resources. It's as if we predicted in 1800 that a type three civilization would have a steam locomotive that would reach the center of the galaxy, rather than anticipating that new types of energy would be discovered or could be used more efficiently, or raw materials could be infinitely recycled, or society could advance by more sophisticated metrics than energy consumption.

What if we came up with a new step-by-step process for advancing civilizations that was more about humanity? Society should be based on how educated, healthy, capable, and actualized its people are, which enables civilization to accelerate its evolution—and in a more positive direction. This transforms our notions of advancement from being primarily about technology to being primarily about human beings, even if their development is empowered by technology. In our new model:

- A type one civilization is post-scarcity: All people have access to the means to survive easily.

- Type two is post-ignorance: All people have information readily available and sense-making tools to accurately understand it.

- Type three is post-trauma: All people have moved beyond asymmetrical and inappropriate behavioral reactions to the situations they encounter in life.

Let's pause here. What do we mean by asymmetrical behavioral reactions? In these cases the amygdala takes over the brain when the frontal lobes and logic should lead. If people's lives are not threatened by a predator's attack or a life-threatening natural disaster, they should not have to feel and react as if that were the case. This fight-or-flight reaction can cloud the mind from understanding the situation on a personal level (becoming infuriated by a minor offense) and societal scale (going to war in response to a political affront). Leaders can manipulate populations by stimulating the collective amygdala to advance support for their political agendas. In our type three civilization, instead of reacting inappropriately, people react appropriately and are not unreasonably traumatized by poverty, abuse, war, or political or economic manipulation, instead using a synthesis of reason, experience, and emotional information to understand and react to situations, unclouded by residual trauma.

If we stretch even further, we can imagine a type four civilization, in which everyone is empowered and has the means to create, innovate, research, and expand their own limits, as well as the limits of their society. Imagine what we could accomplish and how exciting it would be to live in a type four civilization. People could collaborate and communicate much more effectively, leading to rapid innovation, better adaptation to change, and more fulfilled lives. People would not be stuck in PTSD from trauma, so they could see situations for what they really are. The question then becomes not what *could* we achieve, but what *couldn't* we?

This framework of our types one through four would put a more humanistic lens on how we measure the advancement of a civilization, instead of the current standard practice of simply measuring the amount of energy and resources we could consume. If we combined this humanistic framework with measures of circular economy, sustainability, and material wealth, we could measure our advancement even more holistically, to capture both the experience of the human beings within society, as well as the technology and resources available to all of us. This is the path to what we would call utopia today, and hopefully what our future generations would call obvious. In this type of world there would be less risk of terrorism and the societal upheavals that arise due to vast inequalities, unfairness, and injustice. It doesn't mean that we forgo technology; it doesn't mean we forgo "progress." We would actually accelerate progress by having all hands (and brains) on deck, with everyone on board to benefit. That's how we could reach this true potential of human society. In fact, it may be the only way to get there at all.

Achieving Accuracy in Sense-Making

With today's information sphere (mostly on the internet), we have a store of information, but there's no consistent judgment about it and no way to reach a conclusion that doesn't demand the vast majority of our time to deeply research a topic and fact-check every asserted point. Anyone can put out whatever information they want—and can ingest whatever they want and have time for.

People should, of course, be free to do this, but if we really want to have better sense-making, then we need the ability to, at the most basic level, filter what's demonstrably true and what's false. We've recently had a collective recognition of the social consequences of echo chambers and tribal information acceptance or rejection, and how disinformation can cause division at best, and even lead to civil war at worst. We're seeing the beginning of widespread fact-checking with Facebook, Twitter, and Google, starting with putting notifications on posts that are suspected to be false. Naturally there are concerns about these tech giants' potential power and influence if we trust them to interpret what truth is for us. Let's assume, for the sake of argument, that this could be done transparently and accurately to deserve our trust. We have solved only the simplest problem: fact-checking true or false information.

A more complex issue is distortion, especially in disinformation campaigns that base their narratives on true information but flood their audience with *selective* true information taken out of context to make trends and truth appear different from what they actually are. For example, selective or disproportionate reporting of violent crimes, especially when races and ethnicity are in the headlines, while ignoring the vast majority of crimes that don't have the same demographics, creates a false impression.

If you read far-right newspapers, you might think that Minneapolis is overrun by Somali immigrant men who are regularly sexually assaulting white women throughout the city, and the "leftist-controlled media" are involved in a coverup of this rampant problem for the sake of political correctness. Research will tell you that perpetrators of sexual assaults in the US are primarily white (57%), and a majority (72%) are committed by someone known to the victim.[10] A similar distortion of statistics about Sweden reported that 80% of sexual assaults were by foreign-born men. However, on looking more closely at the data, we see this is only in cases where the woman did not know the attacker (a small fraction of total cases). Further, sexual assaults in Sweden actually declined by 12% in 2015, when the country admitted its highest numbers of immigrants.[11] Again, this distortion was used to push anti-immigration political agendas in the country, which can often go beyond the policy sphere and result in hate crimes or even genocide.

If these "newspapers" were truly interested in solving the sexual assault problem, instead of using it as a dog whistle for anti-immigration and—let's be frank—racist policies, they would accurately report on these crimes in context of the trends, while providing solutions to the problem. Instead, the artificial narrative feeds a political agenda. They develop these messages, and then, even if they're not putting out fake information, they're emphasizing only the topics that support only the narratives that they want people to believe. It's not only the right that is guilty of this, and most news outlets do this to some degree, even if it is unintentional.

Disinformation is a much harder nut to crack. But with AI and the ability to visually depict information simply to help people process it in context, combined with better education and training for people to better recognize logical fallacies and disinformation, we can improve our collective sense-making and reach a more accurate understanding of how the world around us works—an essential element for the healthy functioning of democratic societies.

The available technology can help to flag disinformation and do some of the heavy lifting in terms of compiling research, synthesizing and analyzing it, and presenting it in a way that helps us better understand it. A solution to this problem would:

1. Break echo chambers and get information from a variety of perspectives.

2. Identify narratives within those perspectives.

3. Discern what is true or false within those narratives, and put the information into context.

4. Identify "weasel words," logical fallacies, and emotional language or imagery meant to override a person's rationality without supplying real evidence to support a viewpoint.

5. Identify who's behind the information and what political or economic interest they might have in presenting a particular narrative to you.

With this more nuanced and sophisticated approach to sense-making, a society could more accurately make the decisions that would lead it down the right path and help the people who make up the society become better citizens and neighbors to each other. Perhaps we will see a return to institutions that can be trusted to provide information in these ways, with transparency in how they analyze the information. Or perhaps entrepreneurs will solve this puzzle with new websites, apps, and rating systems for the information we ingest. Schools should also teach children how to spot logical fallacies and disinformation, inoculating future generations against these kinds of manipulation. The School of Thought is one organization that has excellent resources for any educator interested in tools for teaching this curriculum, including playing cards for logical fallacies and cognitive biases.[12]

Overcoming Existential Threats

It is important for us to be able to use this information to prioritize the most important challenges for us to address as a species at any given moment. The most existential risks to humanity, according to the experts who study this depressing topic in depth, are climate change and ecological collapse, nuclear war, and biotechnology (as either a bioweapon or genetic experimentation that goes wrong). But at the top of the list was AI. If it got out of control, it could decide to systematically eliminate humanity.[13] There are many other threats—such as social dissolution, conventional war, and economic collapse—but the existential threats just listed have real potential to bring about human extinction. If we can galvanize human and material resources to solve these global existential issues, our society will have a much brighter future. However, if we simply chase the next political or tribal dog whistle from low-priority issue to low-priority issue, we will lose not only valuable time that we could have devoted to securing our safety, but also the energy needed to self-actualize and attain our hopes and dreams for the future.

People Power to the People

Empowered people have the means to create, innovate, and research to participate in pushing the limits of society. Without an empowered population, either we will never reach our desired utopia or it will take us much, much longer, giving existential threats more time to wipe us out. This must mean not just technological empowerment, but mental and emotional empowerment as well. Much of the conversation around empowerment focuses on making sure people have the knowledge, education, funding, and technology available to help them succeed. But we also need to heal and strengthen these deeper parts of ourselves to self-actualize before we can really get there safely as a society.

Creating a Nonviolent, Creatively Empowered Society

The importance of creating a nonviolent society goes back to our assertion that technology keeps making it easier for one person to kill a million people. It's very easy for one person to kill one to tens of people in today's world because weapons like semiautomatic and even fully automatic firearms are widely available in many countries. It's harder to kill a hundred people, much more difficult to kill a thousand, and nearly impossible for an individual to kill one million people. However, as people become more empowered by technology, this difficulty is decreasing. A few have access to technology that's more intelligent and has more reach, with the potential to cause massive destruction. Although cyber security and surveillance programs help to thwart would-be terrorists, this approach will go only so far in a free society empowered by deadly technology, without a culture of peace and compassion.

As our society navigates the exponential age we've entered, we have an obligation and responsibility to heal ourselves and fellow human beings to safely reach the technologically empowered society of our future. Even if a tiny fraction of people feel disenfranchised or have trauma, that can motivate them to inflict damage on people; if we don't have a way of helping them heal that trauma, then we basically have two options. The first is a dystopian, authoritarian society of ubiquitous surveillance, strict control, and punishment to prevent any individual citizen from gaining too much dangerous power and threatening the society. Unfortunately, this situation is ripe for political groups to abuse their immense power to our detriment. Let's assume that we all agree the path of authoritarian control is not a desirable option, even if it might make people feel safer from terrorism and disorder. I don't want to live there, and I don't think anybody else does either, but unfortunately it becomes a realistic outcome if we get to this level without healing our individual and societal traumas at scale.

The second, and far better, option is to create a self-actualized society, where people are included, informed, responsible, and compassionate. In other words, a much better world to live in. To reach this outcome, it's critical for our society to get to a level where people can heal from their trauma, make sense of the world around them effectively, and are empowered to seek the actualization of their dreams. It's the only way to truly achieve a civilization that is free, technologically advanced and empowered, and also viable. Otherwise, it's likely to have regular violence, self-destruct, or become an authoritarian society. The choice is easy, even if the execution is not. Just imagine being a person who is surrounded by people who are well-informed, emotionally balanced, compassionate, inspired, and enthusiastically living the lives they choose. Imagine how much easier it would be to create a better future. Designing for and working toward a self-actualized society can help us achieve this seemingly utopian feat, sitting on the foundations of the other met needs in the pyramid, and the shoulders of our ancestors that worked hard to get us this far. The only question is how long and how much work it will take to get there—a choice in prioritizing that is up to us.

Conclusion

The Future Is Created by Those Who Build It

THE LATTER PART OF THIS BOOK HAS ESSENTIALLY been a thought experiment applied to some of the greatest challenges of our time. Its primary goal has been to shake up how we usually think about crises, to empower us to take more effective approaches. By exploring what could go right, we look differently at how things are. Complexity arises when we take a bigger-picture or systems-level view of any change. It's easy to become overwhelmed and to seek comfort in the easy answers of cynicism or resignation. Our outlook can certainly get dire—after all, life can be painful, sometimes unbearably so. But we can shift from feeling overwhelmed and disempowered to seeing opportunity in our challenges. We can apply a fresh take to the current trends and the tools available to us to handle them.

My hope is that this thought experiment provides a good starting point, or launchpad, for you as you jump into making your own impact on the world. This could be the beginning of your journey, or a step along your path of contributing to a world you want to live in. So I want to close by thanking you for investing your time, and by sharing tools and sources of motivation to help you on your journey.

Start by Being Willing to Fail

While many motivational books teach that failure isn't an option—we should succeed at all costs, and never give up, no matter what! I encourage you to use failure to test your vision for your life and the world. Begin by asking yourself: *What is the outcome that I want to achieve?* Then ask why you are doing it: *Is this about getting rich, feeding my ego, or healing some past wound? Or is it something I deeply care about for its own sake?* One way to know is to consider whether, if you tried to achieve this vision and failed at it, you would still be happy that you spent your time working on it.

If you wouldn't be, it's likely the goal is not worth your time. Even if you're successful, make a ton of money, and obtain high social status, but you don't really care about what it is you've done to get there, you still run the risk of regretting the time you spent doing it. So if you're willing to try and fail, and the vision is meaningful to you, you should have the much-needed fuel for motivation along the way. This is a good measure of whether something's worth doing because anything has a possibility of failing. There is pride in working on something that is meaningful to you, regardless of the outcome for you.

Of course, you're not going to achieve your goals if all efforts fail, so to enable your success you must seek learning, improvement, and experience from those failures. Obviously you want to succeed, and need to work hard to do so. Even if you fail, your efforts could contribute in unknown ways to the overall movement forward. Your failure could signal a vital course correction for other people, or in five or fifty years someone could pick up where you left off and make more progress because the time was right. You could provide a contribution, putting your hands in the right place to push society forward so others learn from you. Either way, remaining tenaciously determined to reach your outcome, while keeping a zen-like detachment from the way you reach it, can keep your eyes open to opportunities and paths you might not have otherwise noticed.

The more you are connected to a larger mission and feel a place in the world's communities, the more meaning you will feel in your life. If you really want to be happy, contribute to something greater than yourself. This sounds cliché for a reason, but science backs it up. Whether you're contributing to your family, your community, a company that seeks to do good in the world, a nation that improves the well-being of citizens, your species as a whole, one of the other species that share our world, or the entire organism of the planet— finding a way to work toward a better future will make you happier and more proud of your life.

It can be helpful to ask yourself the scale and personal level on which you'd prefer to work. Would you prefer to work on something that will probably have a small degree of impact on a very large, long-term problem like renewable energy or space exploration? This could mean you never meet the people you are going to help. Or would you rather meet these people face to face, have a large impact on a smaller scale, and see your impact personally? To look the kids you're tutoring in the eye? Help a person heal from abuse or domestic violence? Help someone emerge from a drug addiction? Or act swiftly as a first responder to save lives at an accident? Whatever motivates you and makes you feel inspired needs to come from within you, to combine what the world needs with what will give you meaning and satisfaction—and what you can sustain over time.

The Antidote to Fears That Hold You Back

One of the great ironies of life is that we all may have unlimited desires and potential, but limited time to fulfill them. All of us are on a timeline with a definite end, no matter how good or bad we are in life. Paradoxically, there is liberation in recognizing that we're going to die. The urgency of knowing time is limited releases so much, from primal fears to the social conventions that hold us back from saying the words the world needs to hear. In the context of a limited life, the things we're afraid of become minor, temporary issues, because in the end, none of these fears compare to the ultimate end, nor will they survive it. We must make decisions without ultimately knowing for sure how things will turn out, the meaning of our lives, or why we are here. The French philosopher Albert Camus called this the inherent absurdity of being alive, which liberated him to choose to live a life free from worry.

The Bridge is an emotionally intense documentary that explores the many suicides at the Golden Gate Bridge in San Francisco. It shares the story of a man who tried to end his life by jumping off the bridge, but luckily survived the fall. In an interview, he says that the moment his feet left the platform, he immediately saw solutions to all the problems in his life, except one. While facing the ultimate problem—death—he saw that he had been able to solve the rest of his problems the whole time. Solving personal conflicts seemed trivial in comparison to the impossibility of stopping his fall or taking back his choice to jump. We can learn from his story. We don't need to survive a suicide attempt to have a similar realization.

Awareness of death also liberates us from the temptation to be cynical when it is most alluring: when cynicism is disguised as practical thinking that protects us from misadventures that might threaten our comfort or existence. It's coming, one way or another, whatever you do, whether it's in five minutes or eighty-five years— so acknowledge that your time is limited and precious, and make it something you enjoy and are proud of.

Acknowledging that we are here only temporarily will help us live more humbly and authentically, better understand our true values, and take a stand to advance them. It's terrible to lose someone we love, but when we look at how they feel about the process, it seems that the experience for those who are leaving us is very different. This sounds counterintuitive, but let me explain—a study of blogs by terminally ill people found that as they got closer to death, their writings became more positive and they focused more on friends, family, and community. However, those who were not dying but simply thought about death had more negative things to say about it.[1] We tend to have a more negative view of death when we imagine it than when we're actually close to experiencing it. If you ask the average person to think about death, they will probably have a very negative view of it. There's a disconnect between the real experience and the imagined experience, challenging us to think about death differently.

If you think about death as a part of your life that you're going to experience, you can think about it more clearly. This leads to a more positive take on life as you acknowledge that it is precious and you have limited time to spend with your loved ones and on the projects and visions that you want to accomplish before your time's up. When we think about death more practically and in a positive light, we can experience it similarly to those who are facing it imminently.

This can help us determine what's important and what's not. When we consult that part of ourselves, rather than the part that seeks approval or to meet others' expectations, we find liberation, urgency, and wisdom. This recognition can also help us plan for the longer term in our lives, knowing that, if we are lucky, we can contribute to positive changes that will persist beyond us. Steve Jobs once said, "Remembering that you are going to die is the best way I know to avoid the trap of thinking you have something to lose. You are already naked. There is no reason not to follow your heart."

Let's not get too serious, though. Humorous cynicism can be entertaining, and I enjoy a good joke or ironic observation as much as the next person, because it actually helps us acknowledge and confront our problems. I believe humor can be an early warning system built into our social communication protocols, warning us that we have hidden problems and need to alter our course accordingly, before a comedy becomes a tragedy (Charlie Chaplain's buffoonish depiction of Hitler in his film *The Great Dictator* comes to mind). But defeatist cynicism helps no one—in fact, a cynical worldview can become a self-fulfilling prophecy and can lead us to ignore a bad situation until it's too late, or even take part in building a worse-off world.

It takes real courage for us to be creative, positive, and optimistic in a cynical world. People who can summon that courage are the types of leaders we need to envision and get us to a better world. A fatalistic mindset and cynical leaders will only lead us toward a world more worthy of being cynical about.

So I challenge you to find that courage within yourself. Be the hero your ninety-year-old self would be proud of and your grandchildren will tell stories about. As you reflect in your final days, who do you want to have helped and spent your time with? What do you need to have done, worked toward, and accomplished in order to feel extremely proud of your life? In other words, what would *old you* encourage you to do?

A Motivating State of Mind and a Mission to Focus On

When I was ten years old, I lost my younger brother, and his death shocked me to my core. It made me see the world in a very different way than I had before and made me ask questions that wouldn't have otherwise come to mind. But it also forced me in no uncertain terms to recognize that life is short and limited. Just as acknowledging death can help you overcome cynicism, it can also be an enormous source of motivation.

When considering our mortality, it is easy to go the way of the nihilist. But the classical economist John Maynard Keynes gives us a good example—he embraced it. Most other classical economists imagined humanity as simple, selfish, profit-maximizing machines. But psychological research over the past century has taught us that we are much more egalitarian, complex, irrational, and altruistic than they imagined. These economists said greed ruled the world and that we don't need to help each other during depressions and recessions because the market always comes roaring back in the long term—that is, short-term challenges are evened out by the long-term stability of the market. So in the long run, we're all okay (ignoring the suffering of the underprivileged classes). Keynes famously responded by saying, "This long run is a misleading guide to current affairs. *In the long run, we're all dead.* Economists set themselves too easy, too useless a task, if in tempestuous seasons they can only tell us, that when the storm is long past, the ocean is flat again."[2] Essentially, he pointed out that human beings are what make up an economy, and our experiences and quality of life matter.

Just as Keynes challenged classical economists to think bigger, we should take on his challenge today. We can't just look at charts and graphs while dismissing human needs and impacts—especially those of us in positions of privilege or wealth. When we look people in the eye and see the suffering inherent in our economic policy or structure, it becomes apparent how important it is to put our work into changing the world for the better.

If death is the destination we all share, why shouldn't we just live out our hedonistic earthly desires for the rest of our days? Well, setting aside the financial and bodily exhaustion such an approach would bring after a long bender, we actually live better, happier lives when we have a sense of meaning, purpose, and community. Feeling a responsibility to the future means caring for each other, and when you actually deliver on it, the result is a euphoric state. Researchers from the University of British Columbia and Harvard Business School conducted a study to determine if people felt happier giving to others or buying gifts for themselves, both using their own money and using free money they were given. Across the board, even for people with very little money, the subjects were consistently happier when they *gave* to others.[3] We are a social species, so it instinctually feels great to be working toward helping other people and doing things that are creating a positive impact in the world. Take heed of that instinct, and you will live a happier life.

You have limited time to make an impact, so why not focus your limited time and energy on impacting the world in a positive way and feeling great in the process? Helping other people, spending that time with your loved ones is a winning strategy. Sure, everyone we know is going to die, including us. The sun will engulf the earth in less than one billion years. Maybe before then we will reach other planets and save civilization from this catastrophe. Either way, the universe will continue on for trillions of years as black holes engulf all matter. Maybe it's all just a simulation, as many in Silicon Valley propose. But what's undoubtedly real is you and your experience—in this moment, today.

Until the sun's day of nuclear confetti in the sky, we're each looking for a little piece of life to live and share. All we know is the fact that we are conscious, and we are here. It's most likely that other people around us, including our animal friends, are conscious, aware, and feel as we do, just as much as we do. The one thing we know for certain is that we can impact each other and make the world a better place if we try, carrying on a long legacy of hard work by our ancestors to improve on the world they were handed, generation after generation, leading to the world we enjoy today. This purpose should be a top priority, and it matters, even if all of this world is engulfed in flames in a billion years. Because we know that this moment and the people who lived in it existed, and so will the ones that come after—other people just like us, impacted by the actions that we chose today. Our work may even eventually enable the preservation of consciousness beyond the end of this planet, as we voyage out to the stars.

The number of crises we see in the world around us only underscores the need for people to get inspired and create a better future. Spending energy getting down about the doom and gloom we see in the news doesn't help to overcome it. Instead, envisioning the ideal future you would prefer, sharing and refining that vision with others, and putting your energy into building it is infinitely more empowering and effective. Whether you're struggling with depression or boundlessly happy, there are so many ways available to you to boost your own life and the world around you. By helping to drive positive changes important to the lives that will experience them, you will find and enjoy meaning. Whether you believe the universe to be an intelligently guided, mystical place, or simply made up of tiny billiard balls aimlessly bouncing off of each other—your life is yours to live, guide as you see fit, and bring meaning to. Once you know how to lift cynicism, fatalism, and defeatism from your mindset and turn toward ideal, *What could go right?* visions and actions that lead to a better world, even the sky is no limit. The precarious situations and manifold crises we're facing won't fill you with terror or sadness. Instead, you'll run toward them, eager to help lead us all into a better future. More power to you—and thank you for adding your piece to humanity's puzzle. I wish you all the luck in the world on your journey.

Notes

Chapter 1

1. Simon Sinek, *The Infinite Game* (New York: Portfolio, 2019), https://simon sinek.com/product/the-infinite-game/.

2. James Carse, *Finite and Infinite Games* (New York: Free Press, 2013).

3. Arlin Cuncic, "Amygdala Hijack and the Fight or Flight Response," *Verywell Mind* (updated June 22, 2021), https://www.verywellmind.com/what -happens-during-an-amygdala-hijack-4165944.

4. Yuko Hara, PhD, "Does Stress Worsen Cognitive Functions?" *Cognitive Vitality*, December 17, 2018, https://www.alzdiscovery.org/cognitive-vitality /blog/does-stress-worsen-cognitive-functions.

5. Katie Patrick, "Why Creativity Will Save The World," *Medium*, May 22, 2019, https://medium.com/how-to-save-the-world-by-katie-patrick/why -creativity-will-save-the-world-3c64f2532efd.

6. John F. Magee, "Decision Trees for Decision Making," *Harvard Business Review*, July 1964, https://hbr.org/1964/07/decision-trees-for-decision-making.

7. Simpli, "Maximize Your Team's Potential" (n.d.), https://www.simpli5.com /how-it-works/.

8. Stephanie Vozza, "How Our Brain's Habits Affect How We Get Along With Our Coworkers," *Fast Company*, May 5, 2017, https://www.fastcompany .com/40419701/how-our-brains-habits-affect-how-we-get-along-with-our -coworkers.

Chapter 2

1. For more thorough discussion of this data, see Max Roser, "The Short History of Global Living Conditions and Why It Matters That We Know It," Our World in Data, 2020, https://ourworldindata.org/a-history-of-global -living-conditions-in-5-charts.

2. To see just how significant these trends are in charts, visit Dylan Matthews, "23 Charts and Maps That Show the World Is Getting Much, Much Better," *Vox*, updated October 17, 2018, https://www.vox.com/2014/11/24/7272929 /global-poverty-health-crime-literacy-good-news.

3. John Gramlich, "Voters' Perceptions of Crime Continue to Conflict with Reality," Pew Research, November 16, 2016, https://www.pewresearch.org /fact-tank/2016/11/16/voters-perceptions-of-crime-continue-to-conflict -with-reality/.

4. "Global Study on Homicide 2019," United Nations Office on Drugs and Crime, archived from the original on July 15, 2019, retrieved September 26, 2019.

5. Jake Horton, "US Crime: Is America Seeing a Surge in Violence?" *BBC*, July 7, 2020, https://www.bbc.com/news/57581270.

6. Juliana Menasce Horowitz, Anna Brown, and Kiana Cox, "Race in America 2019," Pew Research Center, April 9, 2019, https://www.pewsocialtrends .org/2019/04/09/race-in-america-2019/.

7. Adeel Hassan, "Hate-Crime Violence Hits 16-Year High, F.B.I. Reports," *New York Times*, November 12, 2019, https://www.nytimes.com/2019/11/12 /us/hate-crimes-fbi-report.html.

8. "Covid 'Hate Crimes' Against Asian Americans on Rise," *BBC News*, May 21, 2021, https://www.bbc.com/news/world-us-canada-56218684.

9. Max Roser, "Most of Us Are Wrong About How the World Has Changed (Especially Those Who Are Pessimistic About the Future)," Our World in Data, July 27, 2018, https://ourworldindata.org/wrong-about-the-world. The full reference of the survey is Chris Jackson, "Global Perceptions of Development Progress: 'Perils of Perceptions' Research,'" Ipsos MORI, September 18, 2017.

10. Our World in Data, "Child Mortality: Share of Children, Born Alive, Dying Before They Are Five Years Old" (1950–2019), https://ourworldindata.org /grapher/child-mortality-around-the-world?country=Least%20developed %20countries~Less%20developed%20regions~More%20developed%20 regions~OWID_WRL.

11. Kathy Mulvey and Seth Shulman, "The Climate Deception Dossiers: Internal Fossil Fuel Industry Memos Reveal Decades of Corporate Disinformation," Union of Concerned Scientists, July 2015, https://www .ucsusa.org/sites/default/files/attach/2015/07/The-Climate-Deception -Dossiers.pdf.

12. "Smoke, Mirrors & Hot Air: How ExxonMobil Uses Big Tobacco's Tactics to 'Manufacture Uncertainty' on Climate Change," Union of Concerned Scientists, July 16, 2007, https://www.ucsusa.org/resources/smoke-mirrors -hot-air#.VQI7Xo7F-WU; Peter C. Frumhoff and Naomi Oreskes, "Fossil Fuel Firms Are Still Bankrolling Climate Denial Lobby Groups," Guardian, March 25, 2015, https://www.theguardian.com/environment/2015/mar/25/fossil-fuel -firms-are-still-bankrolling-climate-denial-lobby-groups.

13. Graham Readfearn, "What Happened to the Lobbyists Who Tried to Reshape the US View of Climate Change?" Guardian, February 27, 2015, https://www.theguardian.com/environment/2015/feb/27/what-happened-to -lobbyists-who-tried-reshape-us-view-climate-change.

14. "Global Climate Science Communications Plan 1998," DocumentCloud (n.d.), https://www.documentcloud.org/documents/1676446-global-climate -science-communications-plan-1998.html.

15. Sanders Institute, "Community Land Trusts, Then and Now," Sanders Institute (n.d.), https://www.sandersinstitute.com/blog/renewable-energy -cheaper-than-coal-and-gas-across-much-of-the-united-states.

16. Michelle Lewis, "Texas Leads the US in Wind Power—And Now It's Ramping Up Solar, Too," Electrek, February 21, 2020, https://electrek. co/2020/02/21/texas-leads-the-us-in-wind-power-and-now-its-ramping-up -solar-too/.

17. Hanna Ziady, "BP Will Slash Oil Production by 40% and Pour Billions into Green Energy," CNN Business, August 4, 2020, https://www.cnn .com/2020/08/04/business/bp-oil-clean-energy/index.html.

18. Jordan Weissmann, "Martin Luther King's Economic Dream: A Guaranteed Income for All Americans," *Atlantic*, August 28, 2013, https://www.theatlantic.com/business/archive/2013/08/martin-luther-kings-economic-dream-a-guaranteed-income-for-all-americans/279147/.

19. History.com editors, "Social Security Act," History, updated January 31, 2020; original January 26, 2018, https://www.history.com/topics/great-depression/social-security-act.

Chapter 3

1. Edd Gent, "Carbon Nanotube Transistors May Soon Give Waning Moore's Law a Boost," SingularityHub, June 01, 2020, https://singularityhub.com/2020/06/01/carbon-nanotube-transistors-may-soon-give-waning-moores-law-a-boost/.

2. Jason Dorrier, "OpenAI Finds Machine Learning Efficiency Is Outpacing Moore's Law," SingularityHub, November 2020, https://singularityhub-com.cdn.ampproject.org/c/s/singularityhub.com/2020/05/17/openai-finds-machine-learning-efficiency-is-outpacing-moores-law/amp/.

3. Joe Carmichael, "Arcade City Is a Blockchain-Based Ride-Sharing Uber Killer," Inverse, March 30, 2016, https://www.inverse.com/article/13500-arcade-city-is-a-blockchain-based-ride-sharing-uber-killer.

4. Gregg Keizer, "The Brave Browser Basics: What It Does, How It Differs from Rivals," *ComputerWorld*, April 8, 2021, https://www.computerworld.com/article/3292619/the-brave-browser-basics-what-it-does-how-it-differs-from-rivals.html.

5. kadavy, "A Writer's Guide to Making Money on the STEEM Blockchain—for Beginners," Steemit (2017), https://steemit.com/steem/@kadavy/a-writer-s-guide-to-making-money-on-the-steem-blockchain-for-beginners.

6. Organization for Economic Co-operation and Development (OECD), "Employment: Time Spent in Paid and Unpaid Work, by Sex" (2021), https://stats.oecd.org/index.aspx?queryid=5475.7.

7. Zack Friedman, "78% of [US] Workers Live Paycheck to Paycheck," *Forbes*, January 11, 2019, https://www.forbes.com/sites/zackfriedman/2019/01/11/live-paycheck-to-paycheck-government-shutdown/#6cfe39d04f10.

8. Rita Paul-Sen Gupta, MSc, Margaret L. de Wit, PhD, and David McKeown, "The Impact of Poverty on the Current and Future Health Status of Children," *Paediatrics Child Health* 12, no. 8 (October 2007): 667–672, https://www.ncbi.nlm.nih.gov/pmc/articles/PMC2528796/.

9. Walter Frick, Welfare Makes America More Entrepreneurial, *Atlantic*, March 26, 2015, https://www.theatlantic.com/politics/archive/2015/03/welfare-makes-america-more-entrepreneurial/388598/.

10. Minda Zetlin, "Survey: 63% of 20-Somethings Want to Start a Business," *Inc.* (n.d.), https://www.inc.com/minda-zetlin/63-percent-of-20-somethings-want-to-own-a-business.html.

11. Deloitte, 2018 Deloitte Millennial Survey, https://www2.deloitte.com/content/dam/Deloitte/at/Documents/human-capital/at-deloitte-millennial-survey-2018.pdf.

12. Howard Marks, "How Crowdfunding Is Disrupting VCs," *Forbes*, June 10, 2018, https://www.forbes.com/sites/howardmarks/2018/06/10/how-crowdfunding-is-disrupting-vcs/#4e91fd264823.

13. Hannah Forbes and Dirk Schaefer, The Growth of Crowdfunding, figure in "Guidelines for Successful Crowdfunding," *Procedia CIRP* 60 (May 2017): 398–403, https://www.researchgate.net/figure/The-growth-of-crowdfunding_fig1_316788666.

14. Satish Kataria, "Year 2016: The Year When Funding Will Become Truly Democratic," Inc42, December 31, 2015, https://inc42.com/resources/year-2016-the-year-when-funding-will-become-truly-democratic/.

15. Maddie Shepherd, "Crowdfunding Statistics (2021): Market Size and Growth," Fundera, December 16, 2020, https://www.fundera.com/resources/crowdfunding-statistics.

16. Ibid.

17. Mark Jahn, "How Do Returns on Private Equity Compare to Other Investment Returns?," Investopedia, January 5, 2021, https://www.investopedia.com/ask/answers/040615/how-do-returns-private-equity-investments-compare-returns-other-types-investments.asp.

18. Zachary Shahan, "Chart: Why Battery Electric Vehicles Beat Hydrogen Electric Vehicles Without Breaking A Sweat," CleanTechnica, February 1, 2021, https://cleantechnica.com/2021/02/01/chart-why-battery-electric-vehicles -beat-hydrogen-electric-vehicles-without-breaking-a-sweat/

19. Idaho National Laboratory, "Advanced Vehicle Testing Activity" (n.d.), https://avt.inl.gov/sites/default/files/pdf/fsev/costs.pdf.

20. Brian Eckhouse, "In Shift to Electric Buses, China Is Ahead of US," Transport Topics, May 15, 2019, https://www.ttnews.com/articles/shift -electric-buses-china-ahead-us.

21. Kristoffer Tigue, "U.S. Electric Bus Demand Outpaces Production as Cities Add to Their Fleets," Inside Climate News, November 14, 2019, https:// insideclimatenews.org/news/14112019/electric-bus-cost-savings-health-fuel -charging.

22. Justin Gerdes, 'Electrification of Everything' Would Spike US Electricity Use, But Lower Final Energy Consumption," gtm (Greentech Media), July 30, 2018, https://www.greentechmedia.com/articles/read/widespread-electrification -could-increase-u-s-electricity-consumption.

23. Elizabeth J. Howell Hanano, "Green for Take Off—Inside the Electric Airplane Industry," Toptal (n.d.), https://www.toptal.com/finance/market -research-analysts/electric-airplanes.

24. International Data Corporation (IDC), "IDC's Global DataSphere Forecast Shows Continued Steady Growth in the Creation and Consumption of Data," IDC, May 8, 2020, https://www.idc.com/getdoc.jsp?containerId= prUS46286020; David Reinsel, John Gantz, and John Rydning, "The Digitization of the World: From Edge to Core," IDC white paper, November 2018, https://www.seagate.com/files/www-content/our-story/trends/files /idc-seagate-dataage-whitepaper.pdf.

25. Lucas Mearian, "CW@50: Data Storage Goes from $1M to 2 Cents per Gigabyte (+Video), Computerworld, March 23, 2017, https://www .computerworld.com/article/3182207/cw50-data-storage-goes-from-1m-to -2-cents-per-gigabyte.html; Cynthia Harvey, "Cloud Storage Pricing of 2022: Compare Cloud Storage Providers," Enterprise Storage Forum, April 26, 2018, https://www.enterprisestorageforum.com/cloud/cloud-storage-pricing /#cloud-storage-pricing-comparison; John C. McCallum, "Memory Prices 1957+," October 20, 2021, https://jcmit.net/memoryprice.htm.

26. Peter Brand, "Downtime in Manufacturing: What's the True Cost?" Oden Technologies, April 2, 2020, https://oden.io/blog/downtime-in-manufacturing-the-true-cost/.

27. Kasey Panetta, "Gartner Top 10 Strategic Technology Trends for 2020," Gartner, October 21, 2019, https://www.gartner.com/smarterwithgartner /gartner-top-10-strategic-technology-trends-for-2020/.

28. Kasey Panetta, "Gartner Top 10 Strategic Technology Trends for 2019," Gartner, October 15, 2018, https://www.gartner.com/smarterwithgartner /gartner-top-10-strategic-technology-trends-for-2019/.

29. Erin Blackwell, Tony Gambell, Varun Marya, and Christoph Schmitz, "The Great Remake: Manufacturing for Modern Times," McKinsey & Company, August 29, 2017, https://www.mckinsey.com/business-functions/operations /our-insights/the-great-remake-manufacturing-for-modern-times.

30. Futurism, "An AI Completed 360,000 Hours of Finance Work in Just Seconds," Futurism.com (n.d.), https://futurism.com/an-ai-completed -360000-hours-of-finance-work-in-just-seconds.

31. Tristan Greene, "Alibaba's New AI System Can Detect Coronavirus in Seconds with 96% Accuracy," thenextweb.com, March 2, 2020, https:// thenextweb.com/neural/2020/03/02/alibabas-new-ai-system-can-detect -coronavirus-in-seconds-with-96-accuracy/.

32. James Manyika, Susan Lund, Michael Chui, Jacques Bughin, Jonathan Woetzel, Parul Batra, Ryan Ko, and Saurabh Sanghvi, "Jobs Lost, Jobs Gained: What the Future of Work Will Mean for Jobs, Skills, and Wages," McKinsey Global Institute, November 28, 2017, https://www.mckinsey.com/featured -insights/future-of-work/jobs-lost-jobs-gained-what-the-future-of-work-will -mean-for-jobs-skills-and-wages.

33. Richard B. Lee, Richard Heywood Daly, and Richard Daly, eds., *Cambridge Encyclopedia of Hunters and Gatherers* (Cambridge, UK: Cambridge University Press, 2001).

34. Thomas Widlok and Wolde Gossa Tadesse, eds., *Ritualization, Sharing, Egalitarianism*, vol. 1 in *Property and Equality* (New York: Berghahn Books, 2004).

35. Michaeleen Doucleff, "Are Hunter-Gatherers The Happiest Humans To Inhabit Earth?" National Public Radio, October 1, 2017, https://www.npr .org/sections/goatsandsoda/2017/10/01/551018759/are-hunter-gatherers-the -happiest-humans-to-inhabit-earth.

36. Sarote Tabcum Jr., "The Sharing Economy Is Still Growing, And Businesses Should Take Note," *Forbes*, March 4, 2019, https://www.forbes .com/sites/forbeslacouncil/2019/03/04/the-sharing-economy-is-still-growing -and-businesses-should-take-note/#1ef93c064c33.

37. Ádám Osztovits, Árpád Kőszegi, Bence Nagy, and Bence Damjanovics, "Sharing or Paring? Growth of the Sharing Economy," PriceWaterhouseCoopers (PwC) (2015), https://www.pwc.com/hu/en /kiadvanyok/assets/pdf/sharing-economy-en.pdf.

38. Mary Hanbury, "Amazon Overtakes Google and Apple to Become the World's Most Valuable Brand," *Business Insider*, June 11, 2019, https://www .businessinsider.com/amazon-overtakes-google-apple-worlds-most-valuable -brand-2019-6.

39. Nick Winkler, "Multichannel Inventory Management: Problems & Solutions," Shopify, May 6, 2020, https://www.shopify.com/enterprise /multi-channel-inventory-management.

40. Dan Pontefract, "Millennials and Gen Z Have Lost Trust and Loyalty with Business," *Forbes*, June 3, 2018, https://www.forbes.com/sites/danpontefract /2018/06/03/millennials-and-gen-z-have-lost-trust-and-loyalty-with-business /#1e1876126145.

41. Statista Research Department, "Resident Population in the United States in 2020, by Generation," September 10, 2021, https://www.statista.com /statistics/797321/us-population-by-generation/.

42. Mission Insight, "Millennials Prefer Brands with Purpose," *Medium*, December 5, 2017, https://medium.com/mission-insight/millennials-prefer -brands-with-purpose-73e72ec4002a.

43. Douglas Beal, Robert Eccles, Gerry Hansell, Rich Lesser, Shalini Unnikrishnan, Wendy Woods, and David Young, "Total Societal Impact: A New Lens for Strategy," BCG Henderson Institute, October 25, 2017, https:// www.bcg.com/publications/2017/total-societal-impact-new-lens-strategy.

44. Geoff Weiss, "Why This Entrepreneur Says Sustainability Is the No. 1 Business Opportunity," *Entrepreneur*, April 16, 2015, https://www.entrepreneur .com/article/245041.

45. Goldman Sachs Research, "Taking the Heat: Making Cities Resilient to Climate Change," Goldman Sachs, September 5, 2019, https://www .goldmansachs.com/insights/pages/taking-the-heat.html.

46. Pippa Stevens, "Sustainable Investing Is Set to Surge in the Wake of the Coronavirus Pandemic," CNBC, June 7, 2020, https://www.cnbc.com/2020/06/07/sustainable-investing-is-set-to-surge-in-the-wake-of-the-coronavirus-pandemic.html.

47. Leslie P. Norton, "Sustainable Companies Are Beating the Market During the Crisis. Will It Last?" *Barron's*, March 26, 2020, https://www.barrons.com/articles/sustainable-companies-are-beating-the-market-during-the-crisis-will-it-last-51585241734.

Chapter 4

1. Jillian Scudder, "The Sun Won't Die for 5 Billion Years, So Why Do Humans Have Only 1 Billion Years Left on Earth?" Phys.org, February 13, 2015, https://phys.org/news/2015-02-sun-wont-die-billion-years.html.

2. RethinkX, *Rethinking Humanity* (n.d.), downloadable book, https://www.rethinkx.com/humanity.

3. Shawn Achor, Andrew Reece, Gabriella Rosen Kellerman, and Alexi Robichaux, "9 Out of 10 People Are Willing to Earn Less Money to Do More-Meaningful Work," *Harvard Business Review*, November 06, 2018, https://hbr.org/2018/11/9-out-of-10-people-are-willing-to-earn-less-money-to-do-more-meaningful-work.

4. Grant Smith and Bill Walker, "Federal Energy Subsidies: What Are We Getting for Our Money?," Environmental Working Group, July 17, 2019, https://www.ewg.org/energy/22777/federal-energy-subsidies-what-are-we-getting-our-money.

5. Zhengquan Gu, Xingping Zhang, Sida Feng, and Haonan Zhang, "The Impacts of Reducing Renewable Energy Subsidies on China's Energy Transition by Using a Hybrid Dynamic Computable General Equilibrium Model," *Frontiers in Energy Research*, March 10, 2020, https://doi.org/10.3389/fenrg.2020.00025, https://www.frontiersin.org/articles/10.3389/fenrg.2020.00025/full.

6. Jon Russell, "China's CCTV Surveillance Network Took Just 7 Minutes to Capture BBC Reporter," TechCrunch+, December 13, 2017, https://techcrunch.com/2017/12/13/china-cctv-bbc-reporter/.

7. "China Undercover," *Frontline*, April 7, 2020, https://www.pbs.org/wgbh/frontline/film/china-undercover/.

8. Debasis Dash, "Facing a Future with Organized Weaponization of Social Media," War Room—U.S. Army War College, May 31, 2019, https://warroom.armywarcollege.edu/articles/organized-weaponization-of-social-media/.

9. Nike Ching and Jeff Seldin, "US Pushes Back Against Russian, Chinese, Iranian Coronavirus Disinformation," *VOA News*, March 27, 2020, update April 16, 2020, https://www.voanews.com/covid-19-pandemic/us-pushes-back-against-russian-chinese-iranian-coronavirus-disinformation.

10. Tim Hains, "BBC's Adam Curtis on the 'Contradictory Vaudeville' of Post-Modern Politics," RealClear Politics, December 31, 2014, https://www.realclearpolitics.com/video/2014/12/31/bbcs_adam_curtis_on_the_contradictory_vaudeville_of_post-modern_politics.html; *HyperNormalisation*, written and directed by Adam Curtis, aired October 16, 2016, on *BBC*, http://www.bbc.co.uk/programmes/p04b183c; Ned Resnikoff, "Trump's Lies Have a Purpose. They Are an Assault on Democracy," ThinkProgress, November 28, 2016, https://archive.thinkprogress.org/when-everything-is-a-lie-power-is-the-only-truth-1e641751d150/.

11. Dheeraj Vaidya, "Revenue Per Employee," WallStreetMojo (n.d.), https://www.wallstreetmojo.com/revenue-per-employee/.

12. *The Corporation*, a film by Mark Achbar, Jennifer Abbott, and Joel Bakan, 2005, https://thecorporation.com/film/synopsis.

13. Marie Boran, "Teenage Clicks: Why We Should Be Concerned About Addictive Smartphone Apps," *Irish Times*, October 31, 2019, https://www.irishtimes.com/business/innovation/teenage-clicks-why-we-should-be-concerned-about-addictive-smartphone-apps-1.4065987.

14. Nir Eyal, *Hooked: How to Build Habit-Forming Products* (New York: Portfolio, 2014), https://www.nirandfar.com/hooked/.

15. Bruce Dominey, "North Korean EMP Attack Would Cause Mass U.S. Starvation, Says Congressional Report," *Forbes*, October 23, 2017, https://www.forbes.com/sites/brucedorminey/2017/10/23/north-korea-emp-attack-would-cause-mass-u-s-starvation-says-congressional-report/#773101f6740a.

16. Lila MacLellan, "Business Travelers Find Their Hopscotching Helps Develop Empathy," The Harris Poll (n.d.), https://theharrispoll.com/business-travelers-find-their-hopscotching-helps-develop-empathy/.

17. Visa Performance Solutions, "Mapping the Future of Global Travel and Tourism," Visa, 2014, https://usa.visa.com/dam/VCOM/global/partner-with-us/documents/global-travel-and-tourism-insights-by-visa.pdf.

18. K.N.C., "How to Increase Empathy and Unite Society," interview with Jamil Zaki, author of *The War for Kindness: Building Empathy in a Fractured World, Economist*, June 7, 2019, https://www.economist.com/open-future/2019/06/07/how-to-increase-empathy-and-unite-society.

19. Graham Allison, "The Thucydides Trap," Foreign Policy, June 9, 2017, https://foreignpolicy.com/2017/06/09/the-thucydides-trap/.

20. Graham Allison, "The Thucydides Trap: Are the U.S. and China Headed for War?" *Atlantic*, September 24, 2015, https://www.theatlantic.com/international/archive/2015/09/united-states-china-war-thucydides-trap/406756/.

21. Sir John Bagot Glubb, The Fate of Empires and Search for Survival," University of North Carolina Wilmington People Server (booklet published 2002), http://people.uncw.edu/kozloffm/glubb.pdf.

22. Sierra Bellows, "The Trouble with Civilization: Ancient Cities Reveal the Vulnerabilities of Modern Societies," *Virginia*, Fall 2010, https://uvamagazine.org/articles/the_trouble_with_civilization.

23. Michael Kavanagh, "Jared Diamond's *Collapse* Traces the Fates of Societies to Their Treatment of the Environment," *Grist*, February 09, 2005, https://grist.org/article/kavanagh-collapse/.

24. Tim Urban, "The Fermi Paradox," Wait But Why, May 21, 2014, https://waitbutwhy.com/2014/05/fermi-paradox.html.

25. Dave Mosher, "The Entire Universe Fits in One Image with a Math Trick," *Business Insider*, June 30, 2017, https://www.businessinsider.com/entire-universe-picture-logarithmic-map-2017-6.

26. The StarChild Team, "How Old Is the Universe?" High Energy Astrophysics Science Archive Research Center (HEASARC), Astrophysics Science Division, NASA, December 2000, https://starchild.gsfc.nasa.gov/docs/StarChild/questions/question28.html.

27. Matt Williams, "Beyond 'Fermi's Paradox' III: What Is the Great Filter?" Universe Today, July 23, 2020, https://www.universetoday.com/145512/beyond-the-fermi-paradox-iii-what-is-the-great-filter/.

28. Alan Yuhas, "The Pentagon Released U.F.O. Videos. Don't Hold Your Breath for a Breakthrough," *New York Times*, April 28, 2020, updated September 1, 2021, https://www.nytimes.com/2020/04/28/us/pentagon-ufo-videos.html.

29. Murray Bookchin, "Utopia, Not Futurism: Why Doing the Impossible Is the Most Rational Thing We Can Do," Uneven Earth, October 2, 2019 (reprint of 1978 speech), https://unevenearth.org/2019/10/bookchin_doing _the_impossible/.

Chapter 5

1. Louis Hyman, "The New Deal Wasn't What You Think," *Atlantic*, March 6, 2019, https://www.theatlantic.com/ideas/archive/2019/03/surprising-truth -about-roosevelts-new-deal/584209/.

2 Yi Wen, "China's Rapid Rise: From Backward Agrarian Society to Industrial Powerhouse in Just 35 Years," Federal Reserve Bank of St. Louis, April 11, 2016, https://www.stlouisfed.org/publications/regional-economist/april-2016 /chinas-rapid-rise-from-backward-agrarian-society-to-industrial-powerhouse -in-just-35-years.

3. Ibid.

4. Ibid.

5. Ryan Hass and Zach Balin, "US-China Relations in the Age of Artificial Intelligence," Brookings Institution, January 10, 2019, https://www.brookings .edu/research/us-china-relations-in-the-age-of-artificial-intelligence/.

6. China Undercover," *Frontline*, April 7, 2020, https://www.pbs.org/wgbh /frontline/film/china-undercover/.

7. Cannix Yau, "Some Four in 10 AmCham Members Considering Leaving Hong Kong over National Security Law Fears, Survey Finds," *South China Morning Post*, August 13, 2020, https://www.scmp.com/news/hong-kong/politics /article/3097257/some-four-10-us-businesses-considering-leaving-hong-kong.

8. Laura Silver, Kat Devlin, and Christine Huang, "Large Majorities Say China Does Not Respect the Personal Freedoms of Its People," Pew Research Center, June 30, 2021, https://www.pewresearch.org/global/2021/06/30/large -majorities-say-china-does-not-respect-the-personal-freedoms-of-its-people/.

9. Cato Institute, Human Freedom Index 2020, https://www.cato.org/human
-freedom-index-new.

10. Numbeo, Quality of Life Index by Country 2021 Mid-Year, https://www
.numbeo.com/quality-of-life/rankings_by_country.jsp.

11. Abdallah Fayyad, "Saudi Arabia Isn't Just Raising Taxes," *Atlantic*, June 11,
2020, https://www.theatlantic.com/international/archive/2020/06/saudi-arabia
-taxes-coronavirus-pandemic/612493/.

12. Josef Taalbi, "What Drives Innovation? Evidence from Economic
History," *Research Policy* 46, no. 8 (October 2017): 1427–1453, https://doi
.org/10.1016/j.respol.2017.06.007.

13. Ibid.

14. Maria Langan-Riekhof, Arex B. Avanni, and Adrienne Janetti, "Sometimes
the World Needs a Crisis: Turning Challenges into Opportunities," Brookings
Institution, April 10, 2017, https://www.brookings.edu/research/sometimes
-the-world-needs-a-crisis-turning-challenges-into-opportunities/.

15. Patrick Worsnip, "Wars Less Deadly Than They Used to Be, Report
Says," *Reuters*, January 20, 2010, https://www.reuters.com/article
/us-war-casualties-report/wars-less-deadly-than-they-used-to-be-report
-says-idUSTRE60J5UG20100120.

Part 2

1. Ursula Barth, "How Many Cells Are in Your Body? Probably More Than
You Think!" Eppendorf Handling Solutions, May 12, 2017, https://handling
-solutions.eppendorf.com/cell-handling/about-cells-and-culture/detailview
/news/how-many-cells-are-in-your-body-probably-more-than-you-think/.

2. Suzana Herculano-Houzel, "The Remarkable, Yet Not Extraordinary,
Human Brain as a Scaled-up Primate Brain and Its Associated Cost," *PNAS*
109 (Supplement 1) (June 26, 2012): 10661–10668, 1201895109, https://
www.pnas.org/content/109/Supplement_1/10661.

Chapter 6

1. Debra Umberson and Jennifer Karas Montez, "Social Relationships and Health: A Flashpoint for Health Policy," *Journal of Health and Social Behavior* 51 (Suppl) (2010): S54–S66, https://www.ncbi.nlm.nih.gov/pmc/articles/PMC3150158/.

2. Health Resources & Services Administration, "The 'Loneliness Epidemic,'" January 2019, https://www.hrsa.gov/enews/past-issues/2019/january-17/loneliness-epidemic.

3. Mayo Clinic Staff, "Self-esteem Check: Too Low or Just Right?," Mayo Clinic, July 14, 2020, https://www.mayoclinic.org/healthy-lifestyle/adult-health/in-depth/self-esteem/art-20047976.

4. Mustafa Kirişçi and Ibrahim Kocaman, "Humiliation is the Key to Understanding Widespread Rebellion," *Political Violence at a Glance*, July 29, 2020, https://politicalviolenceataglance.org/2020/07/29/humiliation-is-the-key-to-understanding-widespread-rebellion/.

5. Justin Bean, "Data for the People: How a Smart State is Driving Social Impact with IoT and Analytics," LinkedIn, April 25, 2019, https://www.linkedin.com/pulse/data-people-how-smart-state-driving-social-impact-iot-justin-bean/.

6. Grant Whittington, "Dallas Houses the Homeless, Saves Taxpayers Money," Triple Pundit, September 1, 2015, https://www.triplepundit.com/story/2015/dallas-houses-homeless-saves-taxpayers-money/32186.

7. United Nations, "World's Population Increasingly Urban with More Than Half Living in Urban Areas," July 10, 2014, https://www.un.org/en/development/desa/news/population/world-urbanization-prospects-2014.html.

Chapter 7

1. Dr. Peter Vincent Pry, "Life Without Electricity: Storm-Induced Blackouts and Implications for EMP Attack," Report to the Commission to Assess the Threat to the United States from Electromagnetic Pulse (EMP) Attack, July 2017, http://www.firstempcommission.org/uploads/1/1/9/5/119571849/life_without_electricity_-_final_april2018.pdf.

2. Futurism, "Congressional Report: A North Korean EMP Attack Would Kill '90% of all Americans'" (n.d.), https://futurism.com/congressional-report-a-north-korean-emp-attack-would-kill-90-of-all-americans.

3. Oxfam International, "5 Natural Disasters That Beg for Climate Action" (n.d.), https://www.oxfam.org/en/5-natural-disasters-beg-climate-action.

4. Adam B. Smith, "2018's Billion Dollar Disasters in Context," Climate.gov, February 7, 2019, updated September 9, 2021, https://www.climate.gov/news-features/blogs/beyond-data/2018s-billion-dollar-disasters-context.

5. World Health Organization, "Climate Change and Health," October 30, 2021, https://www.who.int/news-room/fact-sheets/detail/climate-change-and-health.

6. Environmental Protection Agency, "Sources of Greenhouse Gas Emissions" (n.d.), https://www.epa.gov/ghgemissions/sources-greenhouse-gas-emissions.

7. U.S. Energy Information Administration, "Frequently Asked Questions: How Much Electricity Is Lost in Electricity Transmission and Distribution in the United States?" (n.d.), https://www.eia.gov/tools/faqs/faq.php?id=105&t=3.

8. World Bank, "Electric Power Transmission and Distribution Losses (% of Output)," 2018, https://data.worldbank.org/indicator/EG.ELC.LOSS.ZS.

9. Attila Tamas Vekony, "The Opportunities of Solar Panel Recycling," GreenMatch, March 24, 2021, https://www.greenmatch.co.uk/blog/2017/10/the-opportunities-of-solar-panel-recycling.

10. NovoMoto, "Affordable Solar Electricity for the DR Congo: Rapid Growth Despite COVID-19," Wefunder (n.d.), https://wefunder.com/novomoto.

11. Eva Fox, "Tesla Is a Giant Group of Startups That Will Dominate Each Field," Tesmanian, January 06, 2021, https://www.tesmanian.com/blogs/tesmanian-blog/tesla-is-a-many-technology-startups#:~:text=%E2%80%9CTesla%20should%20really%20be%20thought,else%20what%20his%20company%20is.

Chapter 8

1. Carolyn Centeno Milton, "Fear Shrinks Your Brain and Makes You Less Creative," *Forbes*, April 18, 2018, https://www.forbes.com/sites/carolyncenteno/2018/04/18/fear-shrinks-your-brain-and-makes-you-less-creative/?sh=26aaeab1c6d9.

2. Max Roser and Hannah Ritchie, "Homicides," Our World in Data, July 2013, updated December 2019, https://ourworldindata.org/homicides.

3. Rachel Kleinfeld, "Why Are Some Societies So Violent, and Can They Be Made Safe?," Carnegie Endowment for International Peace, November 19, 2018, https://carnegieendowment.org/2018/11/19/why-are-some-societies-so-violent-and-can-they-be-made-safe-pub-77749.

4. Ibid.

5. Frank Schamalleger, "Causes of Crime Why Does a Person Commit a Crime? What Causes Crime and Deviance? Are People Basically Good? Why Are Some People Violent and Aggressive?," in *Criminal Justice Today: An Introductory Text to the 21st Century* (New York: Pearson Education, 2011), https://slideplayer.com/amp/5887917/.

6. U.S. Department of Justice, "2018 Crime in the United States," Federal Bureau of Investigation, Criminal Justice Information Services Division, 2018, https://ucr.fbi.gov/crime-in-the-u.s/2018/crime-in-the-u.s.-2018/tables/table-12/table-12.xls.

7. Kleinfeld, "Why Are Some Societies So Violent?"

8. Mapping Police Violence, "Police Have Killed 937 People in 2021," https://mappingpoliceviolence.org/.

9. Marc Sallinger, "'My Belief Is That This Is the Future of Policing': STAR Van Responds to Hundreds of 911 Calls Where Police Officers Aren't Needed," 9News, November 12, 2020, https://www.9news.com/article/news/community/voices-of-change/star-van-responds-to-hundreds-of-911-calls-police-officers-arent-needed-at/73-b8a7ac06-f01a-4d37-87b9-5435883efe30#:~:text=DENVER%20%E2%80%94%20Five%20months%20ago%2C%20Denver,nothing%20more%20than%20a%20van.

10. German Lopez, "American Policing Is Broken. Here's How to Fix It," *Vox*, September 1, 2017, https://www.vox.com/policy-and-politics/2016/11/29/12989428/police-shooting-race-crime.

11. Chad Marlow and Jay Stanley, "We're Updating Our Police Body Camera Recommendations for Even Better Accountability and Civil Liberties Protections," ACLU, January 25, 2017, https://www.aclu.org/blog/privacy -technology/surveillance-technologies/were-updating-our-police-body-camera.

12. "The ACLU Responds to Body Cameras Used by the LAPD," Sevens Legal, APC, n.d., https://www.sevenslegal.com/criminal-attorney/aclu -responds-body-cameras-lapd/413/.

13. Matthew Yglesias, "Black Lives Matter Activism Is Working," Vox, June 2, 2020, https://www.vox.com/2020/6/2/21276472/police-killing-statistics-african -american.

14. "Cops in Minneapolis Can No Longer Turn Off Body Cameras Whenever They Want," VICE News, February 3, 2021, https://www.vice.com/en/article /5dp4bx/cops-in-minneapolis-can-no-longer-turn-off-body-cameras-whenever -they-want.

15. Matthew Clarke, "Long-Term Recidivism Studies Show High Arrest Rates," *Prison Legal News*, May 3, 2019, https://www.prisonlegalnews.org /news/2019/may/3/long-term-recidivism-studies-show-high-arrest-rates/.

16. Beatrix Lockwood and Nicole Lewis, "The Hidden Cost of Incarceration," The Marshall Project, December 17, 2019, https://www.themarshallproject .org/2019/12/17/the-hidden-cost-of-incarceration.

17. Niall McCarthy, "How Much Do U.S. Cities Spend Every Year On Policing?," *Forbes*, August 7, 2017, https://www.populardemocracy.org /news-and-publications/how-much-do-us-cities-spend-every-year-policing.

18. "Program Teaches Prisoners How to Code So They Can Get Tech Jobs Once Released," BlackNews.com, January 28, 2020, https://www.blacknews .com/news/last-mile-program-san-quentin-teaches-prisoners-how-to-code -get-tech-jobs-once-released/.

19. Cody T. Ross, "A Multi-Level Bayesian Analysis of Racial Bias in Police Shootings at the County-Level in the United States, 2011–2014," *PLOS One*, November 5, 2015, https://journals.plos.org/plosone/article?id= 10.1371%2Fjournal.pone.0141854.

20. Vittorio Nastasi, "Unnecessary Licensing Laws Are Contributing to the Criminal Justice Crisis," Reason Foundation, July 1, 2020, https://reason.org /commentary/unnecessary-licensing-laws-are-contributing-to-the-criminal -justice-crisis/.

21. Lucy Ash, "The Dutch Prison Crisis: A Shortage of Prisoners," *BBC News*, November 10, 2016, https://www.bbc.com/news/magazine-37904263#:
~:text=While%20the%20UK%20and%20much,slated%20for%20closure%20
next%20year; Danielle Batist, "How the Dutch Are Closing Their Prisons," *U.S. News & World Report*, May 13, 2019, https://www.usnews.com/news
/best-countries/articles/2019-05-13/the-netherlands-is-closing-its-prisons.
22. Ibid.
23. M. K. Anser, Z. Yousaf, A. A. Nassani, et al., "Dynamic Linkages Between Poverty, Inequality, Crime, and Social Expenditures in a Panel of 16 Countries: Two-step GMM Estimates," *Economic Structures* 9, no. 43 (2020), https://doi.org/10.1186/s40008-020-00220-6.
24. Jessica Placzek, "Did the Emptying of Mental Hospitals Contribute to Homelessness?" *The California Report*, KQED, December 8, 2016, https://www
.kqed.org/news/11209729/did-the-emptying-of-mental-hospitals-contribute
-to-homelessness-here.

Chapter 9

1. Iyad Rahwan and Azim Shariff, "Self-Driving Cars Could Save Many Lives. But Mental Roadblocks Stand in the Way," *Wall Street Journal*, April 6, 2021, https://www.wsj.com/articles/self-driving-cars-could-save-many-lives-but
-mental-roadblocks-stand-in-the-way-11617732000.
2. "Congress and the Public," Gallup News (n.d.), https://news.gallup.com
/poll/1600/congress-public.aspx.
3. Amy Fried and Paul Sabin, "How the Left and Right Undermined Trust in Government," Niskanen Center, September 22, 2021, https://www
.niskanencenter.org/how-the-left-and-right-undermined-trust-in-government/.
4. George Dvorsky, "12 Futuristic Forms of Government That Could One Day Rule the World," Gizmodo, June 12, 2014, https://io9.gizmodo.com/12
-futuristic-forms-of-government-that-could-one-day-ru-1589833046.
5. Roman Krznaric, "Why We Need to Reinvent Democracy for the Long-Term," *BBC*, March 18, 2019, https://www.bbc.com/future/article/20190318
-can-we-reinvent-democracy-for-the-long-term.

Chapter 10

1. Greg Rosalsky, "The 'Strange, Unduly Neglected Prophet,'" *Planet Money*, National Public Radio, August 27, 2019, https://www.npr.org/sections/money/2019/08/27/754323652/the-strange-unduly-neglected-prophet.

2. Chapurukha Kusimba, "When—and Why—Did People First Start Using Money?" The Conversation, June 19, 2017, https://theconversation.com/when-and-why-did-people-first-start-using-money-78887.

3. Jacob Jarvis, "Fact Check: TRUTH Social Users Must Agree Not to 'Disparage' the Site," *Newsweek*, October 21, 2021, https://www.newsweek.com/fact-check-truth-social-users-terms-donald-trump-1641183.

4. Jim Clifton, "The World's Broken Workplace," The Chairman's Blog, *Gallup*, June 13, 2017, https://news.gallup.com/opinion/chairman/212045/world-broken-workplace.aspx.

5. Kate Raworth, "Meet the Doughnut: The New Economic Model That Could Help End Inequality," World Economic Forum, April 28, 2017, https://www.weforum.org/agenda/2017/04/the-new-economic-model-that-could-end-inequality-doughnut/.

6. Donna Lu, "Universal Basic Income Seems to Improve Employment and Well-Being," *NewScientist*, May 6, 2020, https://www.newscientist.com/article/2242937-universal-basic-income-seems-to-improve-employment-and-well-being/.

7. TalkPoverty, "Unemployment Benefits Aren't Creating a Labor Shortage, They're Building Worker Power," https://talkpoverty.org/2021/05/14/unemployment-labor-shortage-worker-power/.

8. Jonnelle Marte and Lucia Mutikani, "Share of U.S. Workers Holding Multiple Jobs Is Rising, New Census Report Shows," *Reuters*, February 17, 2021, https://www.reuters.com/article/us-usa-economy-multiple-jobs/share-of-u-s-workers-holding-multiple-jobs-is-rising-new-census-report-shows-idUSKBN2AH2PI.

9. "It Has Been Proven, Less Inequality Means Less Crime," World Bank, September 5, 2014, https://www.worldbank.org/en/news/feature/2014/09/03/latinoamerica-menos-desigualdad-se-reduce-el-crimen; Walter Frick, "Welfare Makes America More Entrepreneurial," *Atlantic*, March 26, 2015, https://www.theatlantic.com/politics/archive/2015/03/welfare-makes-america-more-entrepreneurial/388598/.1

Chapter 11

1. BankMyCell, "How Many Smartphones Are in the World?," March 2022, https://www.bankmycell.com/blog/how-many-phones-are-in-the-world#sources.
2. Newzoo, "Top Countries by Smartphone Users" (n.d.), https://newzoo.com/insights/rankings/top-countries-by-smartphone-penetration-and-users/.
3. Mark Aldrich, "History of Workplace Safety in the United States, 1880-1970," eh.net Encyclopedia, Economic History Association, https://eh.net/encyclopedia/history-of-workplace-safety-in-the-united-states-1880-1970-2/; Occupational Safety and Health Administration, "Commonly Used Statistics," https://www.osha.gov/data/commonstats.
4. Pedro Uria-Recio, "Artificial Intelligence will Make the Workplace More Human, Not Less," *Medium*, August 8, 2019, https://medium.com/@uriarecio/artificial-intelligence-will-make-the-workplace-more-human-not-less-49af1ce6cd0d.
5. Kauffman Foundation, "Visions of the Future," September 2019, https://www.kauffman.org/wp-content/uploads/2019/09/Visions-of-the-Future_v3.pdf.
6. Brandon Busteed, "America's 'No Confidence' Vote on College Grads' Work Readiness," *Gallup*, April 24, 2015, https://news.gallup.com/opinion/gallup/182867/america-no-confidence-vote-college-grads-work-readiness.aspx.
7. Ibid.
8. Brandon Busteed, "Is College Worth It? That Depends," *Gallup*, April 8, 2015, https://www.gallup.com/education/237278/college-worth-depends.aspx.

9. Dalai Lama, November 20, 2020, https://twitter.com/dalailama/status /1329718670679973888; Thekchen Chöling, "Educating the Heart—Discussion with EdCamp Ukraine," October 20, 2020, https://www.dalailama .com/news/2020/educating-the-heart-discussion-with-edcamp-ukraine.

10. *Wall Street Journal*, "How China Is Using Artificial Intelligence in Classrooms," October 1, 2019, https://www.youtube.com/watch?v= JMLsHI8aV0g.

11. Team Leverage Edu, "Finland Education System," Leverage.edu, November 15, 2021, https://leverageedu.com/blog/finland-education-system/.

12. OECD, Education Policy Outlook: Finland, 2020, www.oecd.org/education /policy-outlook/country-profile-Finland-2020.pdf.

13. Anna-Karin Sager, "27 Things Finland is Known For," Hey Explorer, August 16, 2020, https://heyexplorer.com/what-is-finland-known-for/.

Chapter 12

1. Abraham Maslow, *Motivation and Personality* (New York: Harper & Brothers, 1954).

2. Economic Research Service, "What Is Agriculture's Share of the Overall U.S. Economy?" U.S. Department of Agriculture, 2019, https://www.ers.usda .gov/data-products/chart-gallery/gallery/chart-detail/?chartId=58270.

3. Jim Rendon, "How Trauma Can Change You—For the Better," *Time*, July 22, 2015, https://time.com/3967885/how-trauma-can-change-you-for-the-better/.

4. Susan Scutti, "More Money Can Mean Scrooge-like Pride, Study Says," *CNN*, February 28, 2018, https://www.cnn.com/2017/12/18/health/poor-rich -happiness-study/index.html.

5. Vincent P. Clark et al., "TDCS Guided Using fMRI Significantly Accelerates Learning to Identify Concealed Objects," Neuroimage 59, no. 1 (January 2, 2012): 117–128, https://www.ncbi.nlm.nih.gov/pmc/articles/PMC3387543/.

6. Emma Young, "Brain Stimulation: The Military's Mind-Zapping Project," *BBC Future*, June 2, 2014, https://www.bbc.com/future/article/20140603 -brain-zapping-the-future-of-war.

7. Rachael Rettner, "Mind-Tracking Devices: Do 'Brain Wearables' Really Work?" Live Science, February 25, 2016, https://www.livescience.com/53840 -do-brain-wearable-devices-really-work.html.

8. Noor Azuin Suliman et al., "Establishing Natural Nootropics: Recent Molecular Enhancement Influenced by Natural Nootropic," *Evidence-Based Complementary and Alternative Medicine*, August 30, 2013, https://www.ncbi .nlm.nih.gov/pmc/articles/PMC5021479/.

9. Johns Hopkins Center for Psychedelic and Consciousness Research, "Psychedelics Research and Psilocybin Therapy," Psychiatry and Behavioral Sciences, Johns Hopkins Medicine, 2021, https://www.hopkinsmedicine.org /psychiatry/research/psychedelics-research.html.

10. Rape, Abuse & Incest National Network (RAINN), "Perpetrators of Sexual Violence: Statistics" (n.d.), https://www.rainn.org/statistics/perpetrators -sexual-violence.

11. "Sweden Rape: Most Convicted Attackers Foreign-Born, Says TV," *BBC News*, August 22, 2018, https://www.bbc.com/news/world-europe-45269764.

12. thethinkingshop.org.

13. "Existential Risk," Future of Life Institute (n.d.), https://futureoflife.org /background/existential-risk/.

Conclusion

1. Amelia Goranson et al., "Dying Is Unexpectedly Positive," *Psychological Science* (June 1, 2017), https://journals.sagepub.com/doi /full/10.1177/0956797617701186#_i32.

2. John Maynard Keynes, *A Tract on Monetary Reform* (London: London Macmillan and Co., 1923), 80.

3. Elizabeth Dunn and Lara Aknin, "Spending Money on Others Promotes Happiness," *Science* 319, no. 5870 (April 2008): 1687–8, https://www .researchgate.net/publication/5494996_Spending_Money_on_Others _Promotes_Happiness.

CPSIA information can be obtained
at www.ICGtesting.com
Printed in the USA
JSHW052000081122
32853JS00006B/113